P9-ARM-258

WITHDRAWN
No longer the property of the
Boston Public Library.
Sale of this material benefits the Library.

Overland to Starvation Cove

Heinrich Klutschak

OVERLAND
TO
STARVATION
COVE

With the Inuit in Search of Franklin
1878~1880

Translated and edited by
WILLIAM BARR

University of Toronto Press
Toronto Buffalo London

G665
1878
.K613
1987x

© University of Toronto Press 1987
Toronto   Buffalo   London
Printed in Canada

ISBN 0-8020-5762-4

First published as
Als Eskimo unter den Eskimos:
Eine Schilderung der Erlebnisse der Schwatka'schen
Franklin-Aufsuchungs-Expedition in den Jahren 1878–1880
by A. Hartleben Verlag, Vienna 1881

Canadian Cataloguing in Publication Data

Klutschak, Heinrich W.

Overland to Starvation Cove

Translation of: Als Eskimo unter den Eskimos.
Includes bibliographical references and index.
ISBN 0-8020-5762-4
1. Arctic regions – Discovery and exploration – American.
2. Inuit – Canada.
3. Schwatka, Frederick, 1840–1892.
4. Franklin, John, Sir, 1786–1847.
I. Barr, William.   II. Title.
G665 1878.K613 1987   917.19′2′041   C87-094335-9

This book has been published
with the help of a grant from the
Social Science Federation of Canada,
using funds provided by the
Social Sciences and Humanities
Research Council of Canada.

Contents

Acknowledgments

I should first like to acknowledge the financial assistance of the University of Saskatchewan which, through a grant from its President's Social Sciences and Humanities Research Council Fund, enabled me to spend some time in the spring of 1985 at the Scott Polar Research Institute in Cambridge, England, where I worked on the introduction and notes to this translation. I am also very grateful to Dr Owen Beattie for providing the illustrations of present-day King William Island which appear on pages 85, 92, 95, and 96 and for contributing such an apt Afterword.

The comments of the various experts who reviewed the manuscript for both the University of Toronto Press and for the Social Science Federation of Canada were invariably very constructive and thought-provoking and I have attempted to incorporate as many of their suggested modifications as possible. In attempting to cast some light on the rather shadowy figure of Heinrich Klutschak I was able, through the good offices of the Czech embassy in Ottawa and the Czech consulate in Montreal, to obtain some information from Prague. I am particularly indebted to Dr George Strnad of Saskatoon for his invaluable contribution in translating these materials for me.

I should also like to thank Dr Robert G. Williamson and Mrs Karla Williamson of Saskatoon for having advised me on rendering Klutschak's versions of Inuktitut names and terms into currently accepted orthography. It is appropriate to mention that neither Dr nor Mrs Williamson was consulted on the ethnographic content of Klutschak's book. Finally, I am enormously indebted to Mr Keith Bigelow of the Department of Geography, University of Saskatchewan, for his superb contribution in the areas of cartography and photography.

Introduction

At 10:30 A.M. on 19 May 1845 the barque-rigged bomb vessels HMS *Erebus* and *Terror* (370 and 340 tons, respectively) sailed from Greenhithe on the River Thames. Their combined crews totalled 134 officers and men, under the command of Captain Sir John Franklin. Their objective was to sail through the Northwest Passage; having emerged from the Arctic Ocean via Bering Strait they were ordered to proceed to the Sandwich Islands (Hawaii) and return home via Cape Horn (Cyriax, 1939:55).

While in hindsight these instructions may appear to have been ludicrously over-optimistic, on the face of it the task Franklin was being asked to tackle did not seem particularly daunting. In 1819–20, in the ships *Hecla* and *Griper*, Captain William Edward Parry had penetrated as far west along Parry Channel as the southwest corner of Melville Island and had wintered at Winter Harbour (Parry, 1821). In 1829–33, on a private expedition aboard *Victory*, Sir John Ross had penetrated south along Prince Regent Inlet to Felix Harbour on Boothia Isthmus (Ross, 1835), where his ship had wintered. From here in the spring of 1830 his nephew James Clark Ross had sledged west across the isthmus to Spence Bay and explored the north coast of King William Island as far west as Victory Point.

Within the next decade another expedition would almost reach the same point from the west. In the summer of 1839 Peter Dease and Thomas Simpson of the Hudson's Bay Company, travelling by canoe, journeyed east along the mainland coast from the mouth of the Coppermine (Simpson, 1843). Passing through Simpson Strait, they explored the south coast of King William Island and turned back at Castor and Pollux Bay on the west coast of Boothia Peninsula. At Cape John Herschel, they were within 100 km of Victory Point, the most westerly point reached by James Ross; that is, only a 100-km gap remained to be filled to complete the picture of the northern limits of the continent. But it is one thing to travel across tundra and sea ice on foot, hauling sledges, as James Ross had done, or to sail the coastal waters by canoe during the brief weeks of open water in summer, as Dease and Simpson had done, and quite another to battle the ice and try to sail those same waters, studded with shoals and reefs, in ocean-going ships.

Erebus and *Terror* probably represented the best possible type of ship for the job. As bomb vessels they had been designed to carry large mortars capable of hurling large-calibre shells on a high trajectory into coastal towns under siege or into entrenched positions. The mortars rested on extremely strongly built wooden beds amidships, and since there was no mechanism for absorbing the recoil of these terrifying weapons, the ships as a whole were unusually strongly built and hence ideal for withstanding the massive pressures they might encounter in arctic ice. If caught between two large floes driven against each other by wind or current, they were much more likely to survive than an ordinary vessel.

Both ships had already seen a considerable amount of polar service. *Terror*, commanded in 1836 by Captain George Back, had tried to reach Wager Bay, as an intended starting point for an overland attempt at exploring the middle section of the Northwest Passage; caught in the ice off the north coast of Southampton Island, she drifted southeast along the east coast of that island and was released from the ice, badly damaged and leaking, near the west end of Hudson Strait in July 1837 (Back, 1838). Between 1839 and 1843, along with *Erebus*, *Terror* took part in a major expedition to the Antarctic under the command of James Clark Ross (Ross, 1847). They explored the Ross Sea and discovered the Ross Ice Shelf and the active volcano, Mount Erebus. Both ships were quite badly damaged during this epic antarctic voyage.

For their new voyage to the Arctic special adaptations were made to both vessels. They were given additional ice sheathing and their bows were built up to the point where they consisted of a mass of timber almost 2.5 m thick. Their bows were then plated with sheets of iron. For the first time both ships also were provided with steam power for manoeuvring in ice or making progress during calms. Railway engines, with only minimal modification, were mounted athwartships in the holds, a drive shaft extending aft from one of the driving wheels to a two-bladed propeller (Cyriax, 1939:39–40). The engines were only twenty hp and under even the best conditions could move the ships at only 4 knots. However, since with their bluff bows these bomb vessels could achieve a maximum of only 8 knots under sail, this auxiliary power probably proved quite useful. The propellers could be hoisted out of the water via a vertical well if they were in danger of being damaged by ice. Other innovative devices were condensers attached to the galley stoves to produce drinking water from sea water, and hot water heating systems throughout the living quarters.

The ships were provisioned for three years. The stores included some 70 tonnes of flour, 48 tonnes of meat (one-third of this being canned and the rest salt meat), 3684 gallons of liquor, and 3.5 tonnes of tobacco. Antiscorbutics included 4.5 tonnes of lemon juice and 170 gallons of cranberries.

The expedition leader, Sir John Franklin, was fifty-eight years old. Having joined the Navy at the age of fourteen, he had fought aboard HMS *Polyphemus* at the Battle of Copenhagen and as signal midshipman aboard HMS *Bellerophon* at the Battle of Trafalgar (Cyriax, 1939:32). His first arctic experience had been as the commander of HMS *Trent*, which in 1818 along with HMS *Dorothea* under Captain David Buchan had attempted, with little success, to reach the North Pole via a route between Svalbard and Greenland (Beechey, 1843). This was Sir John's only experience of shipborne arctic exploration. By contrast, his experience of overland travel and coastal travel by canoe and small boats in the Arctic was practically unparalleled. In 1819–22, during an expedition which ended in starvation and the death of eleven of his companions, travelling by canoe Franklin had explored the coast from the mouth of the Coppermine to Point Turnagain on Kent Peninsula (Franklin, 1823). On his second expedition in 1825–7, this time travelling by boat, he had explored the coast westward from the Mackenzie Delta to Return Reef, west of Prudhoe Bay; meantime, another component of the expedition, led by Dr John Richardson, travelled eastward by boat from the Mackenzie Delta to the mouth of the Coppermine (Franklin, 1828). Sir John had not been in the Arctic since then and had spent much of the time as an administrator, having served from 1837 until 1843 as governor of Tasmania.

In command of HMS *Terror* was Captain Francis Rawdon Moira Crozier, aged forty-eight, and in terms of shipborne arctic exploration by far the most experienced member of the expedition. He had served as midshipman aboard HMS *Fury* during Parry's second expedition of 1821–3, which had wintered first at Winter Island in Frozen Strait and then at Igloolik (Parry, 1824). During both winterings the expedition members had enjoyed close and generally amicable relations with the Inuit of the area, and it seems probable that Crozier would have acquired a working knowledge of Inuktitut. Then, in 1824–5, Crozier had served as midshipman aboard *Hecla* on Parry's third voyage and thus had wintered again at Port Bowen in Prince Regent Inlet (Parry, 1826). Finally, Crozier had commanded *Terror* on James Ross's epic antarctic voyage (1839–43) and so had vast experience of handling a ship in ice.

By contrast, Commander James Fitzjames, the captain of *Erebus* on the new expedition, had no previous arctic experience, although he had explored the Euphrates River by steamer in 1835 and had commanded a rocket brigade during the hostilities in China in 1841. On the other hand, his first lieutenant aboard *Erebus*, Graham Gore, had been in the Arctic previously. In 1836–7 he had served as mate under Captain George Back aboard *Terror* and hence was only too familiar with the dangers of a winter adrift in the ice. Other officers with arctic experience were Mr Charles Osmer, purser and paymaster aboard *Erebus*, who had accompanied Captain Frederick Beechey to Bering Strait in *Blossom* in 1825–8 (Beechey, 1831). Dr Alexander McDonald, assistant surgeon aboard *Terror*, had previously been to the Arctic aboard whaling ships. And finally, each ship carried an ice-master to advise the captain about navigation in ice. James Reid served in this capacity aboard *Erebus* and Thomas Blanky aboard *Terror*; both had had considerable arctic experience as officers of whaling ships.

Of the total complement of 134 officers and men when the ships sailed from England, five would be invalided home from Greenland. Most of the men were recruited especially for the expedition, mainly from the north of England, and many may well have served previously aboard whalers sailing out of ports such as Hull or Whitby. A few, however, were veterans of the Royal Navy. Everyone, officers and men, was to receive double pay for the duration of the arctic expedition, in keeping with normal Admiralty practice.

The actual route Franklin was directed to attempt through the labyrinth of what is now the Canadian Arctic Archipelago was quite narrowly specified. He was to sail west through Lancaster Sound and Barrow Strait along the latitude of approximately 74°15'N as far as the longitude of Cape Walker (the northeast tip of Russell Island off the north coast of Prince of Wales Island at about 98°W). From there he was to steer southward and westward toward Bering Strait, on as straight a course as ice and/or unknown land would permit. If progress were totally blocked in that direction, however, he was to try northward via Wellington Channel, between Devon and Cornwallis islands (Cyriax, 1939:45–56).

On 25 July 1845 *Erebus* and *Terror* encountered the whalers *Enterprise* (Captain Robert Martin) of Peterhead and *Prince of Wales* (Captain Dannett) of Hull in Melville Bukt in the northern part of Baffin Bay. The four ships kept company among the ice for several days, with men and officers visiting to and fro. When last seen by Captain Martin, *Erebus* and *Terror* were moored to an iceberg. He and his crew were the last whites to see any member of Franklin's expedition alive (Jones, 1969:196).

Sir John Franklin, Captain Crozier, and the other men with arctic experience were well aware of what lay ahead of them. They knew full well that even at the height of summer they were almost certain to encounter sea ice somewhere along their route. If a ship became beset, that is, jammed immobile in the ice, and if the ice were being driven by wind or current, it could be subjected to unimaginable pressures. To the accompaniment of a terrifying cacophony of shrieks, groans, crashes, and rumbles, jumbled masses of shattered ice might pile up against the ship's sides until they toppled over the rails onto the decks. If worse came to the worst, a ship's hull could be crushed like an eggshell in a matter of seconds and the vessel would inevitably sink once the ice slackened its grip again.

It was very unlikely that the ships would be able to get a clear run through the Northwest Passage in one season. Almost certainly they would be barred by ice at some point along the route, in which case the expedition would select a convenient harbour and settle down to spend the winter in the hope that the ice would release the ships to continue their progress the following summer.

This turn of events, of course, would mean experiencing the very real discomforts and potential hazards of an arctic winter. At the latitude of Beechey Island, where the expedition did in fact spend its first winter, the sun disappears around the end of October and does not reappear for four months. While the moon and a certain amount of twilight at either end of this period of darkness permit a certain amount of outdoor activity, the winter darkness undoubtedly would have a serious effect on the morale of the expedition personnel. In addition, life in the cramped quarters of the little ships, lit around the clock by candles and oil lamps producing an almost unbearable fug but very little light, can scarcely have been very pleasant.

Temperatures could be expected to drop to $-40°$ and even $-50°C$, while the frequent gales could produce a wind chill that could kill a man, improperly clad, in a matter of a few hours. Even without the winter darkness, blowing snow during arctic blizzards could reduce visibility to practically zero, rendering even a short excursion away from the ships potentially hazardous.

During spring, summer, and fall, by contrast, conditions could be extremely pleasant. Several months of continuous daylight would allow unimpeded outdoor activity and travel. Temperatures in the shade could be expected to rise to 10^0 and even 15^{0}C. Once the snow had melted off the land, large areas would burst into a riot of colourful flowers and tundra ponds and lakes would swarm with ducks and waders, busy with courtship and nesting during the short summer months. From the experience of past expeditions, the officers and men could expect to encounter caribou, muskoxen, polar bears, and seals, all being of considerable significance as a potential source of fresh meat. And they could expect to meet the Inuit with whom Sir John Ross at Felix Harbour and Captain Parry at Winter Island and Igloolik had established such friendly relations.

One can imagine that aboard *Terror*, either in formal briefing sessions or in casual conversation in the wardroom, Captain Crozier must have given his officers the benefit of his considerable knowledge of the Arctic based on his earlier expeditions. One of the men who probably listened eagerly to these accounts was Lieutenant John Irving, aged thirty. As a boy he had attended the Royal Naval College at Greenwich and in the summer of 1830, at the age of fifteen, he had been awarded the second prize in mathematics. With the award went a large silver medal. After graduating from the Naval College he served as a midshipman in the East Indies aboard the survey vessel *Fly* (O'Byrne, 1849), under Captain Blackwood, and aboard *Favourite*, under Captain Sullivan. Promoted to lieutenant in March 1843, he thereafter served aboard *Volage*, under Captain Sir William Dickson, and aboard *Excellent*, a gunnery ship at Portsmouth, under Captain Sir Thomas Hastings. Finally, on 13 March 1845 he was posted to *Terror* to take part in Sir John Franklin's expedition. He was undoubtedly proud of the medal he had received at the Royal Naval College for it was among his baggage when he joined his new ship.

Some thirty years later, on 27 June 1879, a young man named Heinrich Klutschak spotted a human skull and the scattered bones of a skeleton beside a plundered grave built of flat sandstone slabs near Victory Point on the northwest coast of King William Island. Inside the grave lay some remnants of blue cloth whose buttons indicated that it had once been a British naval officer's uniform. A silk handkerchief lay at the head end of the grave, while on one of the sandstone slabs lay a large silver medal. It bore the inscription: 'Second Mathematical Prize, Royal Navy College. Awarded to John Irving, Midsummer 1830.'

II

Heinrich Wenzl Klutschak was a member of an expedition sponsored by the American Geographical Society and led by Lieutenant Frederick Schwatka, U.S. Third Cavalry, which had reached King William Island in a remarkable overland sledge trip from Hudson Bay in the early months of 1879. The expedition's primary aim was to search for records or relics of Franklin. The translation that follows of Klutschak's account of the trip not only reveals how he came to locate Lieutenant Irving's grave but also goes a long way to clarifying how Irving and his medal had come to be buried in such a remote corner of the Arctic.

Schwatka's was certainly not the first group to set off in search of the missing Franklin Expedition. Nor was it the first to find grisly evidence about what had become of Franklin and his men. But all the previous expeditions had left many important questions unanswered.

No particular concern was felt in Britain when there was no word from Franklin in 1846. But by 1847 some anxiety was developing and plans for the first search expeditions were laid. In 1848, under the auspices of the British Admiralty, Sir John Richardson and Sir John Rae travelled west via the fur-trade route, descended the Mackenzie, and searched the coast eastward to the mouth of the Coppermine River by boat (Richardson, 1851). After wintering at Fort Confidence on Great Bear Lake, Rae resumed his search in 1849 intending to search the coasts of Victoria Island, but ice prevented him from crossing Dolphin and Union Strait (Rich & Johnson, 1953). Also in 1848, HMS *Plover* (Captain Thomas Moore) was dispatched to Bering Strait; she reached her destination in October and wintered on the Siberian side of the strait, the first of many winterings she would spend in the area (Hooper, 1853). Meanwhile, HMS *Herald*, under Captain Henry Kellett, while on a surveying voyage in the Pacific was dispatched northward from Panama in the summer of 1848 to rendezvous with *Plover* in Kotzebue Sound (Seemann, 1853, Vol. 2), but on failing to meet her returned south again.

Meanwhile, an expedition had been dispatched to attempt to follow the same route as outlined in Franklin's instructions. Two ships, HMS *Enterprise* and HMS *Investigator* (Captain Sir James Clark Ross and Captain Edward J. Bird, respectively), sailed from the Thames in May 1848. They wintered at Port Leopold on northeastern Somerset Island

and in the spring of 1849 sledging parties from the ships explored extensive sections of the coasts of Somerset and adjacent islands (Gilpin, 1850). They found no trace of the missing expedition and returned to England late in 1849.

That same year *Herald*, under Captain Henry Kellett, again headed north through Bering Strait, met *Plover* in Kotzebue Sound, and proceeded north to Wainwright Inlet but was there blocked by ice. Heading west, Kellett discovered Ostrov Geral'da (Herald Island) before heading south again to winter in Mexican waters (Seemann, 1853, Vol. 2). Meanwhile a party from *Plover*, travelling in two boats under the command of Lieutenants William Pullen and William Hooper, headed east along the Alaskan coast to the mouth of the Mackenzie (Pullen, 1979).

The following year saw a great flurry of activity in the Arctic, involving both private and naval search expeditions and also including an American component. Four naval vessels, *Resolute* (Captain Horatio Austin), *Assistance* (Captain Erasmus Ommanney), *Intrepid* (Captain Bertie Cator), and *Pioneer* (Captain Sherard Osborn) sailed from England in May (Osborn, 1852). Lady Jane Franklin dispatched a search vessel of her own, *Prince Albert*, under the command of Captain Charles Codrington Forsyth (Snow, 1851). Another private expedition, financed by the Hudson's Bay Company, was organized and led by the arctic veteran Sir John Ross; it sailed aboard *Felix*, with a twelve-ton yacht, *Mary*, as tender (Dodge, 1973; Wilson, 1973). Yet another expedition sailed from Britain that summer; the whaling captain William Penny, sponsored by the British government and with instructions from the Admiralty, led an expedition consisting of *Lady Franklin* and *Sophia* (Sutherland, 1852). Finally the American contribution, consisting of the ships *Advance* (Captain E.J. DeHaven) and *Rescue* (Captain Samuel P. Griffin), sailed from New York, northward bound in May 1850 (Kane, 1854).

All these expeditions sailed into Barrow Strait and all congregated in the area of Beechey Island at the southwestern tip of Devon Island in late August 1850. It was in this area that the first finds of traces of the missing expedition were made. On 23 August, Captain Ommanney of *Assistance*, along with some of his officers, landed on Cape Riley, across Erebus Bay from Beechey Island; they found traces of an encampment 'and collected the remains of materials which evidently prove that some party belonging to Her Majesty's ships have been detained on this spot.' The remains included rope, canvas, wood, and animal bones; having examined the remains and also Captain Ommanney's description, such experts as Captain William Edward Parry, Dr John Richardson, and Colonel Sabine later deduced that a boat party from *Erebus* and *Terror* had camped here, probably to carry out magnetic observations (Great Britain. Parliament, 1851:72–9).

Three days later a boat party from *Lady Franklin*, led by Captain William Penny, found clear traces of another encampment ten km north of Cape Spencer, on the shores of Wellington Channel; they included the remains of a circular stone hut with a neatly paved floor and a litter of soup cans, pieces of casks, charred pieces of firewood, rope, mittens, rags, and a scrap of newspaper dated 1844. Sledge tracks were found nearby (Sutherland, 1852:299–301).

The next day, *Lady Franklin* and *Sophia* dropped anchor in what has since been named Union Bay, between Beechey Island and Cape Spencer. *Felix*, *Advance*, and *Rescue* were already lying at anchor. Parties from the various ships went ashore on Beechey Island and immediately realized that this was where *Erebus* and *Terror* had spent the winter of 1845–6 (Sutherland, 1852:303–8; Kane, 1854:162–5). The most conspicuous and revealing evidence took the form of the headboards of three graves, two of the occupants being from *Erebus* and the other from *Terror*. There were also clear signs of where a smith's forge had stood and a general litter of tin cans, wood chips, fragments of canvas, rope, etc. Captain Osborn of *Pioneer*, which arrived a day later, even found a pair of gloves laid out to dry with stones set on their palms to prevent them from blowing away (Osborn, 1852:109). The most baffling and frustrating aspect, however, was that despite a thorough and determined search not a trace of any type of message was found. The further movements of the missing ships after they left Beechey Island, presumably in the summer of 1846, were still a total mystery.

With these tantalizing clues really contributing little to the ultimate solution of the mystery, the sea-borne search by both Navy and private vessels from both Atlantic and Pacific ends of the Northwest Passage intensified, if that were possible, over the next few years. Sledge parties from wintering ships fanned out over large parts of the Arctic archipelago, much of which was thus mapped for the first time. But the first clues as to the ultimate fate of the expedition were gathered by an overland expedition dispatched by the Hudson's Bay Company and led by the redoubtable traveller Dr John Rae. His objective was to survey the west coast of Boothia Peninsula and the search for the Franklin Expedition was only a secondary goal. Having wintered at Repulse Bay in the winter of 1853–4, on 21 April 1854, near Pelly Bay, Rae and his Inuit companions met an Inuk who reported that in the spring four years before, in 1850, off an island some distance to the west, about forty white men were seen travelling south on the sea ice, dragging a boat and sledges with them (Rich & Johnson, 1953:274–5; Great Britain. Parliament, 1855:831–9). Later that same season some thirty bodies and graves were found at a location on the mainland and five bodies on an island nearby, about a day's journey northwest of the mouth of a large river, which Rae later identified as Back's Great Fish River (now the Back River). Rae purchased from the Pelly Bay people a variety of silver forks and spoons with crests identifiable as those of Robert Orme Sargent, mate aboard *Erebus*, Lieutenant James Fairholme, also of *Erebus*, Captain Francis Crozier of *Terror*, and of Captain Sir John Franklin himself. He also bought a number of coins and assorted pieces of watches. None of the Pelly Bay people had seen the white men themselves, either dead or alive, but had heard the story from others, from whom they had also acquired the various items in trade. It was not until Rae returned to his winter quarters at Repulse Bay that from further questioning of the local Inuit he was able to determine that the disaster had occurred on King William Island and on Adelaide Peninsula. Had he known this earlier, he would presumably have tried to locate the various sites himself.

Rae's report of his discoveries reached the governor and committee of the Hudson's Bay Company in London in late October 1854. The information was immediately passed to the Admiralty and the Lords Commissioners of the Admiralty strongly encouraged the Company to send an expedition down the Back River to its mouth to investigate the details of what Rae had reported (Great Britain. Parliament, 1855:846). As a result, an expedition led by Chief Factor James Anderson and James Stewart, a Company employee, descended the Back River with two canoes in the summer of 1855 (Anderson, 1940–1). On 30 July 1855, just below the rapids at the outlet from Lake Franklin, they met a party of Inuit from whom they understood that a party of white men had starved to death on the coast after their ships had been destroyed. In their tents they found copper and tin kettles. They also found various pieces of poles and boards of ash, oak, white pine, and mahogany and the head of a pair of blacksmith's tongs. Communication was difficult for lack of a competent interpreter, so Anderson learned nothing about documents.

On 2 August, in a cache on Montreal Island, they found a variety of items which had clearly come from the missing ships (Anderson, 1941:10–11); these included a tin kettle, a cold chisel, a shovel, a piece of wood with 'Erebus' on it and another with 'Mr Stanley' inscribed into it (Stanley was *Erebus*'s surgeon). Further progress by canoe was blocked by ice on 6 August and Anderson decided to walk on from this point on the east coast of Ogle Peninsula. Having searched Maconochie Island without success, on 8 August Anderson reluctantly decided to turn back. At this point he was within fifteen km of Starvation Cove, where Schwatka's expedition later would find a wealth of remains and many skeletons.

Despite these promising indications, the Admiralty was not prepared to dispatch any further expeditions, but Lady Franklin was not yet ready to give up and in 1857 she dispatched a private expedition. Captain Francis McClintock sailed from Aberdeen aboard the yacht *Fox* on 2 July 1857 (McClintock, 1859). The ship became beset in the ice of Melville Bukt and drifted south for the full length of Baffin Bay and through Davis Strait over the winter of 1857-8. Once his ship was freed, McClintock headed north again and entered Lancaster Sound; the expedition spent its second winter in winter quarters in Port Kennedy at the east end of Bellot Strait.

During a sledge journey in February-March 1859, McClintock met a group of Inuit at Cape Victoria on the west coast of Boothia Peninsula, who were familiar with the fact that a group of whites had starved to death on an island to the southwest. McClintock bought from them a number of relics, including six silver spoons and forks, a silver medal which had belonged to Alexander McDonald, assistant surgeon aboard *Terror*, and several buttons (McClintock, 1859:233-4). The Inuit also reported that a ship with three masts had been crushed by the ice west of King William Island.

Having returned to his ship, on 2 April McClintock set off once again, accompanied by Lieutenant William Hobson, to search the shores of King William Island. On the west side of Boothia, some distance north of Cape Victoria, they encountered the same group of Inuit whom they had met a few weeks earlier. McClintock purchased some more items which had clearly come from *Erebus* and *Terror*. This time questioning revealed that two ships had been seen west of King William Island: one had been seen to sink in deep water; the other had been driven ashore by the ice.

On reaching Cape Victoria on 24 April, McClintock and Hobson separated; McClintock continued south down the east coast of King William Island, aiming to travel clockwise around the island. Meanwhile, Hobson proceeded directly to the west coast with a view to confirming the report of a ship having been driven ashore. On 7 May, at an Inuit camp on the east side of King William Island, McClintock saw and purchased six silver spoons and forks with crests or initials of Franklin, Crozier, Fairholme, and McDonald and a variety of other

items from the missing ships. At a single snow house off Point Booth
on 10 May he saw eight to ten fir poles, a kayak paddle made from two
oar blades, and two large snow shovels, 1.2 m long, made from what had
probably been the bottom boards of a boat.

McClintock now cut south from Point Ogle to Montreal Island,
which he searched carefully but where he found only a few metal
remains. His party then headed west, crossed Point Ogle and Barrow
Inlet, then cut northwest toward Simpson Strait, emerging a few
kilometres west of Point Richardson. On this last overland leg McClintock must have come within about 10 km of the abundant remains at
Starvation Cove. Crossing the strait on the sea ice, he reached the coast
of King William Island again, just west of the Peffer River. About
midway between Gladman Point and Cape Herschel McClintock found
the first skeleton. From the remains of the clothing he appeared to have
been a steward or officer's servant. The skeleton was later identified as
that of Harry Peglar, captain of the foretop aboard *Terror* (Cyriax &
Jones, 1954).

Reaching Cape Herschel, McClintock easily located the massive
cairn left by Dease and Simpson in the summer of 1839 during their
impressive boat trip along the mainland coast. Some 19 km west of here
McClintock found a cairn which Hobson had left six days earlier. The
most exciting part of the message left in the cairn was the news that he
had found a document in a cairn at Point Victory. In McClintock's
words:

The record paper was one of the printed forms usually supplied to discovery
ships for the purpose of being enclosed in bottles and thrown overboard at sea,
in order to ascertain the set of the currents ... Upon it was written ... as
follows:

28 of May 1847

H.M. ships 'Erebus' and 'Terror' wintered in the ice in lat. 70⁰05'N, long.
98⁰23'W. Having wintered in 1846-7 at Beechey Island, in lat. 76⁰43'28"N,
long. 91⁰39'15"W, after having ascended Wellington Channel to lat. 77⁰, and
returned by the west side of Cornwallis Island.

Sir John Franklin commanding the expedition.

All well.

Party consisting of 2 officers and 6 men left the ships on Monday 24th May,
1847.

Gm. Gore, Lieut.

Chas. F. Des Voeux, Mate (McClintock,

1859:283-4)

As McClintock has pointed out, there is an obvious error in this report since clearly the ships wintered at Beechey Island in 1845-6, not 1846-7. McClintock's description continues:

Round the margin of the paper upon which Lieutenant Gore in 1847 wrote those words of hope and promise, another hand had subsequently written the following words:

April 25, 1848. H.M. ships 'Terror' and 'Erebus' were deserted on the 22nd April, 5 leagues N.N.W. of this, having been beset since 12th September, 1846. The officers and crews, consisting of 105 souls, under the command of Captain F.R.M. Crozier landed here in lat. 69°37'42"N, long. 98°41'W. This paper was found by Lt. Irving under the cairn supposed to have been built by Sir James Ross in 1831, 4 miles to the northward, where it had been deposited by the late Commander Gore in June 1847. Sir James Ross' pillar has not, however, been found, and the paper has been transferred to this position, which is that in which Sir James Ross' pillar was erected.

Sir John Franklin died on the 11th June, 1847; and the total loss by deaths in the expedition has been to this date 9 officers and 15 men.

(Signed) F.R.M. Crozier   James Fitzjames

Captain and Senior Officer   Captain, H.M.S. Erebus

and start tomorrow 26th for Backs Fish River. (McClintock, 1859:286)

Encouraged by this message, McClintock continued his search although his provisions were running low. On 29 May the party reached the western tip of King William Island, which McClintock named Cape Crozier, and on the 30th encamped beside a ship's boat, already discovered by Hobson. It was mounted on a solid, heavy sledge; McClintock estimated the total weight of sledge and boat to be about 1400 lbs. In the boat lay two skeletons, both minus the skull, as well as five watches, two double-barrelled guns, and some small books including a Bible and a copy of *The Vicar of Wakefield*. There was also a large amount of assorted clothing, seven or eight pairs of assorted footwear, and an amazing array of twine, nails, saws, files, bristles, candle ends, sailmakers' palms, powder, bullets, shot, cartridges, wads, a leather cartridge case, clasp knives, dinner knives, needle and thread cases, lengths of slowmatch, several bayonet scabbards cut down into knife sheaths, and two rolls of sheet lead. McClintock was amazed that any sledge party would have attempted to haul so much largely useless dead weight. The only signs of any food were some tea and about forty lbs of chocolate.

In terms of identifying the members of the party which had been associated with the boat, some indication was provided by twenty-six silver spoons and forks; of these eight bore Franklin's own crest while the rest had the initials or crests of Gore, Le Vesconte, Fairholme, Couch, Goodsir, Crozier, Hornby, and Thomas. One of the watches bore the crest of Mr Couch of *Erebus*.

Rather surprisingly, the sledge was pointing to the northeast and McClintock surmised from this that the party hauling it were returning to the ships and that the skeletons were those of two men unable to go any farther, whom their companions had planned to come back for after reaching the ships.

On the morning of 2 June McClintock reached Victory Point, where Hobson had found the note with the meagre outline of the final outcome of the expedition. Here McClintock placed a copy of the all-important record in the cairn, along with records of his own and Hobson's visits. This document would later be found by Schwatka's party. McClintock also buried a message beneath a large rock three m north of the cairn.

Scattered all around was an incredible assortment of abandoned clothing and equipment which suggested that having sledged it all ashore, possibly over a fair length of time, the party had selected what was deemed essential for the sledge trip south and had abandoned everything else here. The assortment included four sets of boat's cooking stoves, pickaxes, shovels, iron hoops, old canvas, a large single block, a small medicine chest, a Robinson dip circle, and a small sextant with the name 'Frederick Hornby' engraved on it. The abandoned clothing formed a huge heap 1.2 m high. Every item was searched but all the pockets were empty and no names were marked on any of the items.

McClintock ended his own search here, although Hobson had earlier found two more cairns and many relics between here and Cape Felix. Both men were convinced that the section of coast from Cape Crozier to Cape Felix had not been visited by the Inuit since the Franklin Expedition had disintegrated here.

The next year yet another expedition set out in search of Franklin relics or survivors. The contrast with McClintock's search, or even more so with the massive Royal Navy search expeditions, could scarcely have been greater. The search was mounted by a single-minded American printer, Charles Francis Hall, who was convinced that some of Franklin's men had survived and were simply waiting to be rescued (Loomis, 1972). Hall's one-man expedition went north aboard the whaler *George and Henry* in the summer of 1860, bound for the

Frobisher Bay area; Hall's intention was to sledge west from there to the general area of King William Island. Unfortunately *George and Henry* was wrecked and Hall was forced to confine himself to a study of the Inuit and the landscape of the Frobisher Bay area (Hall, 1864).

Undaunted, two years later Hall headed north again, this time aboard the whaler *Monticello*, intending to start his search from Repulse Bay. In fact, he was landed from the whaler well south of Wager Bay in the entrance to Roe's Welcome Sound (Loomis, 1972; Nourse, 1879). He was to stay in the Arctic for five years. As early as September 1864 the Inuit at Repulse Bay told him of two ships which had been lost near Boothia Peninsula, and of their crews dying of starvation, although they asserted that four men had not died (Nourse, 1879:64).

It was almost two years later before Hall heard any more news of the Franklin people. In June 1866, at his camp on Repulse Bay he was visited by a group of Inuit from Pelly Bay. One of the men told of how he had visited King William Island three years before. At a location near Pelly Bay he had found a cairn built by whites, with a wooden signpost on top. He had also found another cairn between Port Parry and Cape Sabine, about the height of a tall man. In it he had found a small 'tin cup,' evidently a record cylinder which had contained a paper; it had been given to the children or thrown away as being of no importance to the Inuit (Nourse, 1879:276). Nearby lay a skeleton and a pile of white man's clothing.

It was not until 10 April 1869 that Hall finally found some tangible relics of the Franklin Expedition. At a Netsilik encampment at Pelly Bay he found a light pink one-gallon stone jug with a broken handle, a copper *kudlik* (blubber lamp) 75 cm by 30 cm and weighing about 2.5 kg, the end of a sword 10 cm long, and a wooden snow shovel 90 cm long made of pine or spruce which the Inuit said they had made from a plank from a ship near King William Island. The ship had allegedly sunk soon after the Inuit had made a hole in it to get timber out of it. Hall's Netsilik informant, Tungnuk, also reported that when the Inuit had discovered remains of whites on King William Island they observed that arms, legs, etc. had been cut off with a saw, as indicated by the marks on the bones (Nourse, 1879:392).

On reaching the sea at Sheperd Bay on the west coast of Boothia, Hall encountered a further Netsilingmiut encampment; he was shown a large silver spoon with Franklin's eel-head crest, which had come from a large island where many whites had died. In one of the snow houses belonging to a man called In-nook-poo-zhee-jook, Hall was shown a large number of articles from the Franklin ships and their owner drew a map of King William Island and vicinity for Hall. The most interesting features and sites identified on the map were as follows: an island called Kee-wee-woo (O'Reilly Island) off which one of the ships had sunk, at a location known as Ook-joo-lik; a site (Too-noo-nee) on the northwest side of King William Island where In-nook-poo-zhee-jook had found two boats; a small island (Kee-u-na) off the southeast coast of King William Island, possibly one of the Todd Islands, where he had seen the remains of five whites, one of whom he believed was Too-loo-a (the name the Inuit had given to Sir John Ross). This body was wrapped in blankets and was unmutilated, whereas limbs had been severed and flesh cut from the other four. No boat had been found on Montreal Island nor had any whites died there. Finally, a boat and the remains of a large number of whites had been found on a small island on the west shore of the inlet immediately west of Point Richardson (Nourse, 1879:398).

On the basis of these reports Hall decided to make a flying trip to the Todd Islands. En route, at an Inuit camp on the ice south of Booth Point, he found a further significant collection of Franklin relics. They had all come from the shore on the south side of Ook-joo-lik, a bay on O'Reilly Island.

On 11 May, Hall camped on one of the Todd Islands where the Inuit said five men had been buried, although Poo-yet-ta, one of the Inuit accompanying Hall, now reported that when he had first seen them the remains had been lying close to each other on the surface, fully dressed and unmutilated. Unfortunately, the island now lay under a deep mantle of snow and Hall was able to find only part of a human thigh bone.

He next crossed to King William Island, where two more of Franklin's men were said to be buried. Near the mouth of the Peffer River the Inuit uncovered a skeleton after digging away the snow. Hall hoisted the Stars and Stripes to half-mast, built a cairn 1.5 m high, and fired a salute over the remains (Nourse, 1879:401). A strong gale and deep snow inhibited any further search.

On a long, low spit farther east, the Inuit indicated the site where another white man was known to be buried. Again the site lay deep in snow and Hall simply built a cairn without trying to locate the remains. Returning to the Todd Islands, he was shown a site on the southwest end of an island where the bones from some of the five skeletons had been seen. At this point Hall was forced to start back to

Repulse Bay; to his intense frustration his guides simply refused to go any farther.

By careful questioning of the Inuit whom he met Hall was able to establish some very interesting points about the Franklin ships and their crews. A Netsilik who had visited O'Reilly Island told how the local people had found a ship beset in the ice offshore. It had four boats hanging at the sides and another above the quarterdeck. A gangway extended down from the deck to the ice.

In-nook-poo-zhee-jook reported that he too had heard that this ship had sunk a little east of the north end of O'Reilly Island, between it and Wilmot and Crampton Bay. The local Inuit had boarded the deserted ship and begun ransacking it; unable to get below decks they had broken into a cabin. There they had found the corpse of a large, heavy man with very long teeth; it had taken five men to lift him and they had left him where they found him. The sails, rigging, boats, and equipment had all been in perfect order.

The local Netsilingmiut had visited the derelict periodically over a period of time, piling their loot in heaps on board with the intention of sledging it all back to their snow houses later. But on one occasion they reached the spot to find only the mastheads showing above the water; apparently they had made a hole in the hull and with break-up the ship had sunk. Subsequently as the ship broke up a great deal of useful flotsam and jetsam was cast ashore.

A short time later fresh tracks of four men and a dog were found on shore nearby; the tracks were those of booted feet and one of the men had taken very long strides. The Inuit tracked them for a long distance and found where they had killed and eaten a caribou (Nourse, 1879:404–5).

In-nook-poo-zhee-jook also reported having found a second boat on King William Island, a little to the west of the one founded by Hobson and McClintock. It contained a large number of skeletons and also a great deal of paper and numerous books. These had been discarded by the Inuit as being worthless and the wind and weather had soon made short work of them. Nearby stood a tent, also containing a large number of skeletons and skulls. The skeletons had been cleaned fairly effectively by foxes and wolves; however, some of the bones had been cut with a saw and some skulls had holes in them. There were also substantial numbers of books and papers here; these were thrown away by the Inuit, except for one book which was taken home for the children to play with and ultimately was torn to pieces (Nourse, 1879:405).

One of the Inuit whom Hall interviewed had also seen a group of whites dragging a boat on a sledge along the southwest coast of King William Island. They were under the command of a man whom they called Ag-loo-ta, their name for Crozier, whom they knew from his involvement in Parry's expeditions. The group of whites had pitched their tent near the tents of the Inuit and the Inuit saw them shooting geese (it was late spring, possibly July). Ag-loo-ta had made a determined effort to talk to the Inuit, and indicated that he and his men were bound for Repulse Bay. The Inuit descriptions of the men were quite detailed: one of them was very fat but the rest were in poor shape; one of the men was missing his upper teeth, one had marks on the bridge of his nose, and a third squinted or was cross-eyed.

Finally, in conversation with the Inuit at the Todd Islands, Hall heard of a site on the west side of the inlet west of Port Richardson where a boat and many bodies had been found. Many of them had been mutilated, apparently for food. This was almost certainly the site at Starvation Cove where Schwatka and his men would later find similar remains.

Although Hall's discoveries predate Schwatka's expedition by almost a decade, it should be noted that Nourse's edited version of Hall's journal did not appear until after Schwatka had sailed north. Thus one may assume that little if any of the above information was available to Schwatka and his men before they went north. This fact, too, helps to explain Klutschak's rather strange statement (p 11) that 'the accounts which he [Hall] managed to obtain from the local Inuit, are admittedly of little importance ...'

For several years after Hall's return south, interest in the fate of the Franklin Expedition or of its records lapsed somewhat, but then in the mid-1870s there was a marked revival of interest. The cause was information allegedly derived from the Inuit by the American whaling captain, Captain Thomas Barry. He reported that while wintering at Repulse Bay as mate of the whaler *Glacier* in 1871–3 he had heard several of the local Inuit talking of 'a stranger in uniform who had visited them some years before, and who was accompanied by many other white men' (Gilder, 1881:3). The uniformed stranger had left a large quantity of papers in a cairn along with some silver spoons.

A few years later, in 1876, Barry had been wintering aboard the whaler *Ann Houghton* at Marble Island. On seeing Barry writing in his log book one of a group of Inuit visiting the ship reported that 'the great white man who had been among them many years before had kept a similar book' (Gilder, 1881:6). At this point one of the Inuit gave Barry a silver spoon with the word 'Franklin' engraved on it.

Barry reported the incident on his return south and stated that the cairn (with the papers) was alleged to be on an island in the Gulf of Boothia (Stackpole, 1965:13). Ebierbing (Eskimo Joe), the Inuk who had been with Hall on both his searches for Franklin relics or survivors, corroborated the story.

Barry's story resulted in several articles in the *New York Herald* and its influential editor, James Gordon Bennett, conceived the idea of fitting out an expedition to try to find the cairn with the cache of documents. John B. Morrison, of the New York whaling firm Morrison and Brown, offered his schooner *Eothen*, under the command of Captain Barry, to transport the expedition to Hudson Bay. And finally, Judge Charles Daly, president of the American Geographical Society (of which Morrison was a fellow), interviewed Captain Barry and was so impressed that he arranged for the American Geographical Society to sponsor the search expedition (Stackpole, 1965: 14). Thus the expedition to search for records of the Franklin Expedition, which is the subject of Heinrich Klutschak's book, was born.

It was a remarkable expedition in many ways. By adopting Inuit techniques and diet as fully as possible, Klutschak and his companions were able to achieve a sledge journey which surpassed any undertaken by whites previously and has rarely been equalled since. In just under one year they travelled some 5200 km. The return journey across the Keewatin tundra from the Back River to Depot Island was made in the depth of the arctic winter, with temperatures persistently hovering around –50°C. Yet there were no fatalities and not even any serious injuries or ill health.

In terms of its primary objective – to locate records of Franklin – the expedition might be considered to have been a failure. On the other hand it was able to confirm the Inuit accounts, reported earlier by Hall, that documents and papers had been found but had been given to the children to play with or had been left to the mercy of the wind and weather. Therefore Schwatka's expedition did make some contribution, even if negative, in this regard.

The real success of the expedition lay in its discovery of a considerable number of skeletons, partial or complete, on the shores of King William Island and Adelaide Peninsula. Invariably Schwatka and his companions buried these remains and marked the site with a cairn. As Dr Owen Beattie explains in his Afterword in this book, however, these cairns can now rarely be relocated so these skeletal remains are lost forever. Another major success of the expedition was in locating, and in many cases recovering, important relics from the Franklin Expedition. These relics, including as large an object as the stem of one of the boats, were transported back across Keewatin by dog sledge to Depot Island and taken to the United States. They were then returned to England and are now housed in the National Maritime Museum in Greenwich, where they are periodically displayed.

III

While we are provided with a reasonable amount of information in Klutschak's account about the other pivotal members of the expedition, namely Schwatka himself, W.H. Gilder, the *New York Herald* correspondent, and the Inuk interpreter Ebierbing (Eskimo Joe), Klutschak reveals very little about himself. He was born in Prague on 3 May 1848, the son of Franz Klutschak, editor-in-chief and late owner of the magazine *Bohemia*, as well as being editor of a number of other newspapers and journals, both Czech and German. Heinrich studied engineering at the German Technical University and, apparently simultaneously, attended the Artillery College; he was posted to the First Artillery Regiment of the Austro-Hungarian Army on 15 May 1866. He was discharged from the regiment on 7 June 1871, when he emigrated to the United States.

According to his obituary in the *New York Times* (27 March 1890), immediately on his arrival in the United States Klutschak signed aboard a New London whaler for a voyage to Repulse Bay; this accounts for the references to earlier experience with whalers in Klutschak's narrative, and also for the fact that Schwatka should have selected him as a member of the expedition, in that he had had previous experience with the Aivilingmiut and may well have acquired some command of Inuktitut. On his return to the United States Klutschak next signed on for a sealing voyage to South Georgia in the southern Atlantic east of the Falklands aboard *Flying Fish* in 1877; on the basis of this visit he published a detailed description of South Georgia (Klutschak, 1881; Boumphrey, 1967).

For some time after his return to the United States, Klutschak earned his living as an interpreter on transatlantic steamers. Then, as we know, in the summer of 1878 he went north with Schwatka to search for relics and/or records of the Franklin Expedition.

Immediately after the expedition's return Klutschak went on a lecture tour in Austria and Germany, presumably promoting his book. The emperor Franz Josef attended one of his lectures and was so impressed that he presented him with a medal. Unfortunately, the story of the brief remainder of the author's life is rather tragic. Returning to New York, he scraped a living as a clerk, private secretary, and errand boy. His most frequent employer was J.C. Morrison of the whaling company Morrison and Brown; the latter often urged him to make use of his education and obvious artistic talents in order to earn a decent living, but Klutschak refused to follow his advice.

In the final years of his life Klutschak suffered from tuberculosis. In January 1890 influential friends, including Morrison and Judge Daly, president of the American Geographical Society, managed to negotiate his admission to the sailors' home, Sailors' Snug Harbor, on Staten Island. Klutschak delayed moving to the home until late March. He started out from his rooms at 320 Broome Street in a heavy snowstorm but the weather forced him to turn back. He died at Broome Street on 26 March 1890, aged forty-two, penniless. His friends in New York covered the costs of his funeral.

IV

Immediately after the return of the expedition, W.H. Gilder's accounts of its activities appeared in the *New York Herald* and within a year he had published a book (Gilder, 1881). For reasons that are not immediately apparent Schwatka himself did not publish any general account of the expedition; perhaps army duties and preparations for his journey down the Yukon River in the summer of 1883 (Schwatka, 1885) preempted his time. It was not until 1965 that an edited version of his private diary of the expedition appeared in published form (Stackpole, 1965). By contrast, Klutschak produced a description of the expedition, in German, almost immediately, and it is this account which is presented here in English for the first time.

Unlike Gilder and Schwatka, Klutschak had no steady source of income, so he had a strong financial incentive to publish a book about his travels. He was almost certainly aware that there was a considerable market for such a book in that there was much interest in arctic exploration in both Germany and Austro-Hungary. In the case of the latter, the attempt by Karl Weyprecht and Julius Payer to reach the North Pole aboard *Tegetthoff* in 1872-4 (an attempt which led to the discovery of Franz Josef Land instead) received enormous popular support and attention, as did Payer's account of the expedition (Payer,

1878). With regard to German aspirations and activities, the rather modest efforts of the First German Polar Expedition, led by Captain Karl Koldewey in 1868, resulted only in a special supplement to *Petermanns Geographische Mittheilungen* (Koldewey, 1871). Its sequel, the Second German Polar Expedition, again led by Koldewey, ended in the dramatic loss of the *Hansa* in the ice. The even more dramatic story of the crew drifting on ice floes caught the popular imagination (Hartlaub & Kindeman, 1873).

The demand of the German-speaking world for arctic adventures had also been quite well supplied with translations of accounts of the major British expeditions during the Royal Navy's protracted search for the Northwest Passage. Thus German books about John Ross's first and second voyages, Parry's first and second voyages, Franklin's second overland expedition, and Back's journey down the Back River all appeared within a few years (and often within only a few months) of the publication of the English narrative. There had also been earlier accounts by German-speaking participants in two of the British expeditions to the Arctic. Johann Miertsching, a Moravian recruited as Inuktitut interpreter aboard M'Clure's *Investigator* during the latter's search for Franklin, published a book about his experiences within a year of his return to Europe (Miertsching, 1855). Later, A. Becker, who sailed with Sir Allen Young aboard *Pandora* in 1876 during an attempt at the Northwest Passage, published a report of that expedition in the same year that Schwatka's expedition went north (Becker, 1878). The following year, while Klutschak and his companions were still in the Arctic, Emil Bessels, medical doctor and chief scientist on Charles Francis Hall's last expedition aboard *Polaris*, went into print (Bessels, 1879), giving the German public all the dramatic details of Hall's death and of the remarkable drift of Captain Tyson and half the expedition's complement on an ice floe.

Clearly, Klutschak was catering to a well-established demand for arctic exploration literature. Yet it is also worth noting that he was filling a very important gap in the German literature. First of all, no German translation had been produced about McClintock's discoveries of Franklin's remains, skeletal and otherwise, on King William Island in 1859 (McClintock, 1859). Second, and probably more important, Klutschak's book provided the first extensive German-language account of the Inuit of the Canadian Arctic. There had been no German translation of Hall's detailed report on his life with the Inuit of the Frobisher Bay area in 1860–2 (Hall, 1864), and as a result of Hall's death aboard *Polaris* in 1871 even the posthumously produced English-language account of his second expedition to the Repulse Bay and Pelly Bay areas in 1864–9 did not appear until after Klutschak and his party were in the Arctic (Nourse, 1879). In fact, no German version of the book was ever published. Admittedly, John Ross and his companions had spent considerable time among the Inuit of Boothia in 1829–32, while Parry, Lyon, and their fellow officers had spent a great deal of time with the Aivilingmiut of the Repulse Bay and Igloolik areas, an interaction which is dealt with in the German editions of Ross's and Parry's books which appeared in 1835–36 and 1824 respectively. But such interaction was relatively superficial compared to the deliberate near-total immersion in Inuit life on which the success of Schwatka's expedition so largely depended.

The significance of the person to whom Klutschak dedicated his book should not go unnoted. Count Johann Nepomuk von Wilczek was an ardent supporter of polar exploration and research. He had personally financed (to the tune of 40,000 florins) Payer and Weyprecht's Austro-Hungarian North Pole Expedition of 1872–4 (Payer, 1878). In the spring of 1872 he had even made a trip to the Arctic himself aboard the schooner *Isbjørn*, which landed a depot of provisions on the northern tip of Novaya Zemlya for the main expedition aboard *Tegetthoff*, in case her men were forced to retreat there from their attempt at the Pole (Payer, 1878).

After *Tegetthoff*'s return von Wilczek lent his considerable support to Karl Weyprecht in promoting his scheme for a co-ordinated international scientific program in the polar regions, which ultimately came to fruition as the First International Polar Year (Baker, 1982; Corby, 1982; Barr, 1985). Not surprisingly, one of the stations of the First International Polar Year, the one on Jan Mayen Island, was established by Austro-Hungary in 1882 and was again entirely financed by von Wilczek (Wohlgemuth, 1886; Barr, 1985). Indeed he even took part in the voyage of the Austro-Hungarian Navy's *Pola*, which established the station, joining the ship at Bergen. Unfortunately, heavy ice conditions prevented the ship from reaching the island on the first attempt and she was forced to return to Tromsø to refuel. At that point Count von Wilczek was obliged to return south, but at least he had seen arctic ice face-to-face.

Thus in dedicating his book to von Wilczek, Klutschak was honouring a fellow Czech who had generously funded both polar exploration and polar science and had made at least two trips to the Arctic himself as a clear demonstration of his keen interest.

V

It is important to notice the thrust of Klutschak's original title, *Als Eskimo unter den Eskimos* (*As an Inuk among the Inuit*). On his first two expeditions, Hall had demonstrated the enormous advantages to be gained by adopting Inuit food, clothing, habits, and methods of travel. Sir John Rae had taken up Inuit customs even more enthusiastically. But Klutschak was the first writer to introduce the concept to the German-speaking public. It is no exaggeration to state that the remarkable success of this small, minimally funded expedition – an enterprise that achieved the longest known sledge journey undertaken by white men and returned home safely, having considerably increased knowledge about the ultimate fate of the Franklin Expedition – was due entirely to the deliberate decision by Schwatka and his men to adopt Inuit ways as quickly and as fully as possible.

In his preface Klutschak declares that the Inuit will form the major focus of his book, and he follows through on this intention. The result is an anthropological document of enormous value. It was no accident that Franz Boas, widely regarded as the pioneer ethnographer to work among the Inuit of the Canadian Arctic, relied heavily on Klutschak's observations when discussing the various Inuit groups of northeastern Keewatin (Boas, 1888). For instance, Klutschak and his companions were the first white men to spend any amount of time with the Utkuhikhalingmiut. But they met several different Inuit groups, so Klutschak's descriptions are useful for their comparative value. Nowhere does this emerge more strongly than in his remarks about the tensions (which at one stage threatened to erupt into overt hostility) between the Aivilingmiut, with whom they were travelling, and the Netsilingmiut of the Adelaide Peninsula.

Both in anthropological terms and generally, Klutschak's story complements the accounts of the expedition written by Gilder and Schwatka. On two occasions, however, his portrayal of events is the only one available. Only Klutschak wrote about the period from mid-May 1880 until early August, when the expedition members whiled away their time on Depot Island in Hudson Bay waiting for the *George and Mary* to pick them up for the long voyage home. More important, however, during the trip overland, from 6 August 1879 until early December the same year, the group split in two, with Klutschak being in charge of one party and Schwatka the other. Thus only Klutschak describes the Inuit of the Simpson Strait area and only he provides details about the trek south to the rendezvous at the 'Dangerous

Rapids' on the Back River. It was during this journey that Klutschak came upon Starvation Cove. During earlier visits by Schwatka and Gilder the site had still been deep in snow, but now the litter of skeletons and debris could be seen and properly examined for the first time. Starvation Cove, it became clear, was the most southerly point to have been reached by the last desperate survivors of the Franklin Expedition.

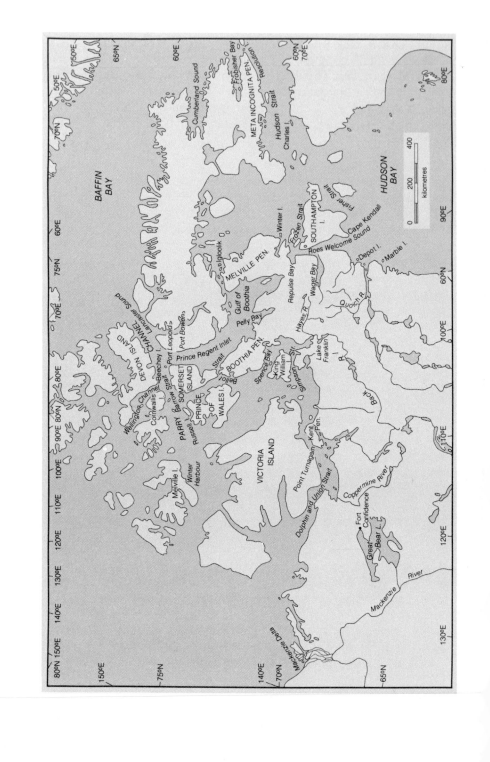

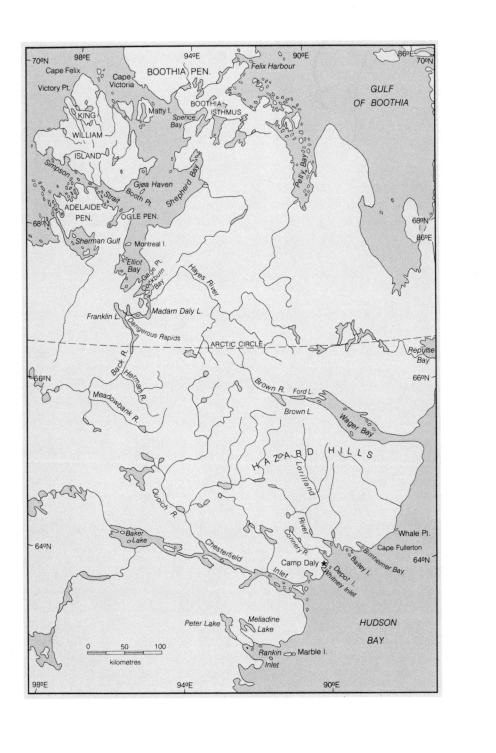

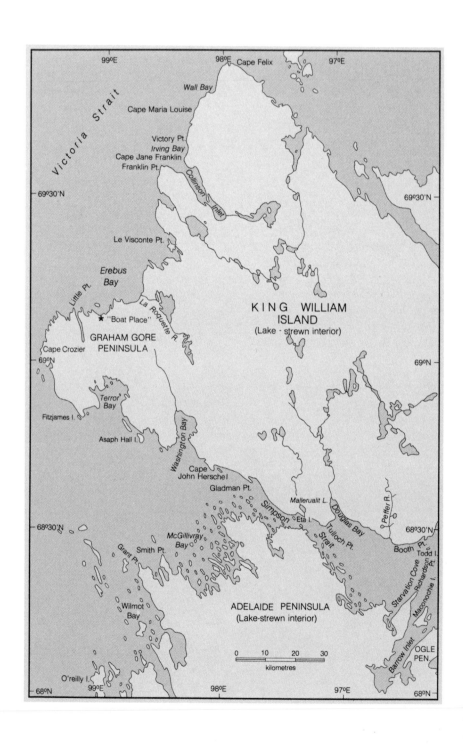

99°E   98°E Cape Felix   97°E

Wall Bay

Cape Maria Louise

Victory Pt.
Irving Bay
Cape Jane Franklin
Franklin Pt.

Victoria Strait

Collinson Inlet

69°30'N   69°30'N

Le Visconte Pt.

Erebus Bay

Little Pt.

La Roquette R.

★ "Boat Place"

GRAHAM GORE PENINSULA

Cape Crozier

KING WILLIAM ISLAND
(Lake · strewn interior)

69°N   69°N

Terror Bay

Fitzjames I.

Asaph Hall I.

Washington Bay

Cape John Herschel

Gladman Pt.

Mallerualit L.

Simpson

Eta I.

Douglas Bay

Tulloch Pt.

Pelter R.

68°30'N   68°30'N

McGillivray Bay

Smith Pt.

Grant Pt.

Strait

Booth Pt.
Todd I.

Starvation Cove
Richardson Pt.

Wilmot Bay

ADELAIDE PENINSULA
(Lake-strewn interior)

Macanochie I.

Barrow Inlet

OGLE PEN.

0 10 20 30
kilometres

O'reilly I.

99°E   98°E   97°E

68°N   68°N

Overland to Starvation Cove

Heinrich Klutschak

Preface

The aim of these pages is to present to the reader by means of maps, words, and pictures the experiences, incidents, and impressions accumulated by the members of the last Franklin Search Expedition on their journey to King William's Land in 1878–80. Far from laying too great an emphasis on the main object of the expedition, the author has made it his task to pay special attention to the inner life of the small party and to make a point of accentuating those moments when the .men struggled with their own resources against the fierce elements of the polar regions. Across the wide snow-and-ice fields of the North lies the route, prepared by Mother Nature for North Pole travellers of the future. Here the adequate animal resources provide the answer to the question of their survival, while the native of the cold zone represents his best and most sterling companion. To become acquainted with the Inuk in his unmodified condition as a child of the North, to demonstrate his capacity for being civilized, and to prove that it is possible to use him to advance geography and the natural sciences, these were the author's particular objectives.

Respectfully dedicated
to
His Excellency
Count Johann Wilczek

Royal/Imperial Privy Councillor and Chamberlain,
Hereditary Member of the Upper House of the Austrian Reichsrat,
Commander of the Imperial Austrian Order of Leopold, etc.

as
a patron and promoter of arctic exploration

The author

The Search for Franklin

The history of the so-called Northwest Passage, that is, a connecting route by sea between the Atlantic and Pacific oceans around the north coast of the American continent, is a theme in the larger history of the world almost as persistent as the history of civilization. Its original basis lay in the struggle between nations for possession of the trade route to India. Columbus died believing that by his discovery among the great waters of the setting sun he had found a new route to the rich Indies. But his lands turned out to be islands off a major continent which spread its bulk through all five latitudinal zones of the earth and appeared to form an obstacle to any route to the still distant East. Unaware of the riches which Columbus had placed in her hands, Spain sent Magellan south; he sailed south around America via the strait now named after him, reached India, and by effecting the first circumnavigation provided proof that the earth is round.

What Spain had achieved through Magellan, England attempted to achieve by sailing around the north of America, and with John Cabot's voyage of 1498[1] began the attempts to discover the Northwest Passage, a major concept which England sought to make a reality with all the well-known energies of the Anglo-Saxons in order to compete with her Iberian rivals. Despite defeats by Drake, Cavendish, and Burroughs the latter managed to maintain their supremacy over the route around Cape Horn even long after England had become the sovereign of the seas. During Napoleon's campaign in Egypt the discovery of the aforementioned passage for the exploitation of the trade with China became a vital matter.

These were the powerful motives which, combined with the love and mysterious lust for adventure and the craving to enrich knowledge, maintained Great Britain in a position to support her arctic explorations so strongly. Cabot's efforts were followed by those of Hudson,[2] Sir John and James Clark Ross,[3] and Parry[4] but it was not until the terrible and still unexplained fate of Sir John Franklin's expedition that his dying men found the last connecting link between the two oceans, which with its colossal icebergs and limitless barriers of eternal icefields will remain eternally impassable for individual ships, and even more so for world trade.

In May 1845 Sir John Franklin ordered the anchors weighed aboard his two expedition ships, *Erebus* and *Terror*, and embarked on his third voyage within the Arctic Circle with 23 officers and 115 men of the British Navy. Off the Whalefish Islands on the west coast of Greenland, along with three men who had become unfit for duty, he transferred the last letters from his crews for dispatch home. His words at this point, in a final message to the British Admiralty: 'I now have provisions for a full three years and am very heavily laden but in view of the proximity of the ice I believe that we can scarcely expect heavy seas,' represent the last report which he was destined to make. On 25 July of that same year the whaler *Prince of Wales*, under Captain Dannett, saw the two ships working their way into the ice of Lancaster Sound, never to sail open waters again. In the fall of 1846, when no news of the expedition had arrived over the summer, Sir John Ross expressed his fears to the Admiralty that the two ships were beset in the ice off the west coast of Melville Island and could proceed neither forward nor back. Time has confirmed how well-founded this view was, but at the time it found no credence and it was felt that these fears were not conclusive enough to send assistance for Franklin so soon after his departure. But when no news was received by the summer of 1847 anxious premonitions compelled the authorities to send four boats with complete crews, with the ships of the Hudson's Bay Company to its trade posts in the northern part of America; having reached the north coast by various routes they were to search for the missing men. With Dr Richardson, Dr Rae, and Messrs Anderson and Stewart[5] began the series of search expeditions which were to be pursued for thirty-three years with courage, skill, and energy, and whose humane efforts and scientific results represent a pearl in the history of our century. In 1847–50 the aforementioned boat expeditions reached the north coast of America via the three large rivers flowing to the Arctic Ocean from the Far North of America, the Mackenzie, Back, and Coppermine, and returned with the certain knowledge that Franklin's ships had never reached that coast.

In the fall of 1847 two ships also sailed with supplies around Cape Horn in order to penetrate through Bering Strait and bring assistance to the expedition in case it executed its plan and returned safely via that strait. At the same time Sir James Clark Ross in the ships *Enterprise* and *Investigator*, following the route specified in the orders of the Franklin Expedition, was to search for it in Wellington Channel and along the coast of North Somerset in 1848 and 1849. After this second expedition had placed its ships in suitable winter quarters, sledge trips were made in various directions, depots were established, and everything possible was done to make some contact with the missing men. The ingenious commander went so far as to have foxes trapped, pieces of paper with messages attached to their tails and necks in such a way that they could not easily be pulled off, and then had them released again. But in vain. Not the slightest success crowned the efforts of these philanthropic hands. Private parties were also cruising the northern waters to the same end. Thus a Captain Thomas Moore in the ship *Plover*, Captain Robert Sheddon in his private yacht, *Nancy Dawson*, and Captain Kellett in the ship *Herald* had penetrated through Bering Strait from the Pacific while Dr Goodsir (a brother of A.D. Goodsir, who was assistant surgeon aboard *Erebus* of the Franklin Expedition) with Captain Penny in the *Advice* and Captain Kennedy in the *Albert*, were searching for the missing men from the Atlantic side. What joy the bold, tireless searchers experienced when some small sign seemed to indicate the proximity of those they sought, and what fearful disappointment so frequently followed due to the malicious tricks of the northern environment. Thus one sunny day Dr Goodsir was scrutinizing the coast of the nearby land with close attention, telescope in hand, when he thought he spotted an upright post on a point. It had to be; his eyes could not be deceiving him. A seaman also saw the same post through the telescope. The ship altered course and all eyes were rivetted on the point; great was the joy and jubilation at finally being on the track of the missing men. But the sun had now ceased to play its malicious trick and where the supposed post had stood there was in reality only a pointed piece of ice. With experiences such as this Dr Goodsir returned home, just as they all had returned home, unsuccessfully; but these results did not weaken the desire of the public to find the missing sailors. On the contrary, they simply forced the government to pursue the outfitting of further search expeditions with abundant funds.

The two warships *Enterprise* and *Investigator*, under the command of Captain Collinson and Captain M'Clure, were entrusted for a second time with their earlier mission and were dispatched around Cape Horn and north through Bering Strait, while *Resolute* and *Assistance*, with two smaller ships under Captain Horatio Austin, Captain Ommanney, and Lieutenants Sherard Osborn and Bertie Cator, attempted to raise the mysterious veil which had concealed Franklin's fate via Baffin Bay. This squadron was joined by *Lady Franklin* under Captain Penny, *Sophia* under Captain Stewart, *Felix* under Sir John Ross, as well as by *Advance* and *Rescue* under Lieutenants De Haven and Griffin; the latter ships, sent by the United States, were known as the 'First Grinnell Expedition.'

Captain Ommanney found traces of the missing ships and on 27 August 1850 Captain Penny, who distinguished himself from all the others by his energy and activity, succeeded in actually finding the first winter quarters of the Franklin expedition at a small harbour on Beechey Island. Among other traces there were in particular three graves; on headboards which served as gravestones were inscribed the names and dates of three men who had died here in the winter of 1845–6. But this information marked the limits of the squadron's achievements.

In 1852 another fleet set off, under the command of Sir Edward Belcher. It consisted of the ships *Resolute*, *Assistance*, *North Star*, *Pioneer*, and *Intrepid*, and if possible was to penetrate to the Parry Islands since there was a strong possibility that Franklin had sought a passage west via that route. Of all these search expeditions this was the least fortunate; not only did it fail to reach its goal but it had to abandon all the above-named vessels, beset in the ice, with the exception of the *North Star*. The latter also took the crew of the *Investigator*, which also had been abandoned in the ice in 1852, back to England. Almost incredibly, *Resolute* drifted south with the ice, was taken in tow by a whaling captain in Davis Strait, was restored, and given back to the Queen of England by the United States under the name of the *Anglo-American*. As is well known, a desk was recently constructed from parts of this historically remarkable ship and was sent to the President of the United States from England.

After the loss of so many ships and so much money, the British government found itself compelled to abandon further searches and declared Sir John Franklin and his companions to be lost without hope. The public thought otherwise; they were convinced that further attempts had to be made; it was even thought that some of the men might still be alive, waiting for help. But even if not it was felt that the search for clues as to their fate, and for the place where the heroes had found their last resting place, should continue.

To this period, too, belongs the Second Grinnell Expedition aboard the *Advance*, under Dr Elisha Kent Kane, who had taken part in the

First Grinnell Expedition as medical doctor and was of the view that Franklin had possibly sought a route to the west, northward from Lancaster Sound. He was the first to conceive of the theory of an open polar sea. The loss of his ship, his sojourn in the North, and his adventurous return will still be remembered by many of my readers.

How small was the hope for the continued existence of Franklin and his people was proved by oral reports and by items which Dr Rae received from Inuit families when he was sent north by the Hudson's Bay Company on his second search for Franklin in 1851–4. 'White men,' he was told, 'were seen alive by Inuit, just as they were in the process of reaching a major river with a view to heading south up it to reach their own people.' Years later, on an island near or in the mouth of Back's River, the natives found many corpses and many items which proved incontestably that these could only be the remains of the lost expedition.

But in England they would not be appeased even with this news; the expedition commander's noble-minded widow, Lady Jane Franklin, appealed several times to the British Admiralty to fit out further search expeditions and when no attention was paid to her petitions she resolved on fitting out her own expedition yacht, the *Fox*, with the last of her private funds which had already been significantly reduced by her generous contributions toward that same goal. Captain (now Admiral) Sir Leopold McClintock took command and men of arctic experience such as Captain Young, Lieutenant Hobson, and Dr Walker voluntarily joined the undertaking without expecting payment. The successes of this voyage were so great and will have to be referred to so often in the following pages that they cannot be passed over cursorily. Captain McClintock left Aberdeen on 1 July 1857 but became beset in the ice in Baffin Bay. While imprisoned in the ice his ship drifted for 242 days in a zigzag course which covered 1194 miles from 75°24′N to 63°30′N. *Fox* finally reached Bellot Strait on 20 August 1858 and here went into winter quarters. Early in the spring of 1859 sledge trips were undertaken; during one of these the captain made contact with a number of Inuit from whose accounts he was able to determine that he should make the island of King William's Land the focus of his spring activities.

He outfitted one detachment under his own leadership and with two sledges, one man-hauled, the other pulled by dogs, he headed for the northeast coast of King William's Land and travelled southeast along it. Meanwhile his first officer, W. Hobson, headed directly to the most northerly point of the island, Cape Felix; he was to follow the northwest coast of the island with an equally strong party in order to search for the wreck of a ship which supposedly had been found by the natives and for years had satisfied their need for wood, iron, and copper. The wreck could not be found but at Cape Felix, Hobson stumbled onto unmistakable proof that Franklin's men had been here. Despite the stormy spring weather, the party travelled south, cheered by their find of a British ship's flag and many smaller relics; in a cairn Hobson found a small tin box containing the world-renowned document which, however brief, after thirteen years provided the first written news of the missing men, although at the same time it seemed to confirm the fears of the entire interested world as to the fate of all the men. We will have an opportunity later to reproduce a copy of the document verbatim and hence here we will limit ourselves only to presenting its most important points.

Until the beginning of September 1846 everything had gone well; the ships had slowly made their way west but on the 11th of that month, to the north of Cape Felix, ice masses had blocked the ships' progress, locking them in forever and so setting insurmountable limits to the hopeless struggles of the bold seafarers. The first winter passed well and safely, but when the following summer brought no liberation, on 7 June 1847 the commander died. Death took a toll of a further nine officers and 15 men and the dreaded scurvy, the terror of many a northern traveller, seems to have appeared in epidemic proportions. The new commander, Captain Crozier, felt obliged to abandon the ships at the end of April 1848 and with the remaining 105 men to retreat to the river explored by the British naval lieutenant George Back in 1833–5 and named after him (also known as the Great Fish River). By following that river south Crozier hoped to reach one of the Hudson's Bay Company's trading posts. No matter how courageous was this decision to retreat, only a few miles to the south Hobson was to see from an abandoned boat and from the skeletons lying in it how soon the physical strength of this large party began to fail. Meanwhile McClintock was searching in vain on Montreal Island for the traces of the party which had been reported to Dr Rae as having starved to death near the mouth of the Back River. He then travelled along the south coast of King William's Land heading north and west. Despite the deep snow he found a skeleton lying in the sand near the coast of Washington Bay. Its position confirmed the view that illness, exhaustion, and hunger had slackened discipline and that in the process of arbitrary attempts at self-preservation the individual members of

Crozier's command had come to one of the saddest ends which one can find in the whole of history.

Scurvy had appeared as a hindering factor in the state of health of the searchers, too, and this may well have been the main reason that McClintock left the scene of the tragic end of the Franklin Expedition which had been sought for so many years. Notwithstanding the fine results which a summer sojourn on the island must have produced, he returned to his ship, put to sea, and returned to England.

For a long period of years, the matter appeared to have been settled with McClintock's voyage. But then in 1869 Captain C.F. Hall, a private American citizen, stayed among the Inuit of his own volition and, accompanied by them, visited Adelaide Peninsula and also the adjacent part of King William's Land. His finds, and the accounts which he managed to obtain from the local Inuit, are admittedly of little importance, but his trip, lasting only 90 days, provided proof that a sojourn in the area during the summer was the only means of searching for any written records of the Franklin Expedition. This is assuming the premise that Franklin's men, faced with imminent death and with no chance of rescue, buried the treasures they had accumulated for science, for the sake of posterity.

Captain Young had also realized this necessity and in 1875 had attempted to reach King William's Land in the yacht *Pandora*, fitted out through the combined funding of Lady Franklin and James Gordon Bennett, in order to search for such documents. He was obliged to abandon his project 120 miles from his goal and, supplied with provisions for only one year, barely escaped the icefields which threatened to imprison him. This time it was the ship which prevented the execution of a well-prepared plan. If, despite more than thirty years of effort, one were to dare to believe the rumours which the returning whalers had annually been bringing back to the civilized world, and were to send out yet another expedition to complete the long sequence, then it would have to try to reach its goal by means of an overland march from a suitable point in Hudson Bay, totally independent of ships.

Travel overland and a summer sojourn on the site of the catastrophe were thus the two basic principles on which the last Franklin search party of 1878–80, whose activities I shall now discuss, based its plans.

CHAPTER ONE

Schwatka's Franklin Search Party, 1878, 1879, and 1880

Members of the expedition. Lieutenant Frederick Schwatka.
Eskimo Joe. Funds. Contributions. Departure.

A major part of the success of an arctic expedition in general lies in its proper organization and equipment. The party's aim and intention of travelling with sledges hauled by dogs as the sole motive force determined that the number of participants on the trip could only be very small, and that Inuit had to be taken along to perform the necessary work, other than that involving the areas of science and research, that is, as hunters and dog drivers. Naturally, such an expedition could consist only of men with a certain inner drive who, on the one hand, possessed a special interest in the aim of the expedition but, on the other hand, also possessed the necessary physical attributes.

Immediately after the first call of the American Geographical Society which undertook the sponsorship of the new expedition which was to be sent out, Lieutenant Frederick Schwatka of the Third U.S. Cavalry Regiment volunteered to command it. Lieutenant Schwatka was born in the state of Illinois in 1849,[1] a third-generation descendant of Germans who emigrated from Danzig to America. At an early age he had moved with his parents to Salem, Oregon. There, in the thinly populated regions, he enjoyed his first education, but life at an outpost of civilization may have contributed greatly to the fact that he began to seek the goal of his vocation in a military career.[2] At the Military Academy at West Point he received a thorough grounding in that comprehensive knowledge which, while leading his command in the North, earned him the respect of his companions and the admiration and trust of the Inuit. Life on the frontier with the U.S. Army in direct contact with the various Indian tribes encouraged the development in him of those constitutional relations which life in the North demanded, and his interaction with fellow officers and men, both in and

Lieutenant Schwatka

out of uniform, taught him that strict discipline can be achieved if one knows how to lead a command without giving too many orders. He attempted to make use of a fairly long leave in the eastern states to study medicine, but the war with the Sioux prevented completion of this plan.[3] After the end of the war, in which Lieutenant Schwatka took an active part, he volunteered for the leadership of the expedition,[4] and its fortunate success is largely to be ascribed to his wide knowledge, good judgment, energy, and correct handling of his men.

Apart from the recruitment of another three whites, Schwatka asked that an Inuk be hired as interpreter and hunter. William H. Gilder of New York, acting as correspondent for the *New York Herald*,[5] Heinrich W. Klutschak of Prague, who filled the role of artist and surveyor, and Frank F. Melms of Milwaukee, Wisconsin, all took part voluntarily in the execution of the planned operation, while Joseph Ebierbing, known as Eskimo Joe and then living in the United States, was hired to handle the duties mentioned above.

Joe Ebierbing (his real name is Adlala) was born on Cumberland Sound on the west coast of Davis Strait among the Nurrarmiut and (as far as can be determined from his own accounts) first went to England aboard a whaler at the time of the Crimean War. He stayed there for a winter, and his wife learned English so quickly that after their return home Captain Charles F. Hall retained the family as his permanent companions during his first sojourn in the North.[6] Accompanying this gentleman, Joe and his family saw the United States for the first time, but after a winter had elapsed they returned to the North in order to accompany Captain Hall on his journey to King William's Land.[7] After yet another return to the United States the Inuit family accompanied the American *Polaris* expedition. After the death of the commander, C.F. Hall, the crew, along with the ice, became separated from the ship in a storm. Joe and his family found themselves with this party, led by Captain Tyson, and were thus involved in its famous southward drift of 1500 miles on an ice floe.[8] The kudos for having fed and kept alive eighteen people through that severe winter largely belongs to Joe and when, after his return to New York, the American people presented him with a home in Groton near New London, Connecticut, it was doing nothing more than rewarding, as right and conscience demanded, the loyalty and discretion of a man who had proved himself so brave, and who had contributed so greatly to American arctic exploration. But even now Joe did not remain unemployed; in 1873 he accompanied the naval steamer *Juniata* on her voyage to rescue the survivors of *Polaris*'s crew, and in 1874 Joe took part in the voyage of *Pandora*, whose goal of King William's Land was unfortunately not attained.[9] Thus in total Joe had accompanied two North Pole trips and three Franklin expeditions. He had already begun to feel at home in America but when death robbed him of his wife and a twelve-year-old daughter and when, during his stay in the North with Schwatka's party he found a new wife who did not want to follow him to the United States, he left his home and the comforts of civilization in order to make his real home his place of residence for his last days.

Outfitting the expedition demanded no great amount of funds, indeed only $450 in cash, which was subscribed by private individuals. All the greater and more appreciated were the contributions in kind which, within only a few days, placed the expedition in a position to be adequately, even abundantly provided with the means which it most needed to achieve its task. The supply of provisions for the period of our sojourn in Hudson Bay both prior to beginning the overland journey as well as after our return there, until we started for home, was easily purchased with our quite limited funds. But for the trip itself no supplies of foodstuffs could be taken along, or certainly not enough for the entire duration of the trip, due to the limited means of transport. But since it was intended from the start that the numbers of our party would be reinforced by Inuit, and since we anticipated the need to obtain their good will by means of their well-known preferred treat of bread and molasses, we first ensured that we had a good supply of both and used the cash contributions to buy these items.

Other items of foodstuffs which were donated included: 200 lbs of their famous corned beef from Wilson and Co. of Chicago; 500 lbs of hardtack from the Wilson bakery in New York; and also 400 lbs of margarine, which turned out to be very suitable, and even was preferable to butter in terms of its keeping qualities in a very cold climate.

With regard to canned goods we had been given apples, tomatoes, and other fruits to try. Arctic expeditions should be advised, however, that if they have no means of preventing such items from freezing, they should take them only for the initial period. After the first thawing occurs the contents quickly go bad, and hence after the first wintering they are worthless if they have been kept outside the ship. In our case condensed milk was the exception. The last cans, which we used on 16 June 1879 on King William's Land, were just as good as the first ones in the summer of 1878 before they froze, although they had been stored with the other items.

The greatest care was taken in equipping the expedition with firearms and ammunition. Donations in this area included: two Winchester magazine rifles with 1000 centre-fire metal shells and the necessary percussion caps and apparatus for reloading them from Winchester and Co.; two Remington army rifles, 1000 shells and similar accessories from Remington and Co.; from Whitney and Co. one fine Treadmore target rifle worth $115.00, 1000 shells and 1000 extra bullets ready moulded and with all the accessories for Joe, our Inuit interpreter; from the Merwin Co. one Evans 26-shot magazine rifle with 500 shells and accessories for special testing by Lieutenant Schwatka; also two Russian Army revolvers (Smith and Weston) with 500 shells. For each of these rifles separate lock and breech components were also donated and the various metal shell companies also made significant contributions.

The Commissariat of the Weapons Administration of the Militia of the State of New York also gave the party 20 muzzle-loading rifles with spare parts for trade with the natives. Other donations included 600 lbs of various types of shot, 1000 lbs of lead in pigs from the Newark Lead Company, and 300 lbs of powder of various types from various companies. Contributions of hunting necessities and percussion caps (40,000), etc. were also received; the expedition was very well provided with everything both quantitatively and qualitatively. We were also well supplied, through donations, with needles, fish-hooks, tin dishes, mugs, china dishes, headbands, etc. for trading, and the Lorillard Company gave the expedition the magnificent quantity of 600 lbs of tobacco.

In terms of instruments, James Gordon Bennett donated a Negus pocket chronometer worth $350, a sextant worth $85, and an aneroid barometer worth $50 as well as nautical almanacs. The firm of C.J. Tagliabue of New York donated six alcohol thermometers with Fahrenheit scales. In terms of medicines we took only a small bottle of opium and some eyedrops. Wood for building dogsleds was donated by the W. Poillon Co. of Brooklyn.

Transport of the expedition and its equipment to its destination was undertaken by the firm of Morrison and Brown of New York. That company commissioned Captain Thomas F. Barry to take the expedition north with him in his schooner *Eothen*, which was departing on a whaling voyage to Hudson Bay, and to land it at a point convenient to the commander.

The steamer *Fletcher* took the *Eothen* in tow at noon on 17 June 1879, and accompanied by numerous friends of the expedition members, many members of the American Geographical Society, and some gentlemen from the British Embassy, our expedition set off, for a stay of at least 2½ years in the North on the basis of the very small total outlay of barely $5000.

Sojourn in Hudson Bay from August 1878 to 1 April 1879 as an Acclimatization Period

The sea voyage. Resolution Island. The first Inuit. Landing the party. Establishing camp. Activities at Camp Daly. A great success at imitation. The Aivilingmiut. First hunting trips. The Inuit on the fall hunt. Five days on Bailey Island. The transition to winter. A blizzard inside the tent. An ice house. The sleeping bag. Skin clothing. The first snow house. Christmas. New Year. Northern lights. The first sledge trip. An unpleasant situation. Marble Island. Whaling ships in winter quarters. Scurvy. Return to Camp Daly. Preparations for our departure.

A sea voyage in a small sailing ship has little new to offer. We were shaken out of the monotonous daily routine of seamen's activities, in which we gladly took part in order to alleviate the boredom, at least as long as we had nothing special to do, by the sight of the first iceberg. This year it hove into view long after we had passed the usual ice belt, which extends far southward to the Grand Banks off the coast of America. It was sketched and discussed, but to our great discomfiture Captain Barry was a man who considered it a matter of seamanlike efficiency to give icebergs as wide a berth as possible,[1] and often went too far in this respect. All the icebergs which hove into view were counted and entered into the journals with scrupulous accuracy, and it would be much too troublesome to quote all the references from the journals, entries made as being important at the start of a protracted voyage. Each of my readers will have had his own experiences in this area and no matter how accurate and strict one may be initially in keeping a journal, despite one's good intentions, if it is not one's profession or special duty the final pages are often deficient or, even more often, completely blank.

After a lengthy period of hoping and wishing on 20 July we finally passed Resolution Island at the entrance to Hudson Strait, having tried for almost a week in thick fog to negotiate the ice fields which were blocking the entrance to Hudson Strait. As regards the character of the island, its appearance in late July–early August was sufficient to give us an impression of the North. Quite insignificant both as to size and height, its barren granite hills, still snow-covered in places, rose from a mass of ice floes; the occasional iceberg grounded on its shores was, with its vast size, by far the most beautiful feature of the view. The north coast of Hudson Strait had the same characteristics and only our fairly long sojourn at sea, out of sight of land, could allow us to find any pleasure in watching the passing panorama of the land, from one headland to the next.

Around 10 P.M., as we were lying motionless in a flat calm in a sort of twilight about three nautical miles from Meta Incognita, waiting for a favourable wind and attentively watching our sails, we spotted three small dots near the land, which were soon heading toward us with amazing speed. They revealed themselves to be Inuit in kayaks (sealskin boats). Greatly amazed at being greeted in their own language when Joe shouted 'Saimu!' (an Inuit greeting), they came aboard and asked the captain to wait until a larger, so-called women's boat (*kuni umiak*),[2] made from wood and walrus hide, could arrive. Apart from several natives it contained supplies of meat and clothing which they wanted to trade to meet their needs in terms of ammunition, etc. And indeed it was not long before, with slow oar strokes a box filled with people arrived, whose only claim to the description 'boat' was that it floated in the water. Its Inuit occupants quickly clambered aboard. The reader would himself have to be in a position to experience a first meeting with these people, and to survive the experiences which utterly shook our so-called civilized sensibilities, in order to appreciate the scene which developed that night on *Eothen*'s deck. The scene was quite indescribable and quite a lengthy period elapsed before both parties engaged in bartering. The selection of items offered for sale was not great; the most important items traded were three dogs which Joe selected for the expedition from the animals brought along.[3] Even more sparing were the words used in this trading operation, for lack of any extensive knowledge of each other's language. The word *pilite* (give)[4] played a major role; then, following both the display of the item and of the price and after both parties had agreed, either *aamila* (yes) or *atgai* (no). With this the deal was concluded. We will have more to cover in the course of these pages and hence for now we must take a rapid departure from these Inuit and take advantage of the favourable breeze which arose to sail on, heading west across Hudson Bay to reach our goal.

In view of the expedition's objectives a favourable point for us to land would have been Repulse Bay on the east coast of the American mainland (66°30'N, 84-5°W), but this bay possessed the unpleasant feature that both it and the straits linking it to Hudson Bay, namely Roes Welcome (between the mainland and Southampton Island) and Frozen Strait (between Melville Peninsula and Southampton Island) are made impassable by pack ice for the bulk of the year. In order to learn about ice conditions we visited the natives living in the vicinity of Cape Fullerton (64°N) on the mainland and held a consultation with them.[5] After a brief discussion it transpired that a point at or south of Cape Fullerton possessed exactly the same advantages and fewer disadvantages, as compared to Repulse Bay if one intended using the Back or Great Fish River as a travel route to King William's Land.

Between 63° and 66° the west coast of Hudson Bay possesses two deep inlets, namely Wager Bay and Chesterfield Inlet. In the spring both provide a good routeway across the smooth sea ice, and it requires only a relatively short overland march to reach the Back River, whose lower course again promises to provide a good sledging route to the northeast and north. But also, with regard to the Inuit who were to accompany the party and thereby support and strengthen it, it was essential to select a spot which lay near a native settlement in order to buy dogs and local clothing. The mainland near Depot Island was such a location, and *Eothen* dropped anchor in the harbour between the island and the mainland coast at 9:00 P.M. on 6 August 1878.[6] Next morning we began landing the expedition's belongings and the natives, who annually trade with the whalers who call here, diligently lent a hand.

We only put ashore such provisions as were necessary to last the party through the winter. The rest was handed over to the ship's captain for caching under his supervision in the interim.

At 3:00 P.M. on 9 August the expedition members went ashore and began erecting their primitive, but perfectly functional housing.[7] By 11:00 P.M. our tent was already pitched and for the time being we had moved our stores above high water mark and covered them with a spare sail borrowed from the ship. A short sleep on solid ground in the land of our desires strengthened us for work next morning, and when we awoke we saw *Eothen* slowly disappearing over the horizon. We were alone, cut off from civilization among a people who were new to us, in

Schwatka's summer camp

that a group of Inuit had moved across from Cape Fullerton and had pitched their tents near ours.

The first few days were used to arrange our place of residence as practically and comfortably as possible given the circumstances, and each of us undertook his share in trying to achieve the goal of a well-regulated household. Gilder, a regular Jack-of-all-trades, assumed the position of honorary carpenter and immediately tackled the job of making a table, etc. from the wood from a whaling ship wrecked on the rocky coast, which he had found on the beach. Melms took over the administration of our supply of ammunition, and by unanimous vote the provisions were turned over to me with the duty of satisfying five stomachs to the best of my abilities. Such a multifaceted job as mine, that is, artist, geometer, meteorologist, and cook certainly has its idyllic side, but it seemed best to me in the morning and evening when I was bustling about with pots and pans in my stone-built, roofless kitchen. After my work was finished I could enjoy watching the superb appetites of my boarders.

A summer sojourn in the North is magnificent. For a short period of 6-8 weeks Mother Nature adorns this area of solid granite formations with her show, unfolding a rich splendour with a great range of pleasant variations despite modest means.

In general the daily schedule of our party was dictated by a desire to achieve and by curiosity. Immediately after we had finished breakfast, which consisted of a good caribou steak, the pancakes so customary in America, and coffee which bore little resemblance to the Arabian beverage, everybody dispersed at his discretion. Immediately after we had successfully organized our place of residence, we measured a baseline for a triangulation survey with the maximum possible accuracy given our very modest means. From this we began work on a coastal survey which at least would be better than the one which formed the basis of the available maps. We always carried rifles with us, and almost daily we would kill some geese or ducks which swarmed on the numerous larger and smaller ponds nearby. Many of my most interesting landscape sketches derive from this initial period of our stay at Camp Daly, as we had named the site of our camp, in honour of our enthusiastic sponsor, the President of the American Geographical Society, Mr Charles P. Daly of New York. Many comical events were interspersed with our normal daily routine. Here is an example.

In terms of locating our maps accurately the compass was useless due to its great variation, and in order to determine the south point we used the transit of the planet Jupiter across the meridian. It was nighttime. I stood a few hundred feet from Lieutenant Schwatka, holding a light so that I would be visible; he was to direct me to move right or left using a duck-call whistle which imitated the shrill tones of a duck. At first everything went well, but as Jupiter was reaching its culmination and the moment to make our determination arrived, I was confused by a series of calls following rapidly one after the other. Only when Lieutenant Schwatka began laughing loudly did I realize the reason. The ducks on the nearby ponds had wakened, thought they were hearing the morning quacks of one of their own kind, and the entire area began to resound with loud quacking. In the meantime Jupiter crossed the meridian and our south point remained unfixed. The firm of Holberton in New York, from whom we acquired the whistle, may congratulate themselves on the imitative fidelity of their product.

Thus each day brought its pleasant and unpleasant incidents, while the evening always found us in very lively intercourse with the Inuit. They soon moved from their previous campsite to our camp on the mainland and pitched their tents around ours. Thereby Camp Daly became quite lively, and whether inside the tents or outside, this new

Amoustadt (as we jokingly called our village) always offered scenes worthy of contemplation from the standpoint of the ethnographer.

Our Inuit all belonged to the Aivilik group and for the past fourteen years[8] had often come in contact with the whalers; hence they were no strangers to associating with whites. Their original area of residence was around Repulse Bay. But since, as already indicated, that site can only rarely be visited by ships, and then only with difficulty due to the heavy ice conditions, they had moved to this area between the 63rd and 65th parallels, and had made the area between Wager Bay and Chesterfield Inlet their new home. With our arrival two subjects claimed their special attention. The first was our supplies of biscuit and molasses, both of which they consider to be special and unique delicacies. The second was our superb firearms and indeed, after a short stay, it was these which ensured that we would be accompanied on the actual journey by the best and most efficient among them. Inuit were to be found in our tent at all hours of the day; small and large they derived special pleasure from perusing the illustrated newspapers which we showed them. But their curiosity reached its climax over the magazine and breech-loading rifles. They were not satisfied at simply admiring the quick-firing mechanisms but would beseech Lieutenant Schwatka, who in this context was happy to start a conversation which could be led around to the topic of the trip, to strip the rifles down for them. We very quickly learned a simple version of their language, and even if none of us achieved the proficiency of speaking and understanding it perfectly (since the speed of their delivery presented a major obstacle to the latter), we succeeded in learning enough over the course of a few weeks to make ourselves passably understood. Prolonged association with whites had added to their language so-called pidgin-English, that is, a mixture between their own language and English; initially this made comprehension easy, whereas in our later contacts with more northerly Inuit groups still unfamiliar with whites, it turned out to be an obstacle to understanding their language. As the first whites who had established their residence next to those of the natives, we were a special object of instinctive curiosity; but they were for us too, and to an even higher degree, with regard to life-style and customs. But we knew only too well that a primary condition for the execution of our plan was that we should discard our mantle of civilized philosophies of life as much as possible, and acclimatize ourselves to their clothing, food, and style of accommodation, in accordance with the conditions of the country. Whether we were studying the internal arrangements inside one of the Inuit tents or travelling around with the male population while hunting, often all day long, our purpose always remained the same: wherever we were we could learn things that would be of use to us. On trips either with the natives or without them we acclimatized more and more to a certain level of comfort, in terms of food and sleeping arrangements, and by late September we were eating raw meat quite often.

Each of us longed to try his abilities as a caribou hunter, and in early September, as the settlement around us daily became smaller and as the individual Inuit families dispersed into the interior for the productive fall hunt, we took turns at accompanying them. By the end of August the caribou have finished moulting and the pelt is long enough to be suitable for making clothing for the coming winter. Also the animals have been fattening all summer long on the magnificent lichen pastures and at this period the quality of their meat reaches its peak, and because of the abundance of fat it is also most suitable for preserving for winter food supplies.

The dogs had spent the summer on a nearby island where they had been able to procure enough food due to the great tidal range (c. 20 feet) and to the great abundance of smaller fish species in the coastal waters. Now they were fetched from their asylum, and one fine morning one would suddenly see a family break camp and pack the tent and also the

Inuit departing for their hunting grounds

most essential implements partly on the backs of the dogs, just as one would load a mule, and partly on their own backs. Items which were not taken along, eg, the blubber lamps, were simply covered with rocks on a conspicuous point, and in case deep snow covered the spot it was made easily recognizable by a small stone cairn, if it had to be relocated in winter. Cairns of this type, which from a distance look like a man, are also often found deep in the interior; they serve either as a sort of signpost for the natives, when they are called *inuksuk* (singular), or are erected over a cache of caribou meat and are then called *tuktuksuk*. In the latter case the animal's antlers project from among the rocks to make it more easily recognizable. Laden in the manner described, the Inuit set off for the interior. If they catch sight of caribou the woman stays behind to watch the dogs, while the man drops his load and sets off after the game. If he is lucky and kills one or more caribou the tent is pitched right on the spot and stays there for as long as the surrounding area can supply food. If the caribou become scarce the Inuit move on again; only when the snow falls does the family settle at some point which is known to be rich in game.

Under such circumstances one's night's rest is well-regulated, comfortable, and quite bearable. A tent like this is still a passable place of refuge as compared to the campsites which the Inuit seek out when they are alone, unaccompanied by their women. If one has been running all day long from hillock to hillock, spying for game and if, as a result of standing or sitting has progressed from a sweating condition to a sort of trembling, then shortly after sunset a shelter against the wind is built from a few large rocks, a cover or skin is stretched across the two parallel walls thus erected, the irregularities of the interior are somewhat levelled out with moss, and the campsite for the night is ready. The first nights which we spent in such quarters alongside our snoring Inuit companions were nothing more than rest periods. But we soon got used to ignoring the cold, which was already very noticeable at night.

Our tent at Camp Daily became perceptibly more comfortable each time we returned, but we would scarcely have been home a few days when we would be driven to go out hunting again. On 5 August we received a visit from the captains of three whalers which had just arrived.[9] Uninformed as to our presence, they were not a little amazed to find whites living for the summer in what they had assumed was an Inuit tent. Their visit produced the advantage for us that they placed a boat at our disposal so that we could make more extensive trips. The first purpose of these trips was to make a proper survey of the coast

Inuksuk

Tuktuksuk

eastward and northward, but this was not achieved since an equinoctial gale which blew up drove us onto a rocky reef (Bailey Island) in the leaking boat and pinned us down there for a full five days.[10] Here we experienced the first unpleasant days of our northern sojourn. The three of us, Lieutenant Schwatka, Melms, and myself, lay on top of a boat sail within sight of our tent at Camp Daly, our clothes totally soaked, beneath a tent which was also saturated by the violently driving rain. By the end of this period we had consumed the last remnants of our supply of biscuits and had boiled our coffee beans for a second time; a crow which Melms had accidentally shot the previous day was the only item we could list on the menu. But it was our boat which gave us the greatest concern. The island was so small and rocky that despite our small number we had only a very limited space in order to secure the boat. Moreover this was only at half-tide; at every high tide we had to go out and frequently had to battle the waves for possession of the boat. Finally, on the sixth day wind and water abated and we reached Camp Daly, where Gilder was just about to send out a search party for us.

With the onset of the abovementioned gale and of a period of rainy weather which lasted almost three weeks, the fine northern summer had come to an end. The cold began to be perceptible; it hailed, then snowed. The ponds froze over and ice also began to form along the coast. Winter had arrived. It ceased to be very cheerful living in just a canvas tent; my ink froze and my fingers were too stiff to write and soon conditions were making apparent the unsuitability of our civilized clothing and of our accommodations. Since there was absolutely nothing outside to tempt one to linger there, one only got up when breakfast time had arrived, and froze until dinner was ready. After each meal, in order to get warm quickly one crawled back under the few muskox hides which we had been lucky enough to buy from the Inuit. But our tent was quite a unique dwelling. Our breath adhered firmly to the walls and roof of the tent. This frost crust grew to a thickness of one inch and when a storm began blasting over hill and dale, shaking the tent pole and the canvas, we would be subjected to a real snowstorm inside. Now we had to make a start at altering our life-style completely. We had to become Inuit and every day we would look carefully across at our neighbours' dwellings. Two families still remained with us and were having to struggle with the same unpleasant conditions as ourselves; we wanted to be able to duplicate as quickly as possible what they were doing. Thus far they were still hesitating, probably afraid of a thaw but on the morning of 27 October,

when there was a particularly noticeable cold snap and our thermometer dropped to -27^0F (-23^0R[11] or -29^0C), they went to work.

Slabs of ice 7 feet long and 4 feet wide were cut from the ice of a
nearby pond, which was about 8 inches thick; these were placed
together in a circle about 14 feet in diameter, in such a way that the
longer edges came together, with the individual slabs inclined slightly
inward. Water-soaked snow served as mortar and did its job superbly,
while an opening 2 feet high and 2 feet wide was made to serve as the
entrance. A sort of flat roof-frame, made from a couple of posts, was laid
across the upper part, an old sail was stretched across this and the new
ice house was complete.[12]

To give a more practical appearance to the whole, some small
additions, not unlike dog kennels, were added to the main structure to
provide separate sleeping chambers, the old tent was repitched as a
store and kitchen directly in front of the entrance and connected to the
whole by a sort of antechamber. Gilder had made a door from a couple
of planks; although it was not very airtight it closed the entrance. We
moved into our new residence with our belongings on 1 November and
after two days had elapsed we began to feel at home. Everything was
stowed securely, even including a barrel of chalk and a little cask of
arsenic, both of which had been contributed by an unknown donor for
some unknown purpose. But the item which most belonged in an ice
house, our beer, was not taken inside, since the seven or so bottles
which we had brought ashore had been emptied with the advent of the
first frosts to save them from freezing. Our dwelling was heated by two
Inuit lamps, carved from soapstone; they had wicks of moss and burned
blubber and they raised the temperature significantly as compared to
that outside. We sometimes also cooked on this type of lamp and
everything that required it was dried over another one which was
brought in for just that purpose. But the main cooking apparatus used
by the party during this period was a gasoline stove, which was
superbly suitable for a permanent base but which might be inappropri-
ate for taking on a sledge journey because of its fragility.

With our change in dwelling we were also faced with the need for
acquiring warmer clothes and especially more suitable bedding. The
necessary skins were provided by the many caribou which the Inuit
who had stayed with us had killed on the hunts they made from Camp
Daly, and with these Lieutenant Schwatka ordered sleeping bags made.
For their bedding the Inuit use untanned, dried caribou skins beneath
them and a *qipik* (a large blanket made from the best, well-tanned
skins, which covers the entire family) as their top covering. We had a

Camp Daly in winter

type of sleeping bag made from well-tanned skins, narrow at the bottom and widening upward, and with a fringe cut from caribou skin at the top. As with the *qipik* this could be pulled close around one's face, resulting in a better fit. The Inuit call such a sleeping bag a *snikpuk*[13] (from *sinikpuq*, he, she, or it sleeps), and as we would have abundant opportunity to experience, for the northern traveller it is a treasure which, next to his rifle, he should always be very careful to maintain in a good, dry condition.

But using the sleeping bags is very closely associated wth abandoning every civilized item of clothing, no matter what type of material it is made from. No matter how low the temperature may be, one always sweats when walking in furs and if one wears cloth shirts they become damp. If one then has to sit quietly one feels one's damp underclothing freezing. And if one crawls into one's sleeping bag in a damp shirt, it too becomes damp and can be dried only slowly and with great difficulty. The opposite applies if one lays one's shirt aside until a warmer season and dresses exclusively in furs. Adoption of this adjustment to the style and cut of the Inuit offers the only guarantee of effective clothing. At home one wears an *attigik*, an over-parka with attached hood with the skin side against one's bare body. The pants (*qarliiq*) are wide, reach only to the knee, and are also worn skin-side inside: footwear consists of two pairs of stockings, the inner pair with the hair side inside, the outer pair the reverse. Over the latter one wears a pair of boots of caribou hide if the weather is cold and completely dry. Otherwise one wears sealskin boots. For a sojourn outdoors one wears a second suit with the hair side outside. All items of clothing are sewn with cords of plaited caribou sinew, which takes the place of our thread. Along the edges of the garments where the air can easily reach one's body are sewn fringes, also cut from caribou skin. On the one hand they break the wind; and on the other they permit air ventilation and make it impossible to become sweaty.

But this clothing also has other advantages. It is extremely light and comfortable, allows one completely free movement, and permits one to dress and undress rapidly, something which, as we will see later, is an advantage not to be overlooked in snow houses.

In such an outfit, at least as far as the outer man was concerned, we began to see ourselves making the slow, gradual, progressive transformation into Inuit; immediately, of our own volition we began making trips in our new clothing. But the more one learns the more one recognizes how little one knows; this truth became very obvious to us on our excursions. Each of us accumulated his own experiences. Here is an example of this.

One day, as a consequence of a small bet that with the south wind which was prevailing there should be caribou in the vicinity, Lieutenant Schwatka and I set off on a hunting trip. A secondary purpose was to check whether an inlet running about eight miles into the interior[14] was the mouth of a river or not. Despite low-hanging clouds we set off, having first wrapped our sleeping bags in oil cloth and strapped them on our backs, stowed a few pieces of biscuit in our pockets, and slung our rifles over our shoulders. Lieutenant Schwatka had decided that today was the day scheduled for our departure and when he got up he had pulled on his travelling outfit, and hence the weather had not troubled him at all. He set off, and I with him. Half an hour later it began to snow. We just had time to reach the inlet when a blizzard obscured both shores, and without us giving any thought to caribou we were suddenly so close to them that they spotted us and fled before we could take aim. One shot cracked out, but the noise it made was the only success it achieved. Around midnight we reached the head of the inlet. The snow was now heavier than ever, and since we could see nothing we either had to turn back or find shelter. The latter seemed preferable. Assisted by a small boy whom we had taken with us, and who was delighted at being allowed to carry a rifle, we set about building a snow house. Slowly and extremely clumsily we arranged one block of snow on top of another; the higher the structure rose the greater the care we had to take. A snow house (and by this I mean one built by Inuit and not our effort) is a dome built of snow blocks set on top of each other in a spiral arrangement, built without any internal support whatsoever. An Inuk places one block on top of the other with such precision and sureness that it is a joy to watch him; he places the final horizontal keystone in place with equal skill. In most cases the symmetry leaves nothing to be desired. Moreover, the time he takes is relatively short, in relation to the work. But in our case things were different. Long before we reached the stage of inserting the keystone the blocks began collapsing, and only after great effort could we persuade the keystone to remain hanging in the ceiling. At 4:00 P.M. we spread our sleeping bags on a sort of wax cloth to protect them from getting wet from the snow, and began getting undressed. Our hut resembled a large bell rather than a dome, and this shape instilled a certain caution in us, in that we took care not to knock against the walls. To get enough room to manoeuvre we each waited outside the snowhouse until the others had undressed in turn. The temperature had been around zero all day and hence the snow had been melting on our clothes and especially our footwear, and had soaked them completely. But snce we had no worries about a sudden change in temperature we either placed them under our sleeping bags or used them as pillows. Finally we all crawled safely into our bags, the lieutenant on his own and the boy and I sharing a bag. Some refreshment, a smoke, a chat, and our day was over.

In the grey morning light we stuck our heads out of our sleeping bags and felt a cold wind blowing into the snow house; we scarcely dared look for the cause. But when it came time for us to continue our journey, and we made energetic preparations for getting up, what a pitiful sight our residence presented! The snow had settled; wide, gaping cracks had developed in the walls, the roof had sunk, and the keystone hung like a sword of Damocles above our heads. Furthermore the wind had swung into the north and had swept the newly fallen snow in through the numerous chinks and hence we were lying in a small snowdrift. Even through our sleeping bags we could feel that the snow immediately next to us had been melted by our body heat; it began to feel unpleasant inside our skins and it would be really uncomfortable when we tried crawling out, digging our clothes out from under the snow in our birthday suits and then struggling into them. The shape of the snow house admonished us to hurry; it could not possibly survive for long, and hence we finally began pulling on our frozen garments. Although each of us was fully occupied with this task neither of us could restrain his laughter whenever a glance at his neighbour made him aware of the strenuous convolutions in which the other was engaged in his attempts to pull his stockings on. This lasted for about a good half hour, until we finally reached the outside world again, on all fours via the small entrance to the snow house. Our first thought was: where to now? The snow lay 1½ to 2 feet deep; blowing snow obscured the distant view, and hence there was really no choice but to start back. We ploughed along with great effort, and it will come as no surprise to anyone who has waded through deep snow that since we had not drunk a drop of water for more than 24 hours we were tormented by a severe thirst. At the head of the inlet we took turns at chopping through the ice, which was about two feet thick, with a large knife. Having broken through the last of the ice the boy uttered the word 'Imiq' (water) as the water came bubbling up in the hole. We each quickly knelt down and gulped down a good mouthful but, alas, the inlet did not represent the mouth of a river – the water was salt. At least we had achieved one of the purposes of the trip, but when we got home, exhausted, we took care not to tell Gilder and Melms how we had procured this information. This trip had taught us a good deal; from then on, when in doubt as to whether we were on fresh water ice or salt water ice, we studied particularly the texture of the ice itself.

Each time we returned from such a trip our ice house seemed more attractive than before and when at the beginning of December we replaced the roof with a snow dome which was both aesthetic and functional, both the design and the value of our accommodation reached the peak of convenience. The auxiliary structures of ice were also demolished and replaced by snow houses, and our residence was thereby expanded in area. The cheerfulness inside was also enhanced by our excellent progress toward acclimatization, and the healthy humour which Lieutenant Schwatka possessed in inexhaustible measure spiced many a meal of which both the content and the mode of cooking left much to be desired. The Inuit gradually came in from their hunting grounds and Camp Daly grew into an impressive village of snow houses. It appeared most beautiful on a dark night; the round shapes of the houses, here and there half covered by snowdrifts, gave the appearance of mounds of earth thrown up by gigantic animals, and yet a light glowed through the slabs of ice from thc well-lit interiors, transposing the amazed observer into the midst of a labyrinth of little crystal palaces. The shadows which darkened the transparent ice slabs here and there revealed a lively amount of activity and busy movement. This was life, indeed a world of its own, and no matter how meagre the conveniences encountered here, such an ice house appears like a palace when a cold northwest wind drives the snow in dense clouds and darkness prevents one from straying outdoors.

Christmas did not pass unmarked, and Eskimo Joe was called upon to impress upon his countrymen the importance of this festival. A Christmas dinner was arranged for both ourselves and the Inuit, a target shooting match was organized, and then we accepted invitations from the Inuit to their houses, where we took part in their sociable games, which will be described in detail later.

A few days later, accompanied by one Inuit family, Lieutenant Schwatka left us to determine personally, by means of a reconnaissance trip, the suitability of the selected route to King William's Land, while the rest of us made preparations for a visit to the ships wintering at Marble Island. We wanted to send home via the ships letters about our initial sojourn, although there was really little to write about.

Not once did we have the opportunity to see the northern lights in their full splendour, which has been described by so many people as being so magnificent and grandiose. And yet almost daily we could clearly see bright patches which looked like clouds in the sky; here and there a few rays would appear and once even several rows of them, but to my knowledge they never attained the full development of the aurora borealis, as Lieutenant Karl von Weyprecht described from his careful observations with the Austro-Hungarian Polar Expedition off the coast of Franz Josef Land, as being so beautiful, colourful, and uniquely striking.

We observed the phenomenon as it slowly developed, gazing intently at the western sky, but our location was too close to the magnetic pole for us to be able to see the aurora borealis unfold in its complete magnificence of colour. All the forms indicated, rather, a corona borealis, but even its development was indistinct.

New Year's Eve came and went, and as the sun climbed we wished that the season would arrive which would allow us to set out for our cherished goal, King William's Land. The various rumours which were to have formed the basis for our searches turned out to be totally groundless. The stories of Captain Thomas F. Barry, who along with the firm of Morrison and Brown, had wanted to fit out a whaler at the expense of our party, revealed themselves to be total falsehoods. Nonetheless, Lieutenant Schwatka opted to pursue the course he had started, with a view either to locate relevant documents, in case such documents had been cached, by means of a summer visit to the site of the Franklin catastrophe, or to establish with certainty, by means of a closely conducted search, that further searches for Franklin, his men, and their fate, would be simply a fruitless exercise. Thorough execution of this plan was our one and only New Year's wish.

On 8 January Gilder and I set off on the trip to Marble Island, accompanied by several Inuit families.[15] Our sledge caravan, consisting of about sixty people, fifty dogs, and eight sledges presented a colourful picture on the wild expanse of ice in the first rays of the morning sun. The clumsy-looking fur outfits of the women with the sack-like, widened appendages at the shoulders and feet of their suits stood out in sharp contrast to the cheerful games of the chldren, who turned somersaults as they ran, leaped on and off the sledges, and played hide-and-seek between them. In this lively scene the shouts of the dog drivers mingled with the howls of the dogs whenever the tip of the long whip whistled too close to their ears. So it continued for seven days, our route being along the coast the whole distance. In the evening we would stop, snow houses would be built, and in the morning we would set off again. One evening the vague outlines of our destination appeared on the horizon, and we had every hope that we would reach it next day. It was still pitch dark when we set off on the 14th; sunrise found us on the north side of the nine-mile-wide channel which separates Marble Island from the mainland. The strong tidal currents through this channel do not permit the ice to form solidly in it until a large bay nearby has frozen over. While the expanses of sea next to the coast are covered by thick ice by the end of November, it is sometimes March before a natural bridge forms across the channel to the island. On this occasion the channel in question was covered only with drifting ice and while one group, to which Gilder had attached himself, began the crossing with their sledges and dogs, the rest of us left ours behind; even the women had to remain on this side of the water. Each armed with a stick, we began the crossing and soon encountered areas of shattered ice over which we had to continue by leaping; elsewhere we had to crawl across thin, newly formed ice, about 2-2½ inches thick, spreading our weight as widely as possible and keeping a fair distance between each other. In contrast to river ice, sea ice is flexible rather than brittle and with every step we could detect the surface sinking resiliently. When we found another ice floe beneath our feet we would rest for a few minutes then continue our trotting run. This continued for about 1½ hours without a break; the island itself began to appear out of the mist but its shapes were concealed by a mass of fog which threatened to transform into reality our fears that there was ice-free water in its vicinity. In fact, the ice now became even thinner, and the group to which Gilder belonged had the misfortune to break through at a weak spot. At a temperature of –41°C an involuntary sea bath is certainly far from being one of the most pleasant surprises, and if Gilder had been alone it could easily have been very dangerous for him, as in the case of Dr Sonntag, Dr Hayes' companion on his 1859–61 polar expedition, who died as a result of breaking through the ice.[16]

Here again an Inuit survival technique was invaluable. Gilder had plunged more than hip-deep into the cold water, and as soon as he had clambered out the natives fell on him and also on a woman who had suffered the same fate, and began to rub them and their clothes with snow. The dry snow easily soaked up the major part of the water, then the mass of snow and ice which had formed as a result of this operation was knocked off again. But Gilder's situation was still serious, especially since his pants were frozen stiff and could not even be removed and replaced with others; naturally they greatly impeded his walking. Yet it was essential that he keep moving constantly so that his body would generate enough heat to offset the chilling effect of his frozen clothing.

Around noon we reached the open water; as we suspected it stretched for a distance of about half a mile between the mobile ice floes and the stationary fast ice of the island. The water was covered with a very thin ice crust but the numerous walrus surfacing through it demonstrated, if nothing else did, that it would not be strong enough to bear us before the flood tide gave way to the ebb. The Inuit accompanying us placed the greatest faith in the reversal of the movement since the drifting ice floes would be pushed from the mainland against the island by the seaward current of the flood tide. But it was still a considerable time to the turn of the tide and this inactive wait on the open ice at such low temperatures was far from pleasant. Hence we sat, stood, or squatted at the edge of the ice and gazed at the rocky shape of the island, which in the rapidly falling darkness seemed to move farther and farther away from us. Thirst tormented us most and we spent most of the time eating snow. But then the Inuktitut shout of *mana* (now) joyfully reached our ears. We stood ready to cross onto the fast ice bordering the island; in the darkness we noticed that the thin ice crust mentioned previously had now been smashed into a porridge between the ice floes as they rammed together. In the pitch black night crossing this dangerous spot demanded some care, but one stride and we were over. We reached a fairly large pond and immediately began licking at splinters of ice which we chopped out with our knives.

Since by preference the Inuit are extremely sociable, even on this occasion they lay down in a circle flat on the pond, with their heads together, and began chopping. They first blew on every little piece before putting it in their mouths, in order to raise the temperature of the parts touching their gums or tongues sufficiently that they would not stick to the ice. One cannot quench one's thirst by eating ice or snow, and especially not with the latter. It is natural that the technique used by most arctic travellers is almost as widely condemned by everyone since the amount of water obtained by melting small quantities of snow or ice in one's mouth is very small in relation to the amount of time devoted to it, and hence only increases one's desire for a good drink. As regards causing cases of illness such as inflammation of the throat, this might only be caused by eating snow and ice if the people involved were accustomed to getting their drinking water by melting snow or ice. In this process the water will usually be drunk at temperatures well above zero. We, however, attempted to obtain our water from beneath the ice cover on ponds wherever possible and hence only drank very cold water. As a result eating snow or ice never produced any symptoms which might have provided some proof of the abovementioned hypothesis.

The remainder of our march across the island, which stretched east-west for about 15 miles,[17] was a very strenuous exercise, especially for Gilder, whose trousers were still totally rigid. We reached the steep, very rocky south coast and, following it west, searched fruitlessly for a long time for the harbour. Since Gilder could no longer keep up with them, we let the Inuit go on ahead and continued the trek on our own. In terms of acclimatization it represented a very fine test of our abilities.

We advanced slowly along a narrow path which followed the coast of the island like a border along the snow-covered ice-foot formed at the high tide mark. Steep rock walls rose on our right; to our left the ice had dropped some twenty feet with the ebbing tide leaving a sheer ice cliff; the grinding produced by the two surfaces rubbing together down there made us realized how essential it was to avoid this abyss. Soon we were faced by a rock face some seventy feet high; this represented a serious obstacle in view of Gilder's limited mobility. Our path did not continue any farther west and we began the task of clambering up the cliff. Moreover, our pocket chronometer chose this time to run down, and we had to take advantage of a stop halfway up the snowbank which we were crawling up, in order to wind it up again. It was a delightful job in the cold and darkness, and the time it took me to find the clock and the key beneath Gilder's furs, and indeed to take care of the job myself in the darkness was quite sufficient to grant my ice-crusted companion whatever rest he could derive, given the conditions. Having reached the top we walked for a few minutes, but then I again had to let my companion rest a few moments and hence it was around 12 midnight before we spotted a red light against the darkest area in the otherwise black, starless sky, which is known as a water sky and always indicates where there is open water in winter. It disappeared, and I had begun to think that I was the victim of an optical illusion when the light reappeared, close enough for us to hear answers to our shouts. The Inuit had reached the ships and some men had been sent out for us. Half an hour later we had reached shelter after an unpleasant, strenuous, and dangerous trip.

Four whaling ships[18] lay in winter quarters in the harbour on Marble Island (which is so named from the whitish, marble-like limestone[19] of which it is composed). In daylight their appearance presented a remarkable picture as they all lay, without yards, and walled up with snow, alongside or astern of each other.

We had been spotted on the ice that morning and a boat had even been sent across the island to fetch us, in case the ice did not close, but of course we had been carried from the westernmost point of the island to its eastern end; hence, although almost all the officers and men from the ships, totalling 120 men, had gone out to search for us with lanterns, they had only spotted us again now, around midnight.

From a social viewpoint life on Marble Island was very pleasant, especially when the other party, including Lieutenant Schwatka and Melms, reached it.[20] But in terms of acclimatization and health conditions we immediately realized how useful and beneficial the months we had spent at Camp Daly had been. The state of health of the men aboard the ships was really lamentable; scurvy had not only revealed its symptoms but, if I may express myself as a layman, had reached quite epidemic proportions.

Like the majority of shipowners, the whaling owners were concerned more with profit than with the state of health of their employees; hence the latter were instructed to eat raw meat as their sole antidote against scurvy.

Partly due to the large number of wintering ships, partly due to the meagre results of the fall and winter hunts of the Qairnirmiut who live nearby, meat was available only in very small quantities this year.

In particular, the Portuguese (natives of the Azores and Cape Verde islands) aboard one ship were suffering greatly and two of them already lay apparently hopelessly sick. Apart from their robust constitutions they were able to thank only the considerable kill of walrus and seal which began subsequently for their later recovery. Marble Island possesses some historical significance with regard to scurvy, as may be seen most clearly from the small graveyard where, between 1871 and 1880, the number of graves had increased from one to twenty-three.[21] However, the fact that scurvy can be countered is proven by Schwatka's party, which revealed not the slightest symptoms of the disease during a sojourn of more than two years. Our stay aboard the ships was of quite long duration, and in terms of preparations it was used as opportunities presented themselves, for completing our complement of dogs.[22] We also received from the various captains, officers, and crews many small contributions which gave excellent and useful service as trade goods on our later journey.

We started back for Camp Daly on 1 March 1879. Equinoctial gales

Whaling ships in their wintering harbour, Marble Island (Klutschak's original painting). Reproduced by permission of Mystic Seaport Museum, Inc.

howled constantly in our faces for the entire trip. But this arctic storm had lost its terror for us; not only were we dressed in Inuit clothing, but even our hides were toughened against the climate. The nearer the date for our departure for the North approached the more attractive the prospect became. We even renounced the conveniences in which we had sometimes still indulged and tackled the final preparations in a mood of restless activity and with the greatest zeal. Each of us had long since packed the few items which he wanted and was allowed to take along; outside in the cook tent stood chest after chest and barrel after barrel, ready for departure day. King William's Land was the goal to which our every effort was directed, and the subject of every conversation during the last days of our acclimatization period, which had been accomplished with such usefulness and success.

TABLE 1
Temperatures (°C) from 14 August 1878 until 31 March 1899

| Month | Temperature (°C) | | | | |
	Month	First half	Mean for second half	Max.	Min.
1878					
August			8	14	3
September	0	2	–2	8	–6
October	–7	0	–14	9	–30
November	–13	–13	–13	–5	–35
December	–27	–29	–24	–13	–44
1879					
January	–34	–30	–38	–19	–45
February	–26	–29	–23	–14	–51
March	–22	–27	–17	–6	–37

CHAPTER THREE

The Trek to the Arctic Ocean Watershed, 1 April–4 May 1879

The departure. Organization of the travel routine. Sledges and dogs. Provisions. Division of the party. Daily routine. Construction of snow houses. Drilling water holes. Interior arrangement of the snow house. Feeding the dogs. On the march. A hunt. Wolves. Downhill. Wager Bay. A five-day storm. A muskox hunt. A northern desert. Torture for the eyes. Prospect of better regions. The height of land and the Arctic Circle.

1 April had been set as the date of our departure for King William's Land and by 11:00 A.M. all preparations were complete and everything was ready for the departure. The heavily laden sledges, whose total load amounted to 4500–5000 lbs, the dogs harnessed in front of them, and the figures dressed in heavy fur clothing all combined to form a group full of life, such as is rarely to be seen in these regions. Standing around the travellers, and dressed in lighter clothing, were the Inuit of the Aivilik group who had spent the winter in our company; at our departure they shouted a final 'Tavvautit!' (Farewell!) as Lieutenant Schwatka gave the signal and the sledges finally got under way to the cracking of whips, the howling of the dogs, and the strenuous co-operation of everybody present.

We made only very slow progress over the first hill and through the rough shore ice; but as soon as we had passed the latter and the going became smoother, the speed of our little caravan increased. Observation Hill, the site of our Camp Daly observatory and about 300 feet high, disappeared behind the headlands we had already passed. One final glance at the area which had formed our place of residence for eight months, and we left the sea ice to head up the channel of the Connery River,[1] which on his reconnaissance trip at the beginning of January Lieutenant Schwatka had identified as a very practical route for the start of our overland journey. When one is travelling with Inuit the first day's travel is never a long one. Partly because the dogs were unaccustomed to such heavy loads, and partly because of the late hour of departure, we covered only about eight miles, although it was late before we made camp.

The Inuit are a people for whom the prime and only consideration in life is that they have enough to eat; if they see a good quantity of provisions, adequate for a few days on the sledges, as far as they are concerned there is no good reason for hurrying. They do not recognize any purpose or goal, and in order not to scare them off right at the start by demanding great feats of them, for the first few days our commander generally let them have their own way.

Hence for the first while our progress was disorganized and time-consuming; on average our normal daily mileage was only 8–10 miles. The dog drivers gave the excuse that the dogs should not be overtaxed initially. When Lieutenant Schwatka saw that he could get the Inuit to camp in good time in the early hours of the evening by means of a strictly enforced insistence on a definite travel period, he made it clear to them that we had to travel for six hours per day, that after every 1½ hours of travelling he would permit them a rest of half an hour, and that after the specified daily period of travel had elapsed our day's work would be considered to be over no matter what time it was. This arrangement fully achieved its aims.

Let us now take a brief look at the composition and organization of our party. The expedition, totalling seventeen people and forty-two dogs, was divided among the three sledges in such a way that each individual sledge could operate totally independently as regards personnel, dogs, or supplies. Depending on their size and that of the dogs assigned to each, the sledges were hauled by thirteen, twelve, and seventeen dogs respectively.

All three sledges consisted of runners 2 inches thick, 9–12 feet long, and 8–10 inches high, joined together by cross-pieces made from old barrel staves and fastened to each other in such a way that the whole structure possessed sufficient elastic resilience to overcome obstacles. The lower surfaces of the runners were shod with whalebone (parts of the jaws), to which an ice layer was applied daily in order to reduce the friction with the surface.

All the dogs pulled at a single point on the sledge, in such a manner that the lead dog ran some 30 feet ahead of the sledge, and the rest 18–20 feet ahead of it. Each dog was separately connected to the sledge by a line (*arllunarq*) cut from walrus hide. Care was taken, in harnessing the dogs, that the laziest animals were in close proximity to the whip, and they had the shortest traces. From a technical point of view one might object that this arrangement of harnessing resulted in a loss of tractive power, but the natives have always been accustomed to this method, and even if one were to try to introduce a more advantageous technique, the unruliness of the dogs would result in a great loss of time. In our case each individual dog had a harness (anuq) made of woven manila cord, since the harnesses normally used by the Inuit, made of caribou or sealskin, often fell victim to the dogs' appetites.

The supplies on the sledges included about 1000 lbs of biscuit in casks and bags, 200 lbs of salted, precooked pork, 200 lbs of Wilson's corned beef in cans, 40 lbs of margarine, 40 lbs of cornstarch, a cheese weighing about 30 lbs, 20 lbs of ground coffee, 20 lbs of roasted barley as a coffee substitute, 5 lbs of tea, and about 20 gallons of molasses (1 gallon = approximately 4 litres), 50 lbs of salt, and insignificant quantities of pepper and condensed milk.

Forty gallons of rendered seal oil was taken along on the overland trip, while the food we took for our teams consisted of about 1000 lbs of walrus meat and hide. The remainder of the loads consisted of weapons, ammunition, items for trade, as well as our baggage, and a canoe (kayak), consisting of a wooden frame covered with sealskins.

Apart from Lieutenant Schwatka, the first sledge was accompanied by Gilder as the sledge leader and the family of the Inuk, Tulugaq (the raven), consisting of his wife and an eight-year-old boy. In addition, to help ease the work, there was a young fellow of 18–20, called Mitkulik. With the second sledge travelled Klutschak as leader, Eskimo Joe and his wife and two older people, man and wife, along with their fourteen-year-old lad, Kumana. Finally, travelling with the third sledge were Melms as leader, the Inuk, Ikusik (elbow) with his family, consisting of his wife, a five-year-old girl, and a thirteeen-year-old lad called Arunak. Like Mitkulik, travelling with the first sledge, this last-named family belonged to the Netsilik group, who live in the region of King William's Land.

On the second day we passed the still unfrozen rapids of the Connery River and soon left the river valley on its left side, heading north to reach a second major water course, the Lorillard River, which corresponded better to our direction of travel.

But before I describe the trip in geographical and touristic terms permit me to make the reader familiar with our daily routine. At 5 o'clock Klutschak, who was obliged to crawl out of his sleeping bag first in any case to take his meteorological readings, would make his rounds and waken all the residents of the snow houses, in order to give them time to cook their breakfasts. This consisted of coffee, brewed separately over blubber lamps in each snow house, hardtack, and margarine, which adequately substituted for butter. At first pork was also served, but everybody refused this thirst-provoking food for their morning meal. Following Inuit custom breakfast was eaten in bed, but after breakfast the Inuit men would begin icing the sledge runners. For this the sledges are turned over and a crust of water-soaked snow is applied to the entire length of the lower side of the runner. When this first layer is sufficiently frozen, water is taken into the mouth and sprayed onto the icy snow crust, then wiped with a piece of long-haired bear skin so that the surface becomes as smooth as possible. This method is also used when the sledge runners are not shod with whalebone, but in this case finely pounded earth soaked with water is used instead of the initial snow layer. For crossing snow-covered terrain the mud is just as good, but the process is time-consuming, and on rough ice a coating of this type is knocked off much more readily than snow.

While the icing process is under way everyone gets dressed inside the snow houses, rolls up his bed, and lashes it firmly with a string or line to prevent the snow from penetrating into it. Everyone leaves the snow house with all his belongings and scarcely is the last item outside and scarcely has the boy, who until this moment has guarded the low door with a stick against incursions by the dogs, moved away, when the pack of dogs, which has been lying in wait, dashes inside the snow house to appropriate any scraps of meat which have been left behind. Loading the sledge is done by the men, who adjust the load into a well-shaped unit, and secure it with walrus lines. The guns, which in order to protect them from damp are never taken inside the snow houses even in the severest winter, are loaded last; the dogs are harnessed by the women and children, and the journey begins. Our travelling time of six hours was adhered to with pedantic accuracy; every ninety minutes we rested for half an hour, and only after the last of these intermediate rests would we start looking around for a suitable campsite.

A good campsite necessitates good snow and proximity to a pond or river which by its extent or gradient gives the probability that water can still be found beneath the ice cover. A fairly substantial snowdrift, 3–4 feet deep, is the most suitable spot for building snowhouses; however, it is essential that the drift has not accumulated as the product of several storms, since the various layers would result in the disintegration of the snow blocks. Both with regard to quantity and quality the snow is tested by the Inuit by means of an iron rod, such as

Inuit building a snow house

they use for catching seals, or a stick made from a caribou antler. The sledges, which have stopped temporarily, are brought up to the selected site, and the work begins.

If construction of a snow house is to proceed rapidly it involves two men, one cutting the blocks and the other assembling the house. The house itself consists of a dome built of snow blocks, 3 feet long, 1½–2 feet wide, and 6 inches thick; these are not laid in layers but are so arranged that they form an unbroken, continuous spiral. Having practised from childhood the art of building this primitive yet ingenious structure, the Inuk endows the entire structure with a very beautiful shape and inserts the final horizontal block, the keystone of the entire dome, with equal skill. The women also play a role in building a snow house; their task is to strengthen the walls by throwing snow on them. This contributes significantly to making it easier to heat the interior. Once the building is completed the platform on which the beds will be laid out is constructed and an entrance opening two feet high and two feet wide is cut in the south-facing side. While the women are left to look after the further interior arrangements the men build a small porch in front of the entrance, which at the same time will serve as a refuge for the dogs in the prevailing storms, and a second one, similarly abutting right against the main structure, as a storehouse to protect our meat supply.

The upper part of the following illustration (1) represents the cross-section and the lower part (2) the plan view of a snow house. V represents the porch; W the windbreak; T the door; B a snow block used for closing the entrance; M the storehouse mentioned above; K the kettle hanging over the lamp L; and F the spot used for storing meat. The ice block I and the opening F take the place of a window during stays of more than one day.

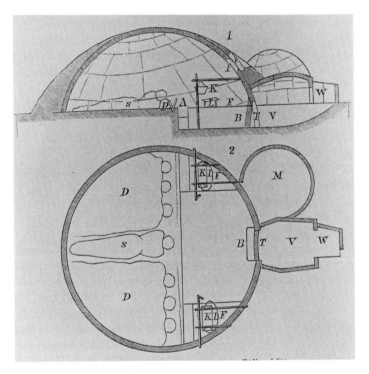

Cross-section and plan of a snow house

While the Inuit were busy building and organizing the snow houses the whites would take it in turn to look after chopping open the water hole. Usually the Inuit would have to identify the most suitable spot for it since from experience the colour of the ice and the appearance of the cracks provide them with a clue to that identification. But despite

Aluut

their experience it would often happen that after chiselling for a long time through ice 4–7½ feet thick, we would run into rocky ground. On such occasions an Inuk will not commit himself to a definite statement. In most cases his predictive comment will be: 'Suugami, amiasuk' (I believe but I do not know exactly).[2] In the event that the drilling is unsuccessful this exempts him from responsibility. A steel chisel is used for chopping the water hole; the ice is chopped out with it, while the loosened ice splinters are removed with a scoop made from the horn of a muskox (*aluut*, also meaning a spoon), fastened to a stick.

But if one does not encounter water at the first attempt, a second and even a third attempt is made at other locations, since water obtained by this method is better in many respects; it saves blubber, which one would have to expend to melt snow, and furthermore, time will be saved in connection with icing the sledge runners next morning. If the drilling is successful, as the last crust of ice is broken through the water comes gushing up almost to the surface of the ice. At the shout of 'Imiq! Imiq!' (Water! Water!) the whole party, large and small, gathers round to quench their thirst, which everyone has been only too well aware of for a long time. Due to the cold it is impossible to transport water with one on the sledge, and reluctantly one has to face up to the decision of carrying a supply of water in sealskin bags, held against one's bare body. Men will adopt this technique only under abnormal circumstances and women, only when they are mothers with small children.

As the last tasks of the day the sledges are turned over and the dogs unharnessed and allowed to run free. For hauling and storing the supply of drinking and cooking water, tin receptacles are not used even when they were available, as in our case; instead the Inuit *qattaq* is used. This is a watertight bucket sewn from sealskin; not only is this material such a poor conductor of heat that it does not allow the water to freeze as fast as metal, but it also offers the advantage that when ice has formed on its sides it can easily be knocked off with a piece of wood without damage to the receptacle.

In this manner everything is finally organized; crawling on all fours everyone disappears through the small door into the snow house and closes it off from the outside world with a snow block set ready for the purpose.

The interior has been arranged by the diligent housewives to the best of their abilities (usually two families live in one snow house, since it it the privilege of only a married woman to be able to tend a lamp). The platform used as the sleeping place is covered with caribou skins; on it lie the whites' sleeping bags as well as the big caribou blankets of the individual families. The lamps and kettles, both hollowed out of soapstone, are set up in the corners; they represent the prized possessions and the pride of the Inuit wife and guarantee her a place on the corner of the sleeping platform. While the snow house is still cold the woman begins lighting her lamp, and arranges the long flame evenly so that it scarcely smokes yet heats the kettle hanging over it most efficiently; the latter is already filled with meat and water. Once the meal is ready she shares the food out and runs the family; she is the first up and the last in bed, the true and unmistakable picture of a good housewife and mother. Our illustration shows such a woman at her simple hearth.

There is only one means of staying warm in a snow house; this involves getting undressed and crawling under the furs, unless the house has been built specially larger for a long stay. The task of undressing is quite complicated since one has to beat all one's clothes with a short stick (anautak) with pedantic thoroughness in order to remove every little flake of snow adhering to them and every little sliver of ice in order to keep them dry. Every article of clothing has its specified place; outer clothing is used to protect the sleeping bag between its lower part and the snow wall, while underclothing are used as a pillow. In order to prevent them from falling down, once the anautak has been used for brushing snow off it is stuck into the edge of the sleeping platform at an angle, to protect one's pillow. Hence even in a snow house it is possible to make oneself comfortable, and having taken these precautions one can go to sleep with the knowledge that the first builder of such a house, and the inventor of the sleeping bag of

Inuit woman tending a blubber lamp

the northern world has probably rendered just as great a service as the one to whom the civilized world is nowadays indebted to the invention of the steam engine.

From the moment we halt until we slip into our sleeping bags the entire process of making camp lasts 2½–3 hours. But if the next day is to be a rest day it takes a little longer since the houses will be built to be more spacious.

Every two days the routine feeding of the dogs occurs; for this purpose the dogs are left harnessed after the sledges have been unloaded. The Inuit men responsible for the respective sledges load their ration of dog food on their sledges, take a knife and an axe each, and head off in opposite directions until they are far enough from the campsite that the dogs of one team cannot see those of another. Once this has been achieved they stop, turn the sledge over, and secure it as firmly as possible so that the dogs, who know very well what all these preparations signify, cannot race off with the sledge. Now the Inuk starts chopping the meat into small pieces, to the accompaniment of a hideous music which one can hear for miles. From the moment the

Inuk begins cutting up the dogfood until the pieces are hurled all together among the unruly pack, there is an endless sequence of howling and fighting and continual attempts by the dogs to tear free from the sledge. If the reader has watched the feeding time at a zoo he has only a vague notion of what twelve to seventeen Inuit dogs can do under similar circumstances. At such moments, whether he uses it conventionally or beats the dogs over the head with the handle, the Inuk's efforts with his long whip are quite fruitless. Only when the feeding begins does silence fall, but only until two or three of the largest dogs fall out over possession of a special morsel; they then end up with torn ears rather than full bellies. Any idea that the weaker dogs get the short end of the stick at feeding time is quite erroneous; due to their stupidity the strong dogs give them an opportunity to look after themselves. Only if enough caribou had been shot on the day the dogs were fed in order to feed all forty–two dogs on the parts less suitable for human consumption were the latter cut into fairly large pieces and left for the dogs to break down into smaller pieces.

This was in general the daily routine which we followed right from the very first days. Until noon on 4 April we were travelling across hilly, rocky terrain which made for difficult travelling, partly because of the steep climbs, partly due to the numerous rocks which were only lightly covered with snow. The latter were a particular problem since they imperceptibly stripped our sledge runners of their ice layer; once this had been removed dogs and men were barely capable of hauling the sledges to the next point where a water hole could be chopped and a new ice skin applied. Freshwater ice completely bare of snow represents just as great an obstacle as rocks, and hence the dog drivers avoid these spots, and the rocks, with great care. On the day mentioned we headed downhill from the last rise and were soon standing on the ice of a fine river, whose wide bed, strewn with numerous small islands, offered us a welcome route for several days. Not until the seventh day after our departure did we allow the dogs the indulgence of a rest day; on that day we determined our latitude from the noon altitude of the sun to be 64⁰29'N. On the eighth day the river, which we had named the Lorillard, swung west and we ascended its right bank.[3] To achieve this we were obliged to haul the sledges up the slope one after the other, using the combined teams. While the Inuit occupied themselves with this time-consuming task we whites had an opportunity to investigate the cause of a magnificent natural spectacle. Even from a great distance we were struck by a glistening wall of ice 60–80 feet high, and on getting closer we thought we were looking at a frozen waterfall.

But a closer investigation revealed that the assumed ice cataract was the overflow from a small hill lake; filled to the brim the previous fall by the frequent late rain showers it had been incapable of containing all the discharge from its catchment. The strata-like layering of the various ice crusts showed clearly the progressive development of this captivating phenomenon.[4]

As soon as we had left the Lorillard River we had to get used to looking for the best of the many routes which offered in a northeasterly direction; in order to make the fastest possible progress we had to be careful to select the most advantageous route across the many ponds and lakes. During the few days of our march the landscape had changed very significantly; the level, undulating highland with gently rising slopes had changed to a higher landscape formed of isolated cones. The snow had become more sparse on these summits and the otherwise flat granite plateaux were covered with talus, which made the going worse. We were standing on the eastern outliers of the Hazard Hills, a low range about 800–1000 feet in height which Lieutenant Schwatka had visited farther west during his reconnaissance trip.[5] They appear to run southwest-northeast between 64^0 and 65^0 and probably reach their highest point in Wheeler Peak (1000–1200 feet). Our route led across some large ponds. As we entered this new type of terrain more reindeer appeared day by day. Naturally these animals appeared all the more desirable to us, since we always had to be prepared for encountering areas later which were relatively short of game, hence making it advisable to haul some reserves of meat with us on the sledges.

We were witnesses of a hunt on the morning of 9 April. Our departure was delayed due to Tulugaq being sick until around 10:00 A.M. Shortly before the dogs were harnessed a herd of caribou appeared on the large lake lying directly in front of us. In an instant the dogs' discipline collapsed and their predatory nature came to the fore in the fullest sense. Forty-two dogs raced after the caribou, and no matter how impatient we were to depart there was nothing left for us to do but to wait calmly until the entire pack returned, panting and unsuccessful, after about an hour. Only two dogs of our entire teams proved themselves to be at all useful at hunting game; in general, the Inuit dog is useless for this purpose because it cannot run fast enough to overtake the caribou, even though the latter is not very fast.

That same day we travelled through the 'Southwest Pass,'[6] named for its alignment. It consisted of the bed of a small stream whose banks consisted of sheer rock walls, which with the snow drifted into their

Southwest Pass

joints presented a very beautiful winter landscape.

In the afternoon there was a heavy snowfall with a strong southeast wind, which also persisted the following day. Thus we elected to stop for a rest day on the tenth day, giving Gilder the chance to catch up with the sledges, which had stayed behind because of the sick man.

Two days later we crossed the divide between Hudson's Bay and Wager Bay; ahead of us lay a beautiful hilly area with abundant game. There was no question of stocking up with enough meat for the entire march to King William's Land, and for our immediate needs we were able to kill enough caribou without having to undertake special hunting trips or to divide up our party and send out subsidiary columns. Tulugaq especially proved himself to be an extremely agile hunter and a good marksman, and when we heard the crack of his Winchester rifle we could immediately send out some dogs in the direction from which the shot came. The dead caribou were hauled back to the sledges by their antlers and loaded on board, then the column would move off again. As the caribou became more numerous wolves also appeared, at first singly then in packs, and even though they did not attack us during the day they followed our tracks and disturbed our dogs at night. On this occasion the donation of a New York company which made signalling lights was particularly useful; when the wolves came slinking around our campsite at night, we made a small hole in the wall of the snow house from the inside and lit one of the flares, used on board ship for signalling for a pilot and which burned with alternating white, red, and white colours.

The nights were still dark and this bright illumination did not seem to please the wolves particularly. They started slowly to withdraw at the first change to the red light, their tails between their legs, and when the white colour again appeared they raced away at top speed. In this fashion we got rid of our troublesome companions. When Mr Coston patented his marine signal flares he certainly can scarcely have anticipated such a use!

The terrain descended steeply and we were often obliged to travel down a steep slope. On these occasions the dogs were unharnessed and raced after the sledges, which were each left in the control of just two men. Once in motion the sledge shoots down the smooth snow surface at a fearful speed due simply to gravity and the drivers reach the bottom in every possible position, having remained with the sledge only to avoid a collision as far as possible. But if the slope is particularly long and steep the Inuit use a coiled walrus-hide line as a brake, throwing it over the front end of the sledge runner at a suitable moment in order to increase the friction.

The deep embayment of the sea marked on the British Admiralty charts[7] was probably crossed, as far as we could tell from our determinations of position, but it is in reality only a combination of larger and smaller ponds. The term 'river' is misplaced here; the term 'Wager Gulf' would be more correct. The sources of the Quoich River lie too far to the east to provide room for such a large river as the gulf is at its mouth, or even sixty miles west of it. This map error and the inappropriateness of the name derive from an error resulting from the first survey.

The weather had been fair up until now, but on 19 April a very sharp southwest wind began to blow and made the three hours which it took us to pitch camp very unpleasant for us. All day long the snow had been whirling in the air in such a fashion that we had great difficulty in maintaining a northwesterly bearing on the basis of the sun, since it was only occasionally visible. But in the evening the storm rose to gale-force. After only a few minutes dogs and sledges were buried in a snowdrift while the women and children squatted behind the sledges,

Inuit braking a sled

which we had set transverse to the wind, the little ones pressed tightly
to their bodies. The men had very great difficulty in placing one snow
block atop another; the most diligent attempts on our part to assist the
Inuit in building the houses were a failure, since every snow block
which we attempted to set up was blown away like a piece of paper
before we could set the next ones in place. In weather like today's the
three or four hours spent waiting until our snow houses were completed seemed to be particularly long but this time, after this period
had elapsed, we were sheltered for a full five days. This was how long
we found ourselves forced to stay literally inside the houses, passing
the time as best we could. We made observations of a curious sort.
Among others, Gilder and I discovered irregularities on the inner
surface of the snow blocks, which in the peculiar light penetrating
through from the outside, threw shadows whose groupings appeared as
beautiful landscapes and figure drawings of infinite variety. We both
spent many otherwise long hours of inactivity in a pleasant fashion,
sketching these pictures. It was also particularly stormy days which
gave rise to quite long discussions in our diaries, and the material

which was lacking in terms of special incidents was made up for by the variety of our thoughts and by our conversation, which often ranged widely across the various spheres of human knowledge.

But on the 28th our line of march took us into terrain different from the previous areas. The slowly rising ground was covered by a vast number of large and small granite blocks and was badly dissected. These regions should have been a suitable habitat for muskoxen; we searched constantly for their tracks but found none until the evening when Iquisik spotted a small herd from a hilltop with the aid of our telescope. Hunting muskoxen had long been our greatest wish. Since it was already late but also since muskoxen do not travel far at night unless startled, we decided to postpone pursuing them until next morning.

On the morning of the 29th a dense fog blanketed the entire region and not until it disappeared, around 9:00 A.M., did the entire male population of the party settle themselves on the sledges, which were being held ready and to which thirty-five dogs were harnessed. We then headed for the area which, from yesterday's observations, was thought to be the best starting point for our hunt. The party moved silently across the smooth snow surface. The driver did not use his whip at all, and even the dogs seemed to know that any noise would startle the animals, since they obeyed the gentle *Ahu, Jihu* (Right, Left)[8] of their driver with remarkable quietness. Around 11 o'clock we reached the first muskox tracks; we stopped and the dogs were unharnessed. Each of us tied two dogs to his waist by their traces and then led them to the clearly visible tracks in the snow. Their heads sunk low to the ground the dogs began following the trail; the sole task of the men was to stay on their feet. Each of us had the opportunity to experience how difficult this was. The irregularity of the terrain on the one hand, and the white snow surface, blinding one's eyes, on the other, had the result that one would reach the bottom of a slope part standing, part sitting, sometimes lying and even rolling, and would attain the crest of a hill out of breath. We went through thick and thin, as they say, but always following the trail along which the dogs remorselessly pulled their masters, to whom they were irrevocably attached, with a strength which mocked any resistance. Not a sound was to be heard, but neither did the muskoxen show themselves. Pursuing these animals may provide a special pleasure for passionate hunting enthusiasts the first few times, but I have to admit that to keep up with Inuit who are used to this type of hunting, harnessed behind two dogs for a distance of three miles is too much of a good thing for a layman, no

A muskox hunt

matter how agile he may be. On reaching yet another hilltop we spotted some dark, black spots; very soon they spotted us too and took to flight. The moment for releasing the dogs had arrived; only too gladly did we release the hounds from assisting us further and they now raced after the muskoxen en masse. The latter are very good hill climbers; neither man nor dog can follow them on very steep terrain, but on level gound they were soon overtaken and encircled. Four in number, they stood together for protection, their heads outward. While earlier it had been the dogs which competed to be first, now it was the hunters who each wanted to shoot a muskox. Once they had approached to within twenty-five paces more shots were fired than were necessary. Once surrounded by the dogs a herd is totally at the mercy of the hunter. The animals lay sprawled on the ground; the hunt was over, and while the dogs still tugged here and there at a hoof or at the dreaded horns we indulged in a short rest. Parseniak, one of our best hunting dogs, had come too close to the horns of one of the animals and had taken an involuntary flight through the air. But scarcely had he hit the ground when he continued his attack, uninjured and with renewed energy. Now he lay contentedly beside the animal and repeatedly bit its nose.

In build the muskox is very similar to the American buffalo, but smaller, with very long hair and sharply curved horns which lie close to the side of the head. The horns extend right across the entire upper part of the skull with the bosses approaching very close together. Muskoxen live in fairly small family herds, numbering up to thirty head; they feed on the mosses occurring in the arctic regions, and in terms of vigilance represent one of the most observant species. For the northern traveller its occurrence in the highest latitudes (up to 80° on the West Greenland coast) is important, since its flesh is tough and hence represents a much more nutritious food for the dogs than caribou or seal meat. For man the meat of the muskox represents a sought-after food item only in case of necessity, due to its strong flavour of musk. By contrast its fat is highly prized by the Inuit as a delicacy in winter.

The four muskoxen we had killed[9] were skinned, dismembered, and the entrails, etc. immediately fed to the dogs right on the spot. Part of the meat was loaded on the sledge, part was lashed in the hides and in this fashion hauled home by some of the dogs. Hence every part was utilized and after our departure only a small pool of blood marked the spot where earlier a herd of these long-haired animals had stood. According to the Inuit, however, even this small remainder would be sufficient to keep every other herd away from this spot for two years. Of course the writer accepts no responsibility for this statement by the Inuit, no matter how wary muskoxen may be.

From 30 April until 4 May we were crossing a large upland plateau which due to its striking lack of water and its total lack of animal life deserves to be described as a small arctic desert. But our progress across it was unpleasant in another respect. The temperature had risen significantly during the month of April and it was now a burden to wear fur clothing, yet because of the cold mornings we did not dare wear any other type of clothing. Those parts of our faces exposed to the sharp spring weather experienced slight frost-bite and hence the skin peeled off. Yet the sun was also making itself felt now, and when it shone on our faces around noon, these two totally extreme processes made our noses in particular look like onions, in view of the multiple skin layers exposed, and like graters in view of their many warts and spots.

Bright sunshine was quite beneficial to the eyes compared to slightly overcast or faintly hazy weather. In sunshine individual snowdrifts cast small shadows and it was these which brought relief to the eyes, due to the contrast which they introduced into the monotonous white. But if the sun's rays could not penetrate with their full strength, then the entire surface from horizon to horizon was a uniform, shimmering snow surface without a rock and without any colour variation, a white so flat that it was both painful to the eyes and unpleasant for the traveller.

Even the green and blue goggles which we had taken along for both ourselves and the Inuit accompanying us contributed little toward relieving the torment. In the case of the Inuit this made itself felt as a burning pain, that is, the affliction known as snow-blindness, but in our case it was a feeling which is very difficult to describe. We suffered no pain and could see things at a distance but could not distinguish individual snowdrifts at close range.

On 4 May a dark chain of hills finally appeared in the distance and when we reached and climbed it a panorama lay before us whose appearance alone compensated us for the travail of the last few days. Hill chains visible a long way off, the many lakes spread before us, and the hill summits covered with a dark moss, where the granite rocks were blown clear of snow, represented a balm to the eye. We were standing on the highest point of the entire landscape and ahead of us the land sloped downhill. Today we had not only reached the divide between Hudson Bay and the Arctic Ocean, but we had also crossed the Arctic Circle itself (66°33′N).

CHAPTER FOUR

From the Area of the Back River to King William's Land, 5 May–12 June 1879

A new daily routine. A caribou hunt. Hilly terrain.
The Hayes River. Abundant animal life. Signs of man.
The Utkuhikhalingmiut. A dreary existence. The first relics.
Hospitality. Hearsay report of Ikinilik-Petulak. On the Back
River. Montreal Island. Ogle Peninsula. An Inuit flag of truce.
Netsilik Inuit. Their reports on the Franklin catastrophe. Relics.
Meetings with the Netsilingmiut. Communication. Maps.
Counting. The first cairn. We reach King William's Land.

By comparison with the areas we had been travelling across in late April and early May, we were now in a real paradise, which completely met all the demands we could possibly make of any landscape. There were ponds and lakes in abundance, caribou in great numbers, while to economize on our diminishing reserves of oil for possible later needs, we used as fuel the dry hair-moss*[1] (*tingaujak*) which grew profusely on the snow-free hill tops.

Due to the higher temperatures the snow was becoming softer and softer around noon, making travel difficult; the icing on the sledge runners was no longer holding properly and hence we would leave our campsite very early in order to be able to camp before the onset of the 'noon heat,' as we referred to midday temperatures of 2–3⁰C. The distinction between day and night had disappeared; one could scarcely talk of darkness any more. Our timely arrival on King William's Land depended entirely on our reaching the good travelling on the Back or Great Fish River in good time. We encountered caribou almost daily,

---

*Hair moss is a very dense, dark green, almost black species of moss which often extends in a turf-like carpet from 4 to inches thick over wide areas, and forms the main food source for caribou and muskoxen.

not just singly as earlier, but in large herds, and we rarely let them pass without killing a few head.

Alerted by the restlessness of our teams during a sharp southerly wind which was driving the snow fairly thickly, we spotted a herd of caribou resting on a hill about a mile ahead of us. We immediately halted the sledges; every single male capable of hunting seized his rifle and attempted to surround the herd, leaving the women with the sledges in order to keep the dogs under control. Fifteen minutes passed and nobody appeared, nor did the herd appear to get wind of anything and a bull which had stood up and was keeping watch all around, quietly lay down again. Our hunters were using this time period to get within firing range of the herd, sometimes creeping, sometimes crawling. The Inuit consider firing range to be from 70 to a maximum of 100 paces; they will fire at greater ranges only in case of extreme necessity.

Quiet still reigned; from the sledges one had an overall view of both caribou and hunters to best advantage, amid tense excitement. A shot cracked out; in an instant the herd was on its feet – but too late. It was surrounded, and for a short time the hunters fired at will until ten of the fourteen animals were down.

We soon found a suitable campsite and while the men set about building the snow houses, the dogs, in charge of the boys, hauled the caribou in. At a stopping place like this the men have the greatest fun right after a hunt. Given the rapid rate of fire and the large number of hunters, naturally nobody knows for sure which caribou he has killed, if indeed any at all, but the natives insist on skinning and dressing only those animals which they themselves have killed. Hence the debate over the topic, often continuing for hours in a peaceful manner, was often very interesting to listen to.

From December until the end of June the caribou hides are useless for skin clothing since they quickly lose their hair due to the moult, and also since at this season a vast number of parasites eats through the hide, making the leather useless for any purpose, if the hide were to be used for leather.

From the watershed a faint blue-black line could be seen on the horizon, but as sledge travellers, the thought that there was a mountain chain ahead of us was not a particularly comforting one. Today, 9 May 1879, we reached the immediate proximity of that line, which now assumes the form of quite a massive-looking hill range. It was not the hills and summits which caused us so much concern as to our further

At the source of the Hayes River

progress, but the extremely dissected appearance of the landscape and the snow cover which was too meagre for sledging. The closer we approached the higher the hills seemed; reluctantly we finally unharnessed our dogs in order to let the sledges down a slope in our well-tried manner. But in this case Mother Nature turned out to be particularly co-operative since on reaching the foot of the hill we reached a stream, scarcely twelve feet wide, which flowed into a large pond, then out of it again.

The sun's noon altitude revealed a latitude of 66°47′N for our stopping place at midday, and from all appearances we were at the source of a river which we immediately named the Hayes River,[2] in honour of the then President of the United States.

We gladly followed the narrow stream channel between high, steep mountain slopes; it led us from lake to lake, sometimes in a northwesterly, sometimes in a northeasterly direction.

What effort it would have cost us if we had had to work our way across the surrounding terrain without such a fine route as the smooth ice surface of the little stream provided; how easily we glided along over the smooth surface and how quickly we progressed downstream down the steep gradient. When we occupied our campsite that evening the wildly romantic riverbank scenery had dispelled the worries which we had harboured earlier, and only the impression of grandeur and beauty formed the topic of our last conversation of the day.

From a hill 600–700 feet high, which we named Stewart's Monument and which was crowned with a large black block of granite that offered a fine distant view, one could follow the stream channel for miles to the north. The river itself might either be a tributary of the Great Fish River or might belong to the drainage of the Castor and Pollux River, discovered by Dease and Simpson in 1839 and seen again by Dr Rae in 1854, although only at its mouth. But in either case our discovery represented a contribution to geography.

We were adequately compensated for our failure to maintain our line of march by the enforced deviations. At times the river pressed through between narrow rock walls which rose directly from the ice surface; at times the walls fell back, to circle the shores of beautiful lakes with low hills. This rich variety repeatedly produced magnificent, new landscapes which possessed special qualities beneath the northern sky. And the forms of the individual hill masses offered a variety which reminded us now of the Rhine, now of the Hudson, and we noted many names, such as the Hippodrome, in our journals, from the appearance which the forms and groups recalled. While it had been hilly and rocky on the upper course, with increasing width and decreasing gradient of the river, the landscape along its banks also changed. The banks became lower and lost the character of a stretch of land totally devoid of flood plains.

Caribou which we had missed during the first few days on this river, reappeared, always in considerable herds. Only with great difficulty and by overriding all objections was Lieutenant Schwatka able to lead the party past a herd of some fifty caribou without lettting the men hunt. Our sledges were adequately supplied with meat and any excess load would have been an impediment to rapid progress at this season. But for the Inuit it was, and remained a mystery, that one could let such a fine source of food run past, unexploited. A party of natives not under the energetic command of a white man would simply have settled down here and stayed as long as there was food.

As we penetrated farther, at various spots we sighted rocks placed on top of each other or placed in a circle; we concluded from this that there were people present in the area, either at the present time, or perhaps only in the past. On the 14th we suddenly noticed a freshly cut

snow block which could scarcely have been two days old; on closer
inspection we found a snow house which was only recently abandoned.
From its construction it had been used by hunters for one night's rest.
We found the tracks of two people and several dogs in the snow; they
had been hauling something – probably a supply of meat – downstream, using a hide as a sledge. The stream channel, the alternating
scenery, the many caribou – all these were now incidental; our newly
discovered river was visited at least occasionally by people. This
temporarily monopolized our conversation both during the day and in
our evening hours.

The Inuit were in a particularly high state of excitement, which
betrayed both great curiosity and fear; our interpreter, who for a long
time had been dreaming of the ceremonies associated with meeting a
strange Inuit tribe, was extremely anxious. For the past few days, since
we had crossed the divide, there had been a slight change in the
weather; the southerly winds had ceased and on the 15th a sharp
northwest wind began blowing, accompanied by brief snow squalls. We
had to travel straight into the teeth of this wind, and the blowing snow
blocked any further distant views. Everything was proceeding in the
usual order of march, when the dogs of the leading team suddenly
displayed unease, and they began, unbidden, to run with the sledge,
something which happened very rarely. After a few minutes a small
group of snow houses appeared, and in front of them some human
figures could be seen moving. The people disappeared and we left the
sledges standing half a mile away, in order to observe the customary
formalities on a first meeting with an unknown tribe; Eskimo Joe
would not have it any other way. Our appearance was almost comical
as we strode toward the village with our rifles. Apart from some dogs
which came running toward us there was nothing to be seen. Only
after several requests did we manage to entice the poor people out of
their houses. Displaying the greatest fear they formed up in a line
facing us, armed with spears, bows, and arrows, and asked us about the
purpose of our trip and about our destination. We gladly gave them the
requested information. The assurance that our intentions toward them
were quite friendly began to dispel their mistrust and after a short time
they invited us to build our houses near theirs and to spend a few days
in their company. This invitation was accepted, the sledges were
brought up, and with massive help from our new friends our dwellings
rose up out of the ground with great rapidity. The first mutual
encounter between different Inuit tribes always has a stamp of
mistrust and caution, and no matter how poor their weapons they stay

Encounter with the Utkuhikhalingmiut

in their hands until the parties involved have reached an understanding.

Initially our attention was drawn to the people themselves; it turned out that the Utkuhikhalingmiut are the remnant of a once large tribe, which not so long before had had its home on the west coast of the Adelaide Peninsula. As a result of prolonged fighting with the Ugjulimmiut and the Netsilingmiut now occupying that area, the number of Utkuhikhalingmiut had been greatly reduced, and they found themselves obliged to abandon their hunting grounds and to drag out their lives in this quiet corner. The entire tribe now consisted of only sixteen families, seven of whom lived here and the remainder along the 'Dangerous Rapids' on the Back River.

The reason why these people eke out such a miserable life in a region which is so rich in caribou and muskoxen is in part their poverty and their poor hunting equipment, but also in part the lack of any energy. If the fishing, their most important source of food, turns out to be poor, as happened this year, they struggle all winter unremittingly against hunger in its most frightful form, and their numbers are reduced by death by starvation. Their appearance, especially their hollow cheeks and sunken eyes, speaks clearly of the want and misery which are their constant companions, and if one wants to see simplicity in its most absolute form and a life-style of the most primitive type, one needs only to enter their houses. The clothing and bedding are not sewn from caribou skins but are made entirely from muskox hides, which would leave much to be desired as protection against the cold, even if they were available in sufficient numbers. There was no trace of seal blubber and these people survive the long, cold winter entirely without artificial heat and the long nights without any illumination. But enough of the interiors; no matter how sharp the air is outside one longs to be back out there again, and we preferred to examine the hunting tools and other equipment of these people outside their houses.

Among them we encountered the first relics of objects which once were either parts of the two ships *Erebus* and *Terror* or otherwise belonged to the Franklin expedition. Arrow tips, lances, snow shovels, in brief everything made of wood, copper, and iron, originated from the site of the Franklin catastrophe and had either come into the hands of these people via intermediaries, that is, via other Inuit, or had been found by them directly.

After our snow houses were built the Utkuhikhalingmiut invited us into their houses to share a meal with them. It was certainly a fine display of the hospitality of these people, when one realizes that the 50 lbs of muskox meat which they proposed to set before us represented their sole reserves of food, and that there was no prospect of replenishing it until the start of the fishing gave them promise of further provisions.

Friendship is expressed among the Inuit in communal eating as well as in touching each others' chests with the flat of the hand, during which action the word *ilaga* (my relations) is uttered. Hence no matter how reluctant we were to partake in the little and last that they could offer us, yet we did so in order to honour their fine custom. In return, the large reserves of meat on the white men's sledges more than made up for it. At the request of the lieutenant I also distributed some hardtack spread with molasses among the women and children; but although this was a delicacy for the northern natives elsewhere, this time it was not appreciated at all. Here we were dealing with a natural people, completely undebased and uninfluenced by civilization. Unfortunately, only a few years would suffice to entirely expunge this once powerful tribe from the face of the earth.

From the moment that we encountered the first relics deriving from Franklin and his people it was also our duty to question the people as to their knowledge in this area, and as to the information which had reached them orally. Only one person, a man of 60–70 years by name of Ikinilik-Petulak, had himself come into contact with one of the expedition's ships. He was one of the first people to visit a ship which, beset in the ice, drifted with wind and current to a spot west of Grant Point on Adelaide Peninsula, where some islands halted its drift. On their first visit the people thought they saw whites on board; from the tracks in the snow they concluded there were four of them. This was in the fall; the following spring they visited the spot again and found the ship in the same position. When no sign of the whites or of any other sign of life could be seen, and since they did not know how to get inside the ship, they made a large hole in the ship's side near the ice surface. As a result the ship sank once the ice had melted. According to Ikinilik they had found a corpse in one of the bunks and they found meat in cans in the cabin. Otherwise they had found no trace of whites on the coast of Adelaide Peninsula, apart from a small boat in Wilmot Bay which, however, might have drifted to that spot after the ship sank.

The credibility of these reports was later enhanced when confirmed by similar statements by others. Ikinilik Petulak had seen whites once before, coming down the Great Fish River in two boats. This was Lieutenant Back's exploring party which descended and mapped this river (also called the Back River, after him) in the summer of 1834.[3]

We were encouraged to receive assurances that the Hayes River (Kuujjuak in Inuktitut) was a tributary of the Back River, and that a further four days' travel would suffice to reach its mouth.

In return for all this news, as well as for some of the most important relics, we repaid the people generously with needles, tin plates, headbands, etc., and hired one of the tribe, Nalijau, to accompany us, because of his knowledge of the country, along with his wife and their five-year-old daughter. We also left the people some of our still substantial reserves of meat, and on the 18th we continued our journey down the lower course of the river, having first passed a long, frozen rapid.

Soon the river channel widened considerably; the banks decreased in height and the granite formation gave way to a miserable clay which emerged from the bed of the river in the form of flat islands; the river was bordered on both sides by clay banks with the most varied formations. The beautiful landscapes of the upper course were now succeeded by a boring, desolate, comfortless region which offered no variety. After our day's march we clambered around for hours searching for fossils, but despite all our efforts we had no success. This type of clay appears to be good for nothing at all; from Lieutenant Schwatka's experience in both areas it appears to be the counterpart of the notorious 'badlands of Dakota' in the northern United States. The only consolation which the river provided was that we did not need to chop any more waterholes; we could now get water at any time from the newly formed thin ice. The temperature had already risen to the point that, at least around noon, the snow was beginning to melt and water was beginning to accumulate at the foot of hills and in the river channel on top of the thick ice. Admittedly an ice crust still formed at night in the latter case, but for this season at least we were no longer obliged to earn every mouthful of water the hard way via a hole chopped in the six-foot-thick ice.

On the evening of the 19th we reached a great bend in the river where it swung to the southwest; since we had been alerted about this by the Inuit we left the river at about 67°30′N, climbed the right bank, and headed west to reach the mouth of the Back River. There were many lakes which made for easy travelling, and we made rapid progress; on the 22nd we camped at the foot of a hill which promised a fine view. Despite a dreadful storm which made it impossible to stand on the very summit, we climbed to the top, and sticking just our heads over the final rock ridge, we gazed ahead. The snow had become moist

At the great bend of the Hayes River

during the day again, so whirling snow no longer obscured the view; in front of us lay a strangely beautiful panorama. The great, wide mouth of the Back River lay before us, representing an obstacle-free route to King William's Land. Having safely made an overland trip of 385 miles, all our fears of being baulked in our progress by natural obstacles had turned out to be groundless. Now the snow could melt as fast as it liked; indeed, we gladly greeted the first raindrops which beat on our snow roof as representing the start of a better season.

The east bank of the Back River, which we now followed, was again granite. We encountered a peculiar trick of nature in the form of a large granite rock, exactly spherical in shape, about 8 feet in diameter, and standing on a relatively very small base. The upper part of the sphere was entirely coloured white, as if somebody had poured a receptacle of paint over it. We were just about to subject the whole thing to a really thorough examination when we realized just in time that the colour derived from the guano of sea birds which had accumulated over the years.

Our next objective was Montreal Island, which according to the

A granite sphere

reports of Dr Rae, mentioned in the introduction, is generally seen as a location where some of Franklin's men are supposed to have died. We camped on the eastern part of the island and stayed there the following day, 27 May, in order to search for a cairn which Sir Leopold McClintock is supposed to have erected during his visit in the spring of 1859.[4] He had the habit of always leaving some trifles such as a knife, scissors, fish-hooks, etc. near his cairns; his rationale was that on finding such items the Inuit might be deterred from destroying any documents that might be contained in the cairn. Naturally this had precisely the opposite effect: the Inuit dismantled the cairns right to the ground. This may also have been the case here since although we searched the entire island we found not the slightest trace of a cairn.

Montreal is not as large as depicted on the maps; it is at most six miles long and is not even a single island but an archipelago of small islands. These are separated by narrow arms of the sea which offer good seal hunting in summer. The island is then a favourite resort of the Netsilingmiut, who call it Kajektuaruik, after the *kayak* (sealing boat) which is widely used here. On the 28th we reached Ogle Peninsula and immediately encountered a terrain which was quite different from any we had travelled across previously. Flat, sandy, and clayey, totally devoid of any trace of vegetation, the region is also completely waterless.[5] As a result we had to expend our last reserves of oil in order to obtain drinking water. Ogle Peninsula is so flat and Barrow Gulf so shallow that it was only by careful investigation of the ice that we were able to determine that we had already reached the sea.

Adelaide Peninsula beyond Barrow Gulf provides a more attractive appearance. According to our running travel calculations (known as dead reckoning) we should soon catch sight of Simpson Strait, separating King William's Land from the American mainland. Suddenly we ran across fresh sledge tracks on a fairly large lake. Their width and other peculiarities indicated that they were not made by a sledge made of wood but by a sledge chiselled from a single piece of ice, as the Inuit sometimes do in the absence of other materials.

One of our companions, whom I shall henceforth call Netsilik Joe in view of his Netsilik origins, explained that we were only a short distance from a camp of his countrymen. We stopped on a hill and lined up all the sledges like a battery of guns heading into enemy fire. Ahead of us lay the coast of Adelaide Peninsula, deeply indented by embayments; on an arm of the sea about a mile away stood 13–15 snow houses of the above mentioned Netsilingmiut. Inuit emerged from

A sled made of ice

every house and gazed up at us in amazement. As with every new encounter we left the sledges in the care of the women and walked toward the village. Halfway there, the bearer of a flag-of-truce, in the person of a middle-aged woman, came toward us. The closer she approached our group the slower and shorter her steps became and her features betrayed a certain unease. She carried a small knife as a weapon. However strange this custom of sending a woman to meet strangers may seem, it is always practised by this tribe. Our interpreter let it be known that *qallunaat* (whites) had arrived, and in a few minutes any doubts that Joe's fears and the precautionary measures he had advised were groundless, had been dispelled. The shout of 'Qallunaat!' alone had a magical effect, and the feared Netsilingmiut became our friends. We pitched camp near them and in a council next day began interviewing those individuals whose testimony had been publicized by previous searchers. Our aim was to check the validity of their stories by cross-questioning. We listened two and even three times over to the accounts of every person who in any way had come in contact with Franklin's men or with their possessions. The witnesses

An Inuit bearer of a flag-of-trace

In council with the Netsilingmiut

were heard separately and everything was arranged in order to eliminate any possible humbug and to achieve the absolute truth. Only once
all their statements were exhausted did we announce a large reward for
the finding of papers or written material, or of any other items which
might lead indirectly to useful conclusions.

The natives of the Netsilingmiut group today occupy the entire
coast of the Adelaide Peninsula; but this was certainly not the case in
Franklin's day. Their old hunting grounds are located on Boothia
Isthmus (east of King William's Land) and only occasionally would the
odd family, responding to the nomadic urge, undertake a journey to the
area they now inhabit and to King William's Land. Even now they visit
the latter only in the fall, and even then only the southeastern part.
The northwest coast of the island first became known to them through
the loss of Franklin's crews, and their attention was drawn to this part
of the island by McClintock's visit. We obtained statements from
various people and I shall quote the most noteworthy from my journal,
as they were given by the various witnesses.

Siutiitsuq (earless: so called because he is hard of hearing) is a man of
50–5 years. Years ago he saw a boat somewhat to the west of Richardson
Point and found a skeleton near it.[6] He cannot remember any details

but there is an old woman living in the settlement who was once the finder of this location, and has a better memory. He offers to take our party to the spot where the boat was found, and show us the spot which we later came to know as Starvation Cove.

Tuktutchiak, an old woman belonging to the Pelly Bay band but who has lived for a long time among the Netsilingmiut, related: 'I have never seen Franklin people alive but I found skeletons and a body near the beach in a small inlet.[7] I was then accompanied by my husband, my adopted son Ibro[8] who is here today, and seven other Inuit. The boat we found lay on its keel* and in it were some skeletons, but I cannot recall the number. Outside the boat I saw four skulls and other human bones. Only one body still had some skin and hair (blonde). The last-mentioned person could have died only the previous winter or spring and was well preserved, although foxes and wolves appeared to have been gnawing at the body. I definitely remember that this man had spectacles and snow goggles lying near him; he wore a ring on his finger, ear rings and a watch fastened to them (the ear rings)** by means of a chain.' The witness and her son Ibro refused to admit that they were mistaken about this latter point, and stuck firmly to their statement despite all objections.[9] In the boat itself lay a great variety of articles: watches, spectacles, snow goggles, a small saw, clay pipes, wood, tin, canvas and clothing, a piece of iron with a hole in it which moved when *savik* (metal) was placed close to it (evidently a compass needle). There was also a tin box (one foot wide and two feet long) full of books and written materials, another box with human bones,** and a tin box of tobacco. We took many of the articles with us and gave them to our children as toys, and I believe the boxes, with time, became covered with sand and seaweed. I had associated with whites earlier in the old Netsilingmiut lands.'

The most important witness was Alañak, of the Netsilingmiut, about fifty-five years old, who testified:

'In the company of my husband, who has since died, and two other families, we were on King William's Land to hunt seals (in the vicinity of Washington Bay near Cape Herschel) and met a party of whites walking southeast; they were about ten in number and were pulling a boat on a sledge. At first we were afraid but when some of the whites came up to us, we engaged in conversation with them by sign-language. They all looked thin, starved, and ill; they were black around the eyes

*Other witnesses reported that the boat was overturned.
**Reported variously and ambiguously.

and mouth and were not wearing any fur clothing. We camped together for four days and shared a seal with the whites, for which I received a chopping knife as payment. As far as I can remember the whites were carrying nothing to eat with them, and while we were together some of them slept in the boat, some in a small tent. During that time I was quite often with the whites. The man from whom I got the knife was called Tuluak by the others; he was tall and strongly built and had a black beard flecked with grey. Aglukan (another name given by the Inuit to one of the men they met) was smaller than the man just described, with a reddish-brown beard while Doktuk (clearly the doctor) was a thick-set man who, like the other two, wore spectacles but not snow goggles [the Inuit specifically described spectacles by the fact that they compared the glass in them to ice (sikku)]. We would have stayed longer with the whites but the ice in Simpson Strait began to break up and to become unsafe. After we had left them and had tried unsuccessfully to cross, we went back to the coast of King William's Land and remained there all summer in the vicinity of Gladman Point, but we never saw the whites again. The following spring we were in the vicinity of Terror Bay (all these points were identified by the individuals concerned on a large map spread in front of them), and there on a small hill with extremely little snow on the ground I found a tent with skeletons lying outside. About two of them were covered with sand and small stones. There were also skeletons lying inside the tent, covered with clothes and blankets, as well as various articles such as spoons, knives, and watches scattered around.'

The witness admitted that her people had carried away everything they imagined would be useful and also asserted that they had not opened any graves, although this was contradicted by the fact that she knew two corpses had been buried. The other statements, which due to the slowness of interpretation occupied a considerable time, all pointed to the fact that the Inuit had searched King William's Land from one end to the other, and that by their own admission not only their tribe, but also others, were in the habit of going to the northwestern part of the island in order to recover articles of wood, copper, iron, etc. which were lying around.

These are, in abbreviated form, essentially the reports which we needed as a basis for the planned execution of our search.

As far as we had an opportunity to make an estimate of numbers, the Netsilingmiut tribe appears to be fairly large, but the encampment we encountered first probably forms the main nucleus of the whole. The remainder live in smaller encampments of from two to seven families scattered along the northern and western coasts of Adelaide Peninsula, where these people depend partly on fishing, partly on sealing at this time of year.

News of our arrival spread like wildfire through the nearby encampments and next day the men from those encampments arrived to visit us. Among others a deputation of this type appeared on 1 June around 11 P.M.; in order to satisfy the requirements of Netsilik custom or the customs of the country as Eskimo Joe called them, we had to go outside in order to repeat the boring procedure of lining up in two rows and to answer our visitors' questions.

Today for the first time the sun did not set, but after it had just touched the hills with its lowest edge, began to rise again. By its light around midnight our huts, on which the snow domes had had to be replaced by a covering of old reindeer skins due to the warm weather, the various costumes, the brightly coloured mix of men, women, and children, all presented a colourful and interesting picture. I had taken myself off to a nearby hill with my sketch book, unseen, or so I believed, and began sketching. But I had scarcely made more than a few strokes when the number of people around the huts steadily began to decrease, and I was surrounded by a large circle of curious people. Although they did not immediately realize what I was doing, they at least condescended not to block my view.

During our entire stay at this, the first Netsilik encampment along our line of march, as well as at all subsequent ones, the people brought us relics of various kinds, but none of them had any marks which might have allowed identification. We suspected that for unknown reasons the people were not showing us everything, and indeed when we began to carry out house-searches in all the huts we found several quite significant items. These included a board in which the letters L.F. had been spelled out with copper nails. The site where this board was found lies on the eastern part of a peninsula near which the ship previously mentioned had sunk. This find was interesting in that, if the letters were the initials of a member of the Franklin crews, one could easily establish which of the two ships had come so far south. A tin plate was gladly accepted by the owner as a substitute, and we guarded the board like a treasure for the whole of the remainder of the expedition. But unfortunately it turned out that the letters did not have the presumed significance and hence the board lost its value to us.[10]

The meetings which we organized in every encampment held a double interest for us. We not only picked up clues for our search but also had an opportunity to study the Netsilik character. To hold such a council (see the illustration, p 72) we would choose a spacious snow house; everybody who wanted to attend could do so, and certainly there was no lack of curious faces, intent on catching every word. Two interpreters served to make everything understood, namely Eskimo Joe, who rendered the questions from English, and Netsilik Joe, who was able to make more comprehensible for his countrymen what Eskimo Joe had said than the latter could have achieved given the differences in the dialects of the two groups, although admittedly these were quite minor.

It was only natural that interrogations conducted in this fashion were a very time-consuming operation, but one had to render a favourable verdict, which surpassed all our expectations, with regard to the mental capacities of the Inuit. A good example of this was their comprehension of maps shown to them. For an area which is known to an Inuk from long residence there, a simple map is perfectly adequate in order to pick out certain points. Admittedly he would not worry about a few miles more or less, but where a fairly large bay, a peninsula, or some other noteworthy landmark characterizes the region in question, he will be able to bring his own view of the landscape into complete harmony with that depicted by the map. His drawings of a stretch of coast which is known to him are particularly interesting since he indicates every smallest headland but completely ignores major swings to the various points of the compass, so that one has first to accustom oneself to his straight-line drawings in order to understand them.

His weakest side with regard to mental development involves counting. His system of counting extends only up to 20 and he forms all the numbers up to there from the numbers 1 (atausiq), 2 (marquunik), 3 (pingasut), 4 (sitamanik), 5 (tallimanik), 6 (arriniq), 10 (qulit), and 11 (aqanakpuk).* The number 7 is the second 6, ie, marquini arriniq; 12 is the second 11, ie, marquini aqanakpuk;* and similarly 19 is the fourth sixth 11, ie sitamanik arriniq aqanakpuk,* certainly a long name for such a small number. Twenty is the second ten, hence maqquni qulit; everything above twenty is expressed exactly with the fingers, or simply amisu idli (but so many).

On our journey through the various camps along the north coast of Adelaide Peninsula, among other news we received reports of the existence of an intact cairn, and on 5 June, along with Gilder, Tulugaq,

*Dr R.G. Williamson was unable to decipher what Klutschak intended here.

and an Inuk as guide, Lieutenant Schwatka made a trip to it with a light sledge.

The report proved to be true. C.F. Hall had erected the cairn on 12 May 1869, that is, almost exactly ten years before, over the remains of two persons (unidentified members of the unfortunate expedition) in the presence of some Inuit, and hence they knew that there was nothing to be found inside.[11] The cairn itself is built of flat slabs of siltstone, and one of them bears the following inscription scratched into it: 'Eternal honor to the discoverers of the Northwest Passage.' H., 12 May 1869. With this simple monument its builder, who himself had died on 8 November 1871 in command of the *Polaris* North Pole expedition, provided the proof that he himself had reached the coast of King William's Land, something which had been doubted even by his friends.

As an example of what dog sledges can achieve with regard to speed when driven by an experienced Inuk, it should be mentioned here that the trip just described lasted in total a mere 8½ hours, despite the fact that it covered fifty miles there and back, and included a stop of 1½ hours.

Crossing the narrow Simpson Strait, around noon on 10 June we reached the low coast of King William's Land; as a sign of our safe arrival we carved with a knife the letters 'U.S.F.S. (United States Franklin Search, June 10, 1879). All's well,' in a large slab of siltstone. On the evening of the 12th we reached Cape Herschel.

CHAPTER FIVE

From Cape Herschel to Cape Felix, 12 June–3 July 1879

An old cairn. The party splits up. Our last bread.
Difficult travelling. A surprise. Crossing Erebus Bay. The first
grave. The finds at Irving Bay. Cape Felix. A bear hunt.

In the history of polar travels Cape Herschel is famous for the cairn which the polar explorers Dease and Simpson erected on 25 August 1839 to mark the most northerly point they reached.[1] The cairn had been partially demolished by the Inuit, certainly, yet a suffficiently large part had survived to indicate its location. Although Cape Herschel had never been reported, either by the Inuit or by earlier searchers, as a point specially associated with the Franklin expedition, such an idea was provoked by some twelve or fifteen cairns which stood in the immediate vicinity of the abovementioned cairn, and which looked very much like graves. But since the snow was still deep we could determine nothing specific about them and we had to leave a closer examination of this area to a later period.

With our attainment of Cape Herschel we had reached the starting point of our search. In implementing the search we could not employ the Inuit whom we had brought with us, and Lieutenant Schwatka now left them behind, with instructions to look after their own support, either here or on Adelaide Peninsula, and to accumulate sufficient blubber oil for the return trip to Hudson Bay by means of diligent seal hunting. Only one family was to accompany us. Tulugaq had earned the respect of everyone by his energy and skill, and on the basis of his abilities as a hunter we were certain that he and his repeating rifle (a gift from the company Winchester and Son) were capable of supporting us. We daily saw herds of caribou coming across to the island from the mainland and according to the Netsilingmiut King William's Land suffered from no lack of game in summer.

Eskimo Joe was entrusted with safeguarding our supplies of ammunition, etc. to the best of his abilities, and in the event that, counter to reports, King William's Land turned out to be too poor in game to support the Inuit left behind under his supervision, and that the latter thus found themselves obliged to cross to the mainland, he was to take all our supplies with him with the exception of the kayak. But under any circumstances the sealskin boat was to be left behind at this point in a completely usable condition, while its position would indicate to us the direction in which Joe and the depot were located.

15 June was a memorable day for our party. In the last snow house of the season, the last remains of our supply of hardtack was distributed among the Inuit, who since our departure from Hudson Bay, had been allocated a daily ration of 1 lb per head. We ourselves consumed the last crumbs for supper (see the illustration, p 80). For the next eight months we would have to do without bread, and soon meat would be our only food.

A cheese, 40 lbs of pressed meat, and the same amount of cornstarch represented the total amount of food which lay on the sledge when we left Eskimo Joe and his party on the morning of 17 June. Our plan was to cut across country to reach Cape Felix, the most northerly point of King William's Land, before the snow disappeared. It was tough going to push ahead 10–12 miles every day, and only somebody who has waded, step by step, day after day, through water 12–18 inches deep, or sinking knee-deep in slushy snow, can have some concept of the difficulties of this trip. As far as the sun was concerned there was no distinction between day and night, and even though at times the temperature dropped sufficiently for thin ice crusts to form, summer had arrived in these parts. In view of the level or only slightly undulating terrain the immense snowfields were turning into vast lagoon-like accumulations of water which transformed the mossy meadows which lay beneath the snow, and were now starting to emerge, into almost impassable morasses. Every step was hazardous, and it was especially the apparently bottomless snowdrifts which made progress for man and dog almost impossible. Under these circumstances the distance to Collinson Gulf seemed to us to be much too great; in order to reach it by the shortest possible route acccording to our maps, we had set a north-northwesterly course. But even greater was our amazement when we spotted rough sea ice through the telescope to the north on the evening of the 20th. Could the maps contain such a major discrepancy from the true shape of the island? This certainly did not augur very well for the credibility of the previous cartographic representation of these arctic regions. Yet next

The last snow house at Cape Herschel

day we reached Erebus Bay, which we thought lay farther west, and following the coast we continued our march on the sea ice. On the evening of the 21st we even found, to our great delight, a large piece of driftwood, and hence we could hope that we would find driftwood for cooking our meals.

In our journals 22 June is marked in black, since on that day the miseries of the journey reached their nadir. The ice of Victoria Strait, which washes the northwest coast of the island, was not simply one-year ice formed since last fall; instead it was composed of floes of varying size which had been formed farther north, had drifted south with the current, and had been piled up here in a wild chaos by the autumnal gales before being frozen together. Here and there a small iceberg projected from a group of sharp-edged ice blocks, while between all of them lay soft snowdrifts or pools of water. Only with great effort, and with frequent detours, could we find a half-passable route for the sledges. Tulugaq's wife, who, so as not to have to wade constantly through the water, leaped from ice block to ice block, with great difficulty and extreme effort since she was carrying their well-nourished son on her back, was an object of general sympathy, but it would have been impossible to transport these two on the sledges as we normally did. Repeatedly the sledge would stick fast; the dogs alone would be incapable of moving it even a hair's-breadth when it had run against a hidden ice block half-buried in the snow, or when one of its runners sank into one of the many invisible ice crevices. It was usually Tulugaq who got us out of such predicaments, hacking away a piece of ice with his large knife, then applying his whip, voice, and strong arm. Each of us whites had long since fastened his hauling harness to the sledge, and we lifted, pulled, or pushed with all our strength (see illustration, p 82). This continued for ten long miles. The stony hills of this monotonous coast have never looked more welcome to us than that evening, and a well-cooked evening meal would never have tasted better, but we had smashed our only cooking pot into a useless cripple against a piece of ice. Since leaving Cape Herschel, Tulugaq had brought in a great deal of game from his hunts; ducks, geese, and swans were abundant all around us; the egg-laying season had arrived; driftwood was available for fuel. But alas we had no cooking pot.

The snow had still not entirely melted and hence for the remainder of the trip we no longer needed to hurry. Instead we enjoyed several rest days, which were used for wandering around the region and for preparing to examine it in detail.

In a cairn on Franklin Point which had the appearance of a grave

Crossing Erebus Bay

built above ground, we found a skull which Lieutenant Schwatka immediately identified as that of a white man.[2] After a thorough search of the grave the skull was buried and the spot marked by a small monument. On another occasion, on the 27th, Franz Melms and I were walking along the coast toward Victory Point, where Sir James Ross had erected a stone cairn on one of his journeys. Near the waterline Melms found a strip of canvas (such as is used for hauling a sledge), with the marking T. 11. While he was making a more thorough inspection of the area I spotted a cairn and near it a human skull. It was a grave made of flat slabs of sandstone, like a grave-vault but built above ground.[3] It had once been covered but had obviously been subjected to a search. The skull (indisputably that of a white man) lay outside, along with other human bones. Inside the grave a luxuriant growth of moss was flourishing on some remnants of blue cloth which, judging by the buttons and the fine texture, had once belonged to an English officer's uniform. A silk handkerchief in a remarkably good state of preservation lay at the head end and above it on a rock a silver medal measuring 2½–2¾ inches in diameter lay openly exposed. The fact that this medal had escaped the eyes of the Inuit I can only ascribe to the fact that it had either been hidden by snow, or that the natives' loot was already quite considerable and that they had overlooked this piece of silver in their joy. Even I did not notice it at first glance since it was the same colour as the rock. The solid silver medal bore on one side a bas-relief of the British king with the inscription 'Georgius IIII D.G. Britain. Rex

Lieutenant Irving's grave

1820.' On the other side was a laurel wreath and around the outside of it was engraved the inscription 'Second Mathematical Prize, Royal Naval College,' and inside it 'Awarded to John Irving, Midsummer 1830.' The medal had been placed in the grave along with the dead man (lieutenant on board *Terror*) about thirty years earlier. During this long period it had even left a mark on the rock, and it provided definite proof as to the identity of the person buried here.

Less than a hundred paces from the shore lay the remains of an artificial heap of rocks which had been thrown together, a pile of old clothes, and a large number of objects which clearly belonged to the equipment of an arctic expedition. They included four stoves with pots and other accessories. Along a short stretch of coast lay items of clothing, stockings, and mittens sewed from woollen blankets, razors, etc. as well as a surgeon's tourniquet. An earthenware jug bore the imprint 'R. Wheatley, Wine and Spirit Merchant, Greenhithe, Kent,' while a brush carried the name 'H. Wilks' carved into its wood.

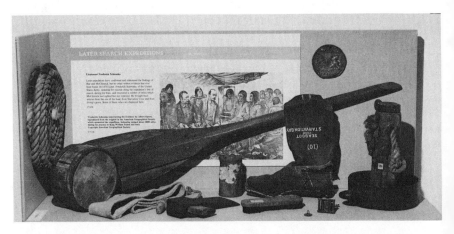

Display of artifacts recovered by the Schwatka expedition from King William Island, now preserved at the National Maritime Museum, Greenwich. Reproduced by permission of the National Maritime Museum

Despite the varied nature of the articles lying around, and although we searched persistently for the next few days, nothing came to the fore which promised to provide any fuller explanation. A simple notebook would have been a find whose significance could have led to great achievements in the search area. But it was too late; thirty-one long

Site of the major cache of abandoned clothing and equipment where the crews
of *Erebus* and *Terror* came ashore, as it appeared in 1982.
Courtesy of Dr Owen Beattie

winters had passed over this spot since Franklin's men camped here for
three days in April 1848.

The historic significance of the site (here I shall anticipate the
chronological order of my description in order to achieve greater
coherence) only became clear to us when we again spent some time on
the site fourteen days later in order to erect a monument on Irving's
grave. Our party took his remains with us for transport back to
England in order to protect them from being disinterred again.

Tulugaq and his better half were looking around the site for further
finds when the latter discovered a paper which turned out to be a letter
from Captain McClintock, between three rocks about 4–5 feet from the
previously mentioned cairn.[4] The letter contained an exact copy of the
original document which Franklin's men had deposited in a cairn here.
It read as follows:

7 May 1859
69°38'N; 98°41'W

This cairn was found yesterday by a party from Lady Franklin's yacht 'Fox,' which at present is wintering in Bellot Strait. It contained a notice of which the following is an exact copy:

'28 of May 1847
H.M. ships 'Erebus' and 'Terror' wintered in the ice in lat. 70°05'N, long. 98°23'W. Having wintered in 1846–47 at Beechey Island, in lat. 74°43'28"N, long. 91°39'15"W, after having ascended Wellington Channel to lat. 77°, and returned by the west side of Cornwallis Island.
Sir John Franklin commanding the expedition.
All well.
Party consisting of 2 officers and 6 men left the ships on Monday 24th May, 1847.

Gm. Gore, Lieut.
Chas. F. Des Voeux, Mate.'

This was written on a printed form which contained in six languages the request that when found the paper should be forwarded to the British Admiralty. Around the edge of the paper was written:

April 25, 1848. H.M. ships 'Terror' and 'Erebus' were deserted on the 22nd April, 5 leagues N.N.W. of this, having been beset since 12th September, 1846. The officers and crew, consisting of 105 souls, under the command of Captain F.R.M. Crozier landed here in lat. 69°37'42"N, long. 98°41'W. This paper was found by Lt. Irving 4 miles to the northward, where it had been deposited by the late Commander Gore in June, 1847. Sir James Ross' pillar has not, however, been found, and the paper has been transferred to this position which is that in which Sir J. Ross' pillar was erected. Sir John Franklin died on the 11th June, 1847; and the total loss by deaths in the expedition has been to this date 9 officers and 15 men.

(Signed)
F.R.M. Crozier,
Captain and Senior Officer

(Signed)
James Fitzjames,
Captain H.M.S. Erebus,
and start on to-morrow, 26th, for Back's Fish River.

Around this monument, which we erected yesterday noon, the last crews appear to have made a selection of travelling materials and to have left everything superfluous lying around the area. I stayed on the site until almost noon today, looking for remains. No other paper was found. It is my intention to follow the coast southwest and search for the wreck of a ship which according to the Eskimos is located on the beach.

Three other cairns were found between here and Cape Felix; they do not contain anything . . .

Signed William R. Hobson
Lieutenant in command of the party.

This paper is a copy of the document left by Captain Crozier as he was retreating to Back's River with the crews of the 'Erebus' and 'Terror.'

The report of the find by Lieutenant R.W. Hobson is intended for me. Since the natives appear to have torn apart a cairn built here in 1831, I intend burying a similar document 10 feet north of the middle of this cairn and one foot underground.

F.L. McClintock,
Captain, Royal Navy.[5]

This paper had lain here since May 1859, ie, a full twenty years, and its discovery threw us into great excitement. Each of us thought we had found a new, previously unknown document and even Tulugaq, who brought us his wife's lucky find, his face beaming with joy, seemed to recognize the significance of a written paper. But (as we learned later) it is just a copy of a well-known document; nonetheless its rediscovery still provides proof, on the one hand, that if properly deposited and especially if they are written in pencil, documents will remain legible, and on the other hand that our search was not just a superficial one.

As we followed the coast further we found the snow largely melted and when on 3 July we were brought to a halt by a second accumulation of relics from the Franklin expedition, the land swung to the east about a mile farther north. We had reached Cape Felix, the most northerly point of the island. Near the coast stood a cairn which had certainly been erected by human hands, but had been partially torn apart again. Around it lay broken, empty beer bottles, a sign that men had once lived better here than we did now. Canvas, woollen blankets, etc. were found mixed up together in wild disorder; from the reports of the McClintock expedition this must also have been the spot where Lieutenant Hobson found a British flag in 1859.

As far as the eye could see the distant view offered nothing but ice, a barren ice surface consisting of a mixture of large and small ice blocks thrown together; beyond it a dark bluish-grey strip on the northwestern horizon identified the coast of Boothia Felix Peninsula.

Since this was the 103rd anniversary of the United States of America we celebrated the 4th of July by hoisting our expedition flag and by killing a large polar bear whose meat promised to provide many good feasts for our dogs. This terrifying neighbour was busy demolishing a seal about six miles out to sea when Tulugaq spotted it through his telescope.

With Franz Melms and a fourteen-year-old boy he immediately set off in pursuit, taking a light sledge hauled by twelve dogs. 'In less than an hour,' my companion recalled, 'we were within 400–500 paces of the bear.' In the presence of its pursuers the bear sought safety in flight, but too late. Tulugaq had already cut the traces of three of his best dogs and these raced after the quarry, while the rest tore after them with the sledge, careening over rough ice blocks and through deep pools of water. Despite its unwieldiness a bear makes fast progress when chased, and if there is open water in the vicinity this is always the goal of its flight. But the sledge was gaining ground; Tulugaq already had his magazine rifle with nine shots ready, and holding his knife in his hands he was whipping his dogs on. The sledge flew through or over every obstacle and the three men sitting on the sledge had their work cut out to stay aboard. Three more dogs were loosed; the bear stopped running, sought a favourable defensive position on a high ice pinnacle, and held the six fierce dogs at bay. The latter tugged at its coat here and there and distracted the bear's attention from the hunter. It was now Tulugaq's turn. He fired his first shot from a range of twenty-five paces, then another; the bear did not drop but scratched itself behind the ears and charged at Tulugaq. The latter leaped back and the dogs sided with their master with renewed fury. Tulugaq hit his opponent in the heart with another shot and stretched it out on the ice. The furious struggle was at an end and, barking and howling, the dogs demanded their share in wild impatience. Our hero extracted a bullet from somewhere in the bear's head; although fired at a range of only twenty-five paces it had not penetrated the bone but had been completely flattened. The skin of the dead bear measured 10′4″ from the snout along the back. The very next day another giant specimen came to within 300 paces of our tent, but was wounded by a rifle shot and took off. Polar bears are far from rare in this area and in winter, will come right up to the snow houses. The Netsilingmiut engage in many courageous hand-to-hand combats with them.

CHAPTER SIX

The Main Search and Its Results, 6 July–6 August 1879

Cape Felix. The party's summer life. Following the line of march
of the Franklin people. Their remains. A memorable location
on Erebus Bay. A beautiful natural spectacle. Ice break-up.
Tedious overland travel. A young bear. Terror Bay.
The lieutenant's first caribou. The results of the search around
Terror Bay and Cape Crozier.

Some 15–20 miles north-northwest and seaward of Cape Felix is the
location where on 12 September 1846 Sir John Franklin's ships were
permanently prevented by the ice from further progress. During a
captivity lasting twenty months their distance off the coast between
Cape Felix and Irving Bay remained approximately the same. Here, too,
the fine hopes of the Franklin expedition collapsed; here began its total
inactivity, the start of every ill; here death demanded numerous
victims in the persons of Sir John Franklin, Lieutenant Graham Gore,
and a further seven officers and fifteen crew members; here the men
were obliged to abandon their ships; and here for the survivors began
those fearful sufferings which ended only in death as a welcome
deliverance. The British flag once found here, as mentioned earlier,
proved that the point at which our party reached its highest latitude
between 3 and 6 July was once visited by the officers and men, while
the varied articles lying around indicated even today that this spot was
used either as a hunting station or as an observatory. Two artificial
cairns located in the vicinity had escaped detection by the natives,
with their passion for destruction, and we subjected them to a
thorough investigation. One of them lay about two miles in the
interior; it was eight feet high and still intact but it contained nothing,
despite the fact that its style of construction, its heavily moss-covered
rocks, and the immediate surroundings left no doubt that it had been
erected by whites.[1]

Cape Felix

Our visit to the second cairn, located on the coast, revealed an old piece of paper which contained a drawing of a life-size pointing hand.[2] Unfortunately its lower end had rotted away under the influence of the elements. The southward-pointing hand certainly must have been pointing at something, but the explanation was no longer available and the only result of this find was an increased attentiveness on our part.

In the event that Franklin's expedition had brought its dead ashore for burial, their burial place would have to be on the stretch of coast between Cape Felix and Irving Bay since terrain conditions were quite suitable here. If they had been built with some care and thought the grave sites should neither have been destroyed by the ravages of time nor by the natives, and all traces of them should not have been permanently erased for an observant and thoughtful searcher.

During our entire sojourn in the area and on the southward march from Cape Felix, that is, from 7 to 24 July, we exercised the greatest care in our search and, so to speak, left no stone unturned which from its location or position seemed at all suspicious to us. Spaced some distance from each other, we covered every smallest indentation or headland on the coast and every second day, without moving our campsite, we made further excursions into the interior to check the view of several earlier searchers that Franklin's men would have deposited more detailed documents farther from the coast.

It was a very tedious task. To the impact of the unaccustomed relatively high temperature was added the unpleasantness of a terrain which was very tiring to the walker. Moreover, the switch to a wholly meat diet made itself felt on our systems in a very unpleasant fashion.

The land forms of King William's Land belong to a fairly recent period; this is a land mass developed on white and grey siltstone strata. The continued formation of these strata would be a profitable field of study for the geologist; but it cannot even escape a carefully observant layman how slowly, but with the exertion of fearful natural forces, the broken ice masses year by year are pushing rock on top of rock from the sea toward the coast. The result is the series of terrace-like steps whose regularity and universal occurrence along the western and southern coasts is so striking.[3] The stretches of land which rise slowly toward the interior display vast areas of water in the interior, while between the magnificent lakes and ponds there stretch for miles the most luxuriant meadows of moss;[4] toward the coast, however, these become increasingly sparse and cease completely at the beach. If there is a little fertile ground lying in a hollow it is covered with a miserable moss, even despised by the caribou; it turns green with the melting snow, blooms with a pale red flower for the duration of the little water puddles, and dies as soon as the sun has sucked up the water, its sole source of life. In the interior the flora is somewhat richer and the famous botanist Professor Dr Moriz Willkomm, Director of the Imperial/Royal Botanical Gardens in Prague, has been good enough to identify, at my request, some of the plants which I picked and brought back, as occurring most frequently on King William's Land. I shall list their names for devotees of botany: *Epilobium latifolium* L., *Saxifraga cernua* L., *Salix Myrxniter* L., *Stellaria humifura* Rottb., *Draba alpina* L., *Rubus chamaemorus* L., *Cineraria congesta* R. Br., an unidentified species of *Potentilla, Oxytropis arctica* R. Br., *Cassiope tetragona* Don., a species related to *Anthemis alpina* L., and *Eriophorum Scheuchzeri* Hoppe.

But even this adornment is quite rare in relation to the little siltstone pebbles, which generally lie with their flat sides up, in colourful confusion. However, they are also often positioned with their sharp edges upward due to frost and cold, thus forming an unpleasant surface for a hiker shod only with thin sealskin soles. A short stretch of

Jagged, abrasive gravels of the raised beaches near Cape Jane Franklin, 1982.
Courtesy of Dr Owen Beattie

sandy coast made a rare, if very welcome change.

Tulugaq, who was driving our sledge along the ice, was battling the same unpleasantness as we whites on land. Even for these colossal ice masses the season was far advanced, and wide, deep cracks were appearing with the melting of the snow. The ice formations were becoming rougher and more angular than before, presenting ever greater obstacles to the sledges' progress. Especially in the evening, when by a prearranged signal we brought the sledge close in to land to make camp, we had many a wet struggle. The masses of water pouring off the land had melted the ice in the immediate vicinity of the coast and only at ebb tide was it possible to bring our things ashore, unless one wanted to wade through deep water.

In June the soft snow had caused us a great deal of unpleasantness; now it was the water which hampered us everywhere. Small watercourses had become roaring rivers, the large flat meadows had become morasses, and every depression in the land, depending on its size, had become a pond or a lake.

Anybody who is afraid of getting his feet wet should not go to King

William's Land in summer; for an entire month we did not know what it was to have dry footwear. In terms of both material and workmanship sealskin boots are completely waterproof, but terrain like this makes fun of the durability of any footwear. Our diligent housewife was busy early and late patching the boots of all six of us, yet none of us had a pair of intact soles.

On the move from morning to evening, we found that we always had a good appetite, for which the country supplied what we needed. There were caribou on the land and seals on the ice and Tulugaq procured an adequate supply of both. We took care of harvesting birds and eggs. There was no lack of the latter, especially; wherever we saw a duck or goose flying up nearby, we would find a free supply of eggs.

There is a remarkable difference between summer and winter in these regions. The former is such a short season, and the transition from winter to summer is so fast. In the wink of an eye animal life is swarming, especially with regard to bird species, where earlier there had been only snow and ice, and where only a polar bear, fox, or snowy owl might survive.

Given our irregular life-style, without any specific divisions of time, there could be no thought of resting at night. There was no night, and even if we were tired enough to sleep in broad daylight, there was another factor which prevented this. In view of the meagre work they were doing our unruly pack of dogs was very well fed and would invariably have disturbed our rest; it would have taken Tulugaq's greatest efforts with his whip and thrown rocks in order to keep them quiet.

Thus we were following a nomadic life in the fullest sense of the word as we followed in the tracks of the retreating men of the Franklin expedition southward from Irving Bay. But we soon saw the number of traces of that expedition decrease. On the point named after Le Vesconte (one of the officers of the expedition) another grave was located,[5] and just as in the case of Lieutenant Irving's grave, the bones from the grave, which had since been disturbed by the natives. But the builders of this grave no longer had the strength to build an above-ground grave out of large rocks. A few stones were all that they had used to cover the corpse and there was nothing to indicate any chance of learning the name of the man buried there.

The route which the unfortunates had taken on their sad march was indicated surely and unmistakably by a series of blue rags and cloth, buttons, and other trifles, while here and there stones laid out in a large quadrilateral demarcated the former site of a tent.

If we had doubted the truth of the Inuit's statements that they had assiduously searched the west coast of King William's Land, we might still have cherished the joyful hope that we would find the key to unravel the secret of this catastrophe; but their statements turned out to be only too truthfully accurate. On Adelaide Peninsula an Inuk had told us that he had found tin cans, barrel staves, an axe, and other articles, but had not taken them with him for lack of transport; instead he had cached them under some rocks. When he came back again he was unable to find these articles again. But even this cache did not escape our searching eyes; we found precisely the articles he had listed, all bearing the broad arrow of the British Queen as a sure sign of their authenticity and hidden, well preserved, under some rocks.

By mid-July the difficulties of making progress on the ice were steadily increasing and the frequent occurrence of fog was having such a disadvantageous impact on our sticking to the sea ice as a route that we now had to hurry to reach at least Cape Crozier, the most westerly point of the island, before the ice broke up completely. But even in this we were disappointed.

After we had crossed the La Roquette River, wading more than hip-deep in water, and had waded knee-deep through the swamps which surrounded it, we did not find our sledge again until around 3:00 A.M. and did not finally have our supper until 5:00 A.M. We broke camp again after 2:30 P.M. on 21 July in order to continue our march. Around 10:00 P.M. Melms spotted three human skulls on the beach quite near the shore and as we approached closer a sad sight presented itself.

We collected no less than seventy-six human bones which, from a superficial examination, let us conclude that at least four people had lost their lives here. These remains were immediately buried beneath a small cairn and a document about the find was placed with them.

Scattered over a surface area of almost a quarter square mile lay the remnants of a large boat[6] and beneath them a wide variety of articles, the most striking of which were some pieces of sacking in which bullets and shot, as well as some percussion caps, were tied up. Without a doubt this was the same spot where in 1859 Captain McClintock had found the boat with the two skeletons, and about whose existence the Inuit had first learned from him.

That same summer they moved here and about a quarter of a mile farther inland they found a second boat, also lashed on a sledge, which had earlier been hidden by a snowdrift. Both boats were dismantled and everything usable taken away. Only the sledges were usable by the natives in their original form, and they still exist; one of them had already been purchased by us on Adelaide Peninsula.

A modern-day hiker making heavy weather of the
muddy surface conditions near La Roquette River.
Courtesy of Dr Owen Beattie

Boot sole found in 1982 at the site where Schwatka's party discovered the
remnants of a boat on the shores of Erebus Bay.
Courtesy of Dr Owen Beattie

Bowl of a clay pipe found in 1982 at the site where Schwatka's party
discovered the remnants of a boat on the shores of Erebus Bay.
Courtesy of Dr Owen Beattie

Captain McClintock was of the view that here the physical strength
of the expedition was so exhausted that they were forced to leave their
boats lying or, if one could derive specific conclusions from the
positions of the sledges, that the men had split up here and that a party
had opted to return to the ships, putting their faith in them and
anticipating that they would be saved when the ice broke up. Admittedly the document tells of a complete abandonment of the ships, but
that the return of such a party must have occurred is proved by the fact
that the Inuit thought they saw people on board the ship stranded off
the west coast of Adelaide Peninsula.

No matter from which side one examines it, the site on which our
party now spent some time is typical of the history of the unfortunate
Franklin expedition, as is the route which they chose to reach safety. In
any case the men who died here must have been sick or for some other
reason incapable of marching. The presence of the individual skeletons
lying scattered around also seems to indicate that discipline in the
party had already slackened under those in command at this point.

We had stopped for quite a long time in order to investigate the site and it was shortly before midnight when we fired the prearranged three signal shots for our sledge, which was travelling along the ice. The night was cold; judging by the little puddles the temperature was a little below freezing yet it was still daylight. The sun was just touching the horizon with the lower edge of its great disc, the horizon being formed by a mass of ice blocks thrown wildly together. It then moved away from it again with great speed and after only a few minutes had begun to climb again. Sunset and sunrise almost ran into each other and the peculiar illumination of the ice, which presented its dark, shadowy sides to us, offered a scene of wonderful natural beauty in comparison to the pale-reddish, matt colour of the sun's disc itself.

From now on the sun would be setting for us too. 'We've beaten the best runners in the world,' said Lieutenant Schwatka, 'having covered 422 miles between sunrise and sunset (1 June to 22 July), counting just our line of march alone.'

But no matter how beautiful the sight of the midnight sun, in terms of majesty and gripping grandeur it was overshadowed by the start of the long-dreaded catastrophe of the final break-up of the ice of our route on 24 July. On that particular day we wanted to continue our march in good time, before the arrival of the high tide, in order to transport our load by sledge at least as far as Cape Crozier, but a strong northwest wind accelerated the flood tide. As we were exerting all our strength to load the sledge we noticed that the ice surface, which previously had been still and motionless, had now begun to rise and fall irregularly.

But even this movement lasted only a short time, since in the next few minutes the ice began to press in from the sea; colossal blocks of ice were thrown up on the land like flints, or pushed over and under each other like shingles. The effect of the water and the storm, which piled up great masses of ice with indescribable speed on the points which projected farthest out to sea, presented a strange sight. The grinding, pressing, shoving, and banging continued for about half an hour, and our sledge, which previously had lain not more than eight feet above sea level, along with the block of ice beneath it, weighing several hundred tonnes, had been picked up by another even more massive slab of ice and heaved about 10–12 feet into the air.

Naturally our first efforts were aimed at saving the sledge. Once it and the items on it had been retrieved by our combined strength, Lieutenant Schwatka declared that we next had to transport all these items, the relics and even the sledge across the tongue of land, some

Break-up of the sea ice

thirteen miles wide, to Terror Bay. This bay is, of course, the site where
the major part of the Franklin expedition found its sad end, according
to Inuit reports, and our task now was to find the spot where the tent
mentioned earlier had once stood. We could then continue our search
westward from Terror Bay around the westernmost part of the island.
The very next day Tulugaq removed the whalebone shoeings from the
sledge runners and each of us took a load on his back and set off with it
on our new line of march. On the third day we moved the last of the
remains and thereby moved our campsite about one mile farther south.
The appearance of our column now possessed the look of a band of
smugglers rather than that of an arctic expedition. Everyone had his
sleeping bag and other items strapped to his back like a knapsack and
carried his rifle and other private belongings in his hand; thus we
slowly advanced.

Tulugaq and his wife carried the boy alternately, while under the
special supervision of Arunak each of the dogs was laden with a
burden. One had the tent on its back, another our meagre supply of
meat; in addition, either a tent pole or a piece of firewood had been

Schwatka's party travelling south overland to Terror Bay

lashed to each one, to be dragged along behind. This means of transport was not very comfortable for anyone, either man or dog; the latter would lie down every moment or, to our great annoyance, would try to wade through the deepest part of every pond. But the worst problems were associated with hauling the sledge. It slid very badly over the gravel and it took the combined efforts of all the men and dogs to move it across the first third of the peninsula. While engaged in this strenuous work we were on short rations for the first time. Although we tied them to large rocks every night our numerous dogs made a lot of noise and scared away the caribou, which were very scarce in any event.

When we pitched camp in the evening our evening meal was usually still running around on four legs, and once we all had to wait thirty-six hours for that meal. We received a special treat thanks to Tulugaq's great skill. He had spotted a large piece of driftwood at a point on Terror Bay which we had just left, and took the dogs with him in order to haul it back to camp. Quite exceptionally he had not taken his rifle with him on this occasion. Reaching the spot he sighted a large female bear with a cub about three or four months old. Before the bears were aware of them Tulugaq loosed all the dogs, pelted the adult bear with rocks, separated her from her cub, and killed the latter simply with his knife. The adult bear had no alternative but to flee from the dogs into the open water; meanwhile our hunter set to work and hauled the bear cub back to us on top of the piece of driftwood. If one has not been spoiled by caribou meat, bear meat is a strong food, even if it is rather greasy for summer. Apart from its tenderness the cub's meat had a particularly piquant taste, and we greatly regretted that the old bear had not had twins.

The southward march was difficult and tedious; not until 4 August did we reach Terror Bay with our bag and baggage, totally tired of carrying it. The sea here was not entirely free of ice; large floes lined the entire length of the horizon and even along the shore individual floes were drifting around in large numbers. During the crossing from the north side to the south side of the large Graham Gore Peninsula a significant difference became discernible. The sharp mudstones ceased, to be replaced as we penetrated farther by meadow areas and numerous lakes. The immediate vicinity of Terror Bay is a true paradise compared to the northern part of King William's Land and possesses a great abundance of caribou. With regard to the quality and tenderness of their meat these animals left nothing to be desired. The good grazing and the relatively small area within which they could move resulted in considerable quantities of fat accumulating on the animals' backs and ribs, and once again we could eat caribou steaks. We made soup from pieces of ribs, and the fat did not just float on it in blobs but accumulated in a thick layer which represented the upper part of each serving. During those few days in Terror Bay we enjoyed by far the best food of the entire expedition. Everyone wanted to shoot caribou and pursued them avidly; but it was the lieutenant who paid most dearly for his first bull.

Following the coast he spotted a magnificent set of antlers behind a hill. He stalked up to the animal and fired. But instead of killing the caribou he smashed one of its hind legs. There was only one escape route for the animal; it headed out into the sea, waded a short distance through the shallow water, then clambered up onto one of the ice floes lying near shore. There the lieutenant's second bullet hit it; it collapsed and died. But it was our custom that when somebody did not immediately bring back the meat of an animal he had killed, but cached it under rocks, he always had to bring back a token of proof, which entitled him to enter one unit in the expedition's hunting results and bag book. The tongue, the liver, or even the ears were sufficient for this purpose.

Lieutenant Schwatka, a good hunter from his experience in the American Far West, could not possibly forego that unit, and certainly not when it was his first caribou, and hence he had to clamber into the water and haul his bull ashore. I was standing at the cooking pot when he appeared over a nearby hill; but I could not understand why he had hung his red handkerchief and some other item from his rifle. In earlier days he had brought home many dozen eggs in that same red handkerchief but now, in August, eggs would scarcely be fit for cooking any more. We all watched and made various suggestions, one being that he had found some relic or other, and meanwhile stared carefully through the telescope. But nobody guessed that the lieutenant would have hung his underpants, which had got wet when he waded through the water, on the barrel of his rifle to dry.

The story of his adventure was funny to listen to, but I would have liked even more to have been an unseen witness of this incident, and to have sketched him as he hauled his quarry by the antlers from the ice floe to land, standing hip-deep in the cold, icy water in his shirt and underpants. But enough of the anecdotes; we were here as a searching party.

The advanced season warned us that we should hurry; we still had to cover a large section of land before the first snowfall, which might bring our work to a rapid conclusion. It was necessary that we split up; in the upcoming chapter I shall permit the reader to accompany my party, but I would like to anticipate the chronological order somewhat and finish the coverage of the western part of King William's Land along with Lieutenant Schwatka and Gilder.

Their coverage was painstakingly executed, but any success can be described in only a few words. Not only was there nothing to be found of the former position of the tent, but further interrogation of the original finder revealed that about six years before (six summers as she expressed it), which was when the woman had last visited the site, every trace had been eradicated.

The search of Cape Crozier was also completed, but apart from the skull of a white man,[7] nothing worthy of note was found, with regard to the aims of our expedition. The two men stayed in the area for a whole month and cached their relics and their sledge in such a way that they could easily be found again at the start of the winter. When Melms and Tulugaq and I returned bringing some much-needed footwear, they headed toward the southeast part of the island.

CHAPTER SEVEN

The Divided Search, 6 August to the End of September 1879

The trek to Gladman Point. King William's Land, geographical ·
conditions, geomorphology, and fauna. Cape Herschel. Fog.
Short rations. Our Inuit. Further finds. Adelaide Peninsula and its
relationship to Franklin's disaster. Probable route of the
unfortunates. Eskimo Joe. Inuit customs. The start of winter.
A new source of food. The crossing to King William's Land.
Arrival of Schwatka's party. The end of the search.

On the morning of 6 August we split into two parties. Lieutenant Schwatka and Gilder stayed on the same spot in order to complete the search in the western part of King William's Land while Melms and I had a double task. On our march we were to cover the coast to the southeast, cross Simpson Strait if our Inuit were not on the island itself, then continue the search on Adelaide Peninsula. Tulugaq, who was to accompany our party, was to return to Terror Bay, with a reinforced number of dogs and with renewed supplies of ammunition, tobacco, and footwear.

There could be no thought of very rapid progress since on the one hand we had to carry all our belongings ourselves, and since on the other hand the region we were traversing for the first few days was very rich in game. In particular the fine caribou skins, whose hair was still quite short, moved Tulugaq to some assiduous hunting. But these rich hunting grounds extended east only to around Cape Herschel; from there on, despite the fine mossy meadows, caribou were only rarely sighted. This transition was an astounding one, and inasmuch as we could not take any extra supplies with us on our dogs, this almost total absence of caribou was very unpleasant for us.

The whole time we stuck mainly to the coast itself and had an opportunity to observe both the horizontal and vertical variations in

the geomorphology of the island. Both in its northwestern and southern parts there is significant coastal evolution going on. Terror Bay,
which extends a distance of only fifteen miles east-west between its
bounding capes which project into the open sea, viz. from Fitzjames
Island to Asaph Hall Island, extends for a distance of ninety-six miles if
one follows the shoreline. With the exception of some extremely short
sandy stretches and the quite level clayey beaches in the southern part
of Erebus Bay and the northern part of Washington Bay, all points from
Cape Felix to Tulloch Point are of the same character.

The coast rises from the very shallow sea in small siltstone formations forming undulating terraces parallel to each other;[1] not until the
fourth or fifth step does a slight trace of vegetative life appear. In the
bays the terraces rise higher and form small hills which in form are
identical to those lying next to the coast. On the various points, for
example, the small peninsulas between Terror Bay and Washington
Bay, the new formation of the land occurs in even more characteristic
fashion.

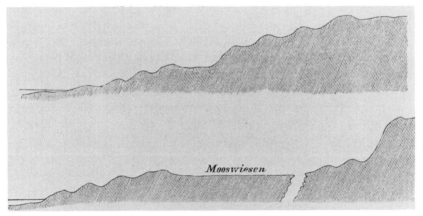

Profiles of the coastal terrain, King William Island
(Mooswiesen = mossy meadows)

Along the sections nearest the coast the terrace forms already
mentioned occur, but behind them at only a small height above sea
level the most magnificent meadows often extend for one to two miles
in width; one often finds remains of driftwood on these. Toward the
interior these moss meadows are bounded by bastion-like belts of hills
which also appear to be composed of siltstone. They are 30–40 feet high
and display a relatively steep slope of 45⁰ to 60⁰ on their seaward side;

indeed in places they drop almost vertically. The illustrations on p 103 present a cross-section through the various vertical landforms, while the drawing on this page illustrates one of the bastion hills.[2]

Whether small or large the siltstone rocks are always flat and display a large number of impressions, of which the three forms illustrated on p 105 occur most commonly.

The uppermost and lowermost are particularly common; one can even say that one of these two forms occurs on one rock in ten.[3] No more significant animal or plant fossils were found either on King William's Land or on Adelaide Peninsula.

The presence of caribou in the various regions is closely linked to the shape of the vertical profile of the land. During the calving period the caribou prefer to remain solitary and away from the coast, and this is greatly facilitated by the land forms of the interior of King William's Land, with its good grazings. In July and early August, by contrast, one finds them near salt water, where a halophitic species of moss grows and commonly occurs in the low meadow lands. To this cause may be ascribed the fact that we saw many caribou west of Cape Herschel, whereas on 13 August, when we reached the cape itself, they disap-

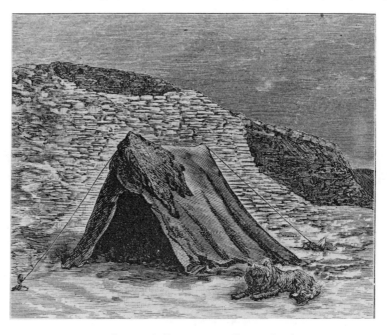

A siltstone hill on King William Island

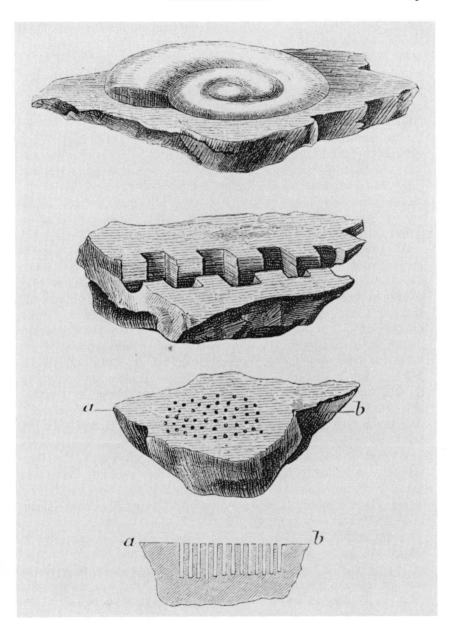

Assorted fossils and features in the siltstone

peared completely. The coastline development from there to Tulloch Point is not very significant; the vertical profile of the land lacks the wide, moss-covered lowlands near the sea and hence this region holds no great attraction for the caribou.[4] To this may also be added the fact that the Netsilingmiut occupy the section we have been talking about at times, and have scared away the caribou, although, as we will see later, they often approach right up to human settlements.

Our long-cherished hopes of finding our Inuit camped at Cape Herschel remained unfulfilled. All that they had left there was the kayak, a large number of seal and bird bones, their stone lamps, and other material which was used only in winter. The position of the kayak pointed to the south-southeast, toward the mainland, and hence we had first to follow the coast in order to cross Simpson Strait at its narrowest point.

Our investigation of the alleged grave site at Cape Herschel, which I mentioned earlier, was not accompanied by the success we had hoped for. The cairns were not graves, but caches, used by the natives for storing blubber and meat. The rocks laid in a circle and the numerous seal bones lying around proved to us that the Inuit stayed here quite often. Even our examination of the old cairn for any possible documents deposited here by Franklin's people was unsuccessful.

On the 15th we got under way at an unusually early hour of the morning, but it was not zeal which motivated Tulugaq to warn us to break camp. It was a distant storm, with hollow thunder but without any lightning, which got our companion's family on the move so early. Was it the rarity of thunder, or was it somehow connected with the Inuit's religious views that such a brave man as Tulugaq indisputably was, could be overpowered by such fear and evident excitement? The reply to that I must leave to the reader, but I can assure him that it was not fifteen minutes before our tent was struck and the dogs packed and Tulugaq was standing ready to march off, carrying his kayak on his head since there was no negotiable water near the coast due to the ice.

On the march to Gladman Point absolutely everything seemed to be conspiring against us. A dense, impenetrable fog had settled over the entire region and obscured every view; it hindered our rapid progress and our hunting was also unsuccessful. After we had pitched the tent each day we would wander around the region for 4–5 hours looking for caribou, but we spotted neither caribou nor the slightest sign of them. We were now experiencing a shortage of food. Thus a duck and a pound of caribou fat once formed the sole meal for our entire party of six people over a period of thirty-six hours. Since the coast was now free of ice, on the 17th Tulugaq undertook the crossing to the mainland to search for our Inuit. He came back without finding them, but he succeeded in shooting a caribou over there and brought its meat back across. Since in this fashion we were provided with food for 2–3 days, he went back across again the following day.

The three days he was absent were very unpleasant for us. The weather was warm and magnificent but we could not take advantage of it; we were barefoot in the fullest sense of the word. The last little piece of sealskin had disappeared during our wanderings, new holes had appeared in our sealskin boots, and we had no material for patching them further. So for three long days we had to spend the whole time in the tent. Here I shall quote a passage from my diary verbatim:

20 July, 1879. Two days have passed since Tulugaq and Arunak (the boy) went to the mainland to look for our natives, but for us it has been an eternity.

The fine arctic summer, of which we have gained some inkling over the past few days, actually seems to exist, judging by today's weather. The fog has dispersed, the sea is like a mirror, and it is terribly hot when one considers the latitude. And yet the boredom! Actually we have not been in such a situation for a long time. No shoes, so we cannot run around; no tobacco, so we cannot smoke; and no large amounts of food so that one cannot pass the time in eating. Yesterday we had two matches, and I intended imitating the Inuit by splitting them in two in order to light two fires with each. But Susy (Tulugaq's wife) had used them for lighting the last remnants of her tobacco and hence there is nothig for us to do but to ponder on whether Tulugaq will find our Inuit or not.

If he were to find at least the supplies of ammunition and tobacco it would be all right. We have already accomplished so much, perhaps we can learn to run around bare-footed on King William's Land's magnificent mosaic paving. Our 12 dogs are giving us the greatest concern. They have been lying here, tied to rocks for seven days now without food, and they cannot stand it for very much longer. But if we were to let them run free they would smell our last leg of caribou and renew their attack on it as they did last night.

I passed the long hours writing down similar comments and when the fog rolled in again in the evening I fired off three signal shots in case Tulugaq were already on his way to us. Another hour passed and we became aware of the light strokes of a paddle in the water. We scrambled joyfully out of the tent, but Tulugaq had already landed and carried a bundle up to the tent on his back. Everything was all right; he had found the other Inuit and the supplies and had made arrangements for transporting us to the other side of the strait.

Next morning his skill and reliability also put an end to the dogs'
problems. Just as we were about to move farther south because there
was a more suitable crossing place there, Tulugaq's wife spotted a
solitary caribou on the crest of a nearby hill. Tulugaq silently grabbed
his rifle and next moment the caribou had disappeared over the
horizon, followed by Tulugaq.

Long minutes of anxious expectation followed. The lives of our dogs
were at stake; if a shot rang out we knew that the animal would be
dead. Tulugaq was such a good shot that he only needed the chance to
get within range and the quarry was his. Half an hour had passed – and
still no shot. Then a single shot cracked out. Melms and I already had
the lines ready for carrying the meat home and we now raced after
Tulugaq, since that single shot was all the evidence we needed that
Tulugaq had been successful. When we reached the spot the animal
was already skinned and soon we had hauled it back to the dogs, which
we fed immediately. Fifteen minutes later there was nothing left except
for a few bones and the hide. We continued our march and in the
evening the Netsilingmiut ferried us across Simpson Strait to the
mainland on two kayaks lashed together.

On the 24th we met Eskimo Joe. First Tulugaq had to be sent to
Terror Bay to deliver the items Lieutenant Schwatka wanted. Melms
volunteered to escort the returning party in that he knew that if they
were unaccompanied by whites the Inuit would gladly loaf around if
they encountered good hunting grounds. Meanwhile the party back at
Terror Bay, waiting anxiously for their arrival especially because of the
gravity of the footwear situation, would simply have to wait. Initially
the prospects of sending any footwear at all did not look very
encouraging. If they have plenty to eat, as was the case here, the women
become lazy; moreover, because of their superstitions they may not sew
sealskins during the best period of caribou hunting. Hence I had no
alternative but to implement a fair system of requisitions and expro-
priated finished sealskin boots, no matter to whom they belonged.
Although unjust, this was the only means at my disposal to protect our
people at Terror Bay from going barefoot.

One could scarcely imagine a more pleasant spot for an arctic
summer residence than that which Eskimo Joe and his newly acquired
father-in-law had located. The two men had pitched their tent near a
small pond on a hill about 400 feet high which overlooked Simpson
Strait to the north and a large part of Adelaide Peninsula to the south.
Caribou are to be found right down to the sea coast here, but were only
hunted when they came close to the tent; in August it is still

somewhat premature to lay in supplies of meat since it spoils easily in the warm weather. There was not another soul for miles around now since the Netsilingmiut were all in the interior, hunting caribou on the large lakes, using their kayaks. They erect rows of stone cairns, which look like men from a distance and which lead toward a hill pass, then chase the caribou through between them and into a large lake located beyond, where the animals are easily overtaken by their pursuers in sealskin boats.

Regions which can permit this type of hunting must certainly be rich in game; for somebody who is familiar with the natural conditions of the area it is all the more incomprehensible how Franklin's men could break down so hopelessly. One could probably make the retort that they visited the various regions at precisely the times when they are very poor in game, as already indicated. But one would have thought that over 100 men, who spent twenty months effectively in inactivity, could not always have been aboard their ships during that period, but would have undertaken hunting and reconnaissance trips. During these, one would have thought, they must have got to know the peculiarities of the country so that they could cope with it during their retreat.

Our Inuit left behind under Joe's supervision had stayed at Cape Herschel where we had left them, until the ice became unsafe, and had then moved with our supplies to Adelaide Peninsula in order to take advantage of the fishing there.

Salmon are encountered in very large numbers, both quantitatively and qualitatively, along the local stretches of coast in late June and early July, since around this time it becomes possible for them to return from the large inland lakes where they spawn in the fall. Their catch of this fish represents a major source of food for the Netsilingmiut. Men position themselves at high tide at cracks and holes which have formed in the ice and use fork-shaped spears (see illustration p 110) to harpoon the fish. For bait they use several little balls of ivory or horn, or even just a collection of small caribou teeth, but they never use any hooks. When a fish approaches it is speared with this fish spear; the long, central prong transfixes the fish, while the two barb-like side prongs, set at an angle, prevent it from escaping. Thousands of fish are caught at the start of the summer in this manner. The heads are kept as dog food, while the remainder of the fish is split along the backbone and dried in the sun on lines stretched between rocks. Thus preserved, the fish are then piled on top of each other, sewed up in sealskins, and cached under rocks to serve as a food reserve for winter.

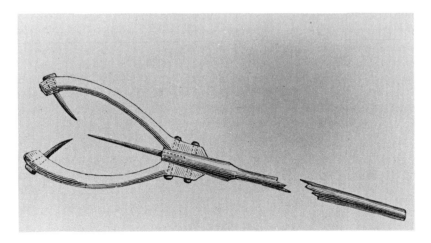

An Inuit fish spear

The presence of our natives, in association with the Netsilingmiut, had resulted in the Adelaide Peninsula being subjected to a search. Eskimo Joe more than fulfilled his duty in this area; he had visited Starvation Cove within his first month on the island. He had not only found bones among the sand and seaweed just above high water mark, but had also dug up pieces of clothing which had probably belonged to officers. Shoes, boots, pieces of uniform, and buttons were still lying around, and he had also found a small silver medal commemorating the launching of a large English steamer by HRH Prince Albert on 23 August 1843, nearby.[5]

Apart from this, only the previous summer the Inuit had found the remains of a Caucasian five miles from Starvation Cove. This find is all we have as proof that the boat found there was pulled up onto the beach by the willpower and strength of its occupants, and not blown ashore at the whim of wind and current. But this conviction also raises the question of what the party who landed here intended doing at this point, assuming that they were still capable of activity. Had they set a course only slightly farther east they would have reached the mouth of the Back River, their original goal, since clearly they had wanted to take advantage of it to travel upstream to the first British trading post. Hence their main reason for landing here could only have been that they were totally incapable of handling their boat, or that they simply

selected the first suitable landing place in the hope of finding an area
where they could hunt.

There could have been no other purpose for their landing, since even
in the event that Adelaide Peninsula was really of some importance to
them as a line of retreat, a better crossing would have offered farther
west, where Simpson Strait is barely three miles wide. There was not
the slightest indication that a party from the unfortunate expedition
had stayed on Adelaide Peninsula; indeed, one can be reasonably
certain that the contrary was the case.

If we examine the party's retreat from Irving Bay we find their
numbers steadily decreasing; first there is the evidence of the disorgan-
ization of the group, still numbering 100 men, at Erebus Bay, then there
was their total dissolution as a disciplined command by the time they
had reached Terror Bay. Judging by the known size of the boats' crews,
the party could not have taken more than three boats from the ships;
moreover, it is established that two were left at Erebus Bay. Hence only
one boat reached Terror Bay with the party, and according to the Inuit
this one was still with the party which they saw near Cape Herschel.
Finally, although I cannot be positive, there is an extremely high
probability that it was seen again at Starvation Cove. But the reader
will recall from Alanak's account in the preceding pages that the ice
was already bad by then (hence it must have been early July) and the
party must have been moving slowly along the coastal leads along the
southeast coast of the island, until break-up permitted them to cross.
The skeletons which C.F. Hall found and buried in 1869 on one of the
three Todd Islands may also have come from this party,[6] while the
isolated remains of whites on the coast of King William's Land
between Washington Bay and Booth Point, unburied prior to their
discovery, derive from the last stages of the men's suffering, just before
they died of starvation. Almost in his last death struggle a man's
willpower asserts itself one last time; summoning his last strength he
struggles to his feet and tries to save himself. This is what may have
happened to Franklin's men; alone, separated, thinking only of saving
themselves, they hurried on, but only for a short time before they
collapsed and died. We know from our experience that there is no game
on that part of the island in July and August.

But this contemplation of the hypothetical route and final end of
Franklin's men also sets limits to any further clarification of the
matter, since there is a total lack of further clues, especially any
supported by adequate proof. A lot of money has been devoted to the
Franklin search; various people have applied great energy, endurance

and ability to it, but for the first twenty years after the catastrophe itself, calm, reflective, intellectual contemplation was totally lacking from the search and this lack of reflection has met with its own reward. The searchers who twenty years ago, and even ten years ago, were right on the site of the deaths of this large number of men, too quickly declared themselves satisfied with easy achievements, instead of following the clues they found to their very uttermost. A halfway-thorough search would certainly have produced something significant then, and perhaps might even have cleared up the entire sequence of events. But in our case, of course, the elapsed interval of thirty-two years had already had too much of an impact.

In view of the already successful search of Adelaide Peninsula by the Netsilingmiut led by Eskimo Joe, I was now master of my free time for the first time. My sole duty and obligation consisted of watching our depots which were buried here and there beneath rocks at points a few miles apart. There was no lack of food here since Joe's father-in-law ensured that there were sufficient supplies. However, Joe himself lay ill with rheumatism for almost a month. Even for an Inuk, participation in two polar expeditions and three Franklin search expeditions has a deleterious effect on the health. But in the meantime there had been a steady improvement in his condition.

But the peace and quiet which I had expected to be able to enjoy did not last long; after two or three days I had to go out hunting. Being on the move had now become a necessity for me. Knowing the weaknesses of whites, Joe warned me most urgently not to go on such trips alone, since I could easily get lost. He had had occasion to mount searches for lost people previously and his anxieties were quite justified. In a country which, in its uniformity, offers no conspicuous landmarks whereby one can orient oneself, and especially when fog, rain, or snow obscures the sun, moon, and stars, the only true signposts in roadless areas, one can very easily become lost. I soon cultivated the habit of always memorizing the direction and distance which I had travelled, and with a picture of the route I had covered in my mind, I easily found my way back.

The purpose of most of my walks was to locate old Inuit camp sites. Small pieces of wood could usually be found lying in their immediate vicinity, mostly remnants of Franklin's missing ships; these had probably been lying there for years as refuse from the working by Inuit of components of the ships into tools and utensils. These wood chips were a treasure for me since there was no driftwood on Adelaide Peninsula and burnable moss occurred only far in the interior. These wood chips remained our only fuel. Often kneeling for hours, I would collect the smallest chips with the greatest patience and attention in order to cook a so-called hot meal with equal thriftiness and care.

Life among the Inuit had gradually become almost second nature to me; I had slowly become used to their customs and indeed almost to their superstitious practices. Just as during the seal hunting season the Inuit are forbidden by traditional dogma to let the dogs gnaw on seal bones when they are being fed, so it is the same with regard to caribou hunting. The dogs, which like the natives themselves look fat and well-fed from doing nothing all summer, are all tied to rocks and on the days when they are fed received only the liver, heart, spleen, etc. of the caribou. Meanwhile the bones are carefully amassed by the housewife until a large amount is accumulated. They are then either buried and weighted down with large rocks, or thrown into a deep river so that they will not fall prey to the dogs.

Another peculiar custom is that, when killed, a caribou must be cut up in such a fashion that no bones are broken. Hence with regard to caribou, the Inuit possess considerable anatomical knowledge and the speed with which they cut up their quarry could be matched only by experienced butchers.

The marrow from the leg bones is an extremely popular delicacy among the natives; we found that it had a taste reminiscent of butter. But now, at this time of year, the Inuit could not smash any bones and at first did not even want me to do so. However, I simply smashed my bones away from the immediate area of the tent; when the Inuit became aware of this they came and asked me to do the same for them. We reached similar compromises in the case of many of their other superstitious customs. But they adhered with great steadfastness to the tradition which prohibited them from making new clothes during the hunting season.

With the arrival of the first days of September, King Winter proclaimed his arrival. The beautiful weather of August was over, and the drop of the temperature below the freezing point gave clear warning of the period ahead when for nine long months snow and ice would cover land and water alike. Rain, hail, and finally snow began to make it unpleasant to stay out in the open. To our great annoyance we found our sealskin boots frozen for the first time one morning. Even the caribou which had appeared in such large numbers near the coast became more scarce, and after a few days they disappeared completely. Our hunters could no longer procure the necessary amount of game for our household from the tent-mouth, as it were, as they had earlier, but had to go out in search of caribou from morning to night. But their successes daily became fewer and finally they returned home with the simple, laconic statement: 'Tuktu piqangituq' (There are no caribou). But Eskimo Joe, who had recovered sufficiently that he could again get around with the aid of a stick, had already found a new source of food.

At the foot of the hill on which we lived there was quite a shallow, but torrential stream which had been of assistance to people previously, to judge by the stone weirs across it. In late August and early September the salmon leave salt water and travel up the rivers and streams into the large lakes of the interior in order to spawn. A short distance from the shore the most powerful current of the river was dammed up, with a sluice gate which was left open at high tide to let the fish in, but which could be closed with a rock. All the other channels were carefully rendered impassable and at the seaward end traps were built out of rocks. These, like a German fish basket, let the fish in but make it impossible for them to escape. When the high tide has reached its peak and the water level begins to drop again, the sluice is closed and the captured fish are driven into the stone traps with a pole. In this manner we caught nineteen fine specimens on one high tide.

But this type of salmon fishing lasts only a short time and the onset of the first cold spell which freezes the shallow stream puts an end to any further catches. I personally was completely happy to have a change from our fish diet. When one gets nothing but a piece of fish cooked in salt water three times per day, and has to suffer this diet for eight straight days, one is quite happy to stroke such a protracted Friday from the calendar. One simply longs for a change.

But game had also become scarce in the interior. The Netsilingmiut were actively moving back to the coast and were crossing to the southeastern part of King William's Land in order to derive their food from the reindeer which were still present there in large numbers.

We crossed the three-mile-wide strait for this same purpose on 17 September. Our original 'ferry boat' was naturally of indigenous construction, consisting of four sealskin kayaks lashed together; for its size it could carry relatively impressive loads. Our party, which consisted in total of seventeen people and thirteen dogs, was transferred to the other shore in two trips. One can imagine how much room each person had from the dimensions of the raft we produced; its load-carrying area was only five feet wide and ten feet long. People, dogs, and baggage lay, sat, and squatted in a close-packed tangle. During the three-hour crossing (the whole craft was powered by only two paddles) the thought struck me (among other fine observations) as to what

At the salmon river

An arctic ferry

would become of us if one or several of the boats happened to spring a leak.

Once across we established our camp on a hill near the coast, from where we had a good view of the country. Next day we began hunting with great success; I shall get around to discussing these activities in the next chapter.

A few days later, on 21 September, I received news via a Netsilik that Lieutenant Schwatka's party had reached our area and had settled into a permanent camp about seven miles west of us, in order to make hunting easier by spreading out the hunting effort.

Fairly frequent snowfalls had covered the ground with white; storms had swept together new snowdrifts; and our search work this month was restricted to burying the bones of a white man which lay at Tulloch Point, and which we were told about by the natives. A well-preserved skull, complete with lower jaw and seventeen assorted pieces of bone, was all of this unfortunate that we were able to commit to the ground after thirty-two years. With this act our summer travels and searches on King William's Land came to a close and our thoughts now turned homeward.

CHAPTER EIGHT

In Permanent Camp, October 1879

Caribou hunting. In permanent camp. Inactive life. Preparation of hides. An Inuit tailor's premises. The Netsilingmiut. Oil supplies. A meal to seal a purchase. A sharp practice. The high priest. String games, an Inuit pastime. A blizzard. Acquiring an Inuit skull. Tuluak fetches our things from Terror Bay. A triple bear hunt. Preparations for depature.

In the fall the southeastern part of King William's Land may justifiably be called a caribou hunter's Eldorado; during a four-year sojourn within and on the borders of the Arctic Circle I have never seen more game at one time than here. The hill on which our tent stood, amid a small Netsilik encampment, provided a panorama with a radius of five or six miles, and during the period from 10 A.M. until 5 P.M. there was not a single moment when we could not count caribou in their hundreds. I have already noted earlier that during the summer they make their home on the northern and western parts of the island and find abundant fodder on the great moss meadows there. But as fall approaches they congregate in great herds which daily reach the seashore, led by majestic bulls. It was not just the quantity but also the quality of the animals which made caribou meat the main item of our diet. The bulls in particular were very fat, the fat on their backs often reaching 2½ inches in thickness. On King William's Land the caribou are confined to a relatively small area and this, in association with the excellent grazings, is the main reason for their fine condition. The fat is the Inuit's only delicacy and I must admit, although with a certain hesitation, that we too found the article in question very fine. Caribou, seal, and duck had been our only food for four months and 'haute cuisine' was a concept of the past as far as we were concerned. We ate purely to live and did not live to eat. There is no wood to be found in these parts of the island, but the *Cassiope tetragona*, mentioned earlier, is available in large quantities and its resin content makes it a particularly good fuel. As long as the snow permitted we would daily go into the interior, led by the Inuit, in order to bring as much of it as possible home in sacks. But when the snow crust became thick we could cook only as much meat as the kettle hanging over the blubber lamp could contain at one time. Raw meat therefore formed our main item of diet and the amount which a person can consume in a day without overeating is in terrible contradiction to the concept of moderation.

Hunting was our main occupation. A bird would scarcely come within one to two miles of the tents and everybody, young and old, Inuk and white, would set off after it. One might think that the Netsilingmiut were not particularly pleased by our presence; this fall they could not adopt their usual strategy of simply lying behind a rock until the bulls arrived following their usual well-known routes. Our excellent firearms had the result that relatively more animals were wounded than would have been the case had we been using muzzle-loaders. Since caribou can 'carry a lot of lead,' to use an old hunting expression, it was on these wounded animals that our Netsilik friends now set their sights, and which they usually all killed. Never before had there been so many caribou running around King William's Land on three legs as this year, and never before had the hunting efforts of the indigenous residents been so productive as this fall. The party's maximum bag for one day was twenty-four caribou.

If a hunter or hunters came within range of the caribou they would use their breech-loaders; once Eskimo Joe killed eight and Tulugaq twelve out of one herd and all twenty fell right there. The Netsiling-miut could have best told us how many more were wounded. The two men just mentioned were in any case the best hunters in the party; while Tulugaq would kill the largest number and at a critical moment, in terms of meat and hunger, was an infallible shot, Eskimo Joe used the least ammunition. With Lieutenant Schwatka's twenty-six-shot Evans magazine rifle he once killed eight caribou with ten shells. A comparison between hunting caribou and hunting American deer species cannot be made since the caribou is inept and clumsy in its movements. If one misses with a shot at a buck it will take to its heels, leaving the hunter staring after it, whereas in the case of a caribou if the first shot does not kill the animal, the hunt is only just beginning. If the hunter knows how to stalk, taking advantage of the lie of the land, a caribou can be followed for hours and the hunter will still have an opportunity to get within firing range. But it is essential that the

Inuit dogs not be used at all, and if they are used for transporting the kill they must be left behind at a suitable distance under the supervision of a second person. Game drives, in our German sense of the term, are unknown to the northern peoples, but I can remember two cases where caribou were pursued by large numbers of hunters.

I have already mentioned the one type and method of hunting caribou, whereby kayaks are used on the inland lakes. The other is only applicable in special cases made possible by the conditions of the country. The following is an example. At the crossing point to the mainland a small island lies just off King William's Land, about three-quarters of a mile offshore. It is called Itah (ie, eating)[1] and when the first ice is forming it quickly becomes connected to the main island by an ice bridge. In their attempts to cross the strait large herds often come onto this island, and this period then provides a rich harvest for the Netsilingmiut. The news would spread through the camp like wildfire and everyone who could run would arm himself with bows, lances, knives, and sticks. The ice bridge would be occupied and the column would advance by rank and file toward the island, taking great pains to make as much noise as possible by shouting, in order to confuse the caribou. At first they would mill around on the island but then would try to break back between their pursuers and would be pushed back by the latter into an area which was well known to them, where the ice was not strong enough to bear the animals. As they broke through the ice terrible confusion would result. This was the moment our hunters had been waiting for; they could then kill the animals one by one, thus being able to kill large numbers of animals in an easy manner.

During the winter itself caribou are rarely the quarry of the Inuit. For groups who, like the Netsilingmiut at the time of our arrival, still possessed no firearms, the adoption of traps is the only possible means of taking them. For this purpose pits are dug in deep snow banks and are covered with a thin crust of snow slabs which are held together by a cement of saturated snow. In order to entice the animals onto the critical spot, dog urine is sprinkled on the snow round about and on the lid of the trap; the caribou are drawn to it because of its salt content. They then break through the cover and thus become the Inuit's quarry.

By 1 October the ice cover on Simpson Strait had become thick enough to support men and animals and during the next few days we saw herd after herd moving to the mainland in order to find better shelter from the northerly storms farther south during the winter. Now, just as in the previous winter, King William's Land was left a desolate snow field, devoid of all life, whose landscape would not even serve to support the arctic wolf. The wolves appear not to like crossing the sea ice, since although we saw many caribou on the island (which on the mainland are always escorted by packs of wolves), during our entire sojourn on the island we saw only a single wolf.

We spent the month of October waiting for an adequate cover of snow and ice; it also gave the Inuit an opportunity to prepare sufficient clothes for a winter march from the thick fall skins, for both us and themselves, and it gave us a chance to make the preparations still necessary for our departure.

Both parties set up permanent camps about seven miles from each other; these were established with all the comforts possible among our Netsilingmiut. Lieutenant Schwatka's group built themselves an ice house near a large lake;[2] with its auxiliary buildings and the masses of skins surrounding it, and the large collection of magnificent caribou antlers, it appeared quite imposing.

From time to time we visited each other but I don't need to stress that our now purposeless sojourn in these regions was no longer any

Schwatka's fall camp on King William Island

great pleasure for us whites. With obvious pleasure we watched the snow get steadily deeper and better in terms of sledge travel. We longed increasingly for the time when we could begin our homeward journey as the sun sank lower and the hours during which the meagre sun's rays shining through the little ice windows of our snow houses brought a pleasant variation in our existence became steadily shorter. That existence was doubly unpleasant due to our inactivity. It was a life without purpose, cheer, or comfort. The long hours crawled past like an eternity and only occasionally was our sleep accompanied by dreams, the pleasant realization of which lay so far in the future.

We had absolutely nothing to read and subjects of conversation with Melms, with whom I occupied a snow house, had long since been exhausted. Thus I occupied myself during the few hours of daylight wholly and entirely with detailed writing of my journal, and with executing my sketches. But even these tasks proceeded only under very unfavourable circumstances. If the house had been occupied for a long time, and if it was packed with people, as it often was with our nearest neighbours the Netsilingmiut, the temperature would rise above the freezing point, the snow roof would start to melt, and the resulting water would drip constantly on my paper. With a drop in temperature the pages of my book would freeze together and when I wanted to start working again I would have to thaw the pages with the warmth of my hands and peel them apart.

Meantime, the natives living at both camps had plenty to do. Old and young, male and female were busy making clothes. According to established custom, tanning of the hides, except for drying them, could begin only once the caribou had left the island and hunting had ended.

Tanning of the hides is carried out without the help of any chemical preparations. In the condition in which the hides are removed from the animal, all particles of fat and meat are removed, then they are stretched out on the snow or on the mossy ground in summer, secured by means of caribou ribs, and in this manner they are dried in the sun. Once this has been achieved the men take a flat stone (slate if this is available) and carefully scrape off the first blood- or meat-coloured layer of the skin. After this task the inner side of the hide is moistened with lukewarm water and is left to lie, rolled up tightly, for twenty-four hours, in order to soften the leather. A further scraping with a caribou shoulder blade or with a scraper made from sheet iron gives the hide its softness and light colour, and it is now passed to the hands of the women for further processing.

At this time of year the interior of a house occupied by Inuit offers a

A typical fall camp on King William Island

scene of great activity. From early morning to late in the evening the women and girls sit needle in hand in front of the brightly burning blubber lamps and busily string the fine threads together. Their unit of measure is a hand-length and their chalk is their teeth; they mark the lines by teeth impressions and cut the material out by following the lines with a semicircular *ulu* (a sort of saddler's knife). The little ones split the caribou sinew for sewing the clothes and only occasionally does the work come to a stop when the housewife takes a piece of caribou meat out of her storeroom and shares it among those present. The Inuit have only two main meals but they take snacks at every hour of the day and night, and the unaccustomedly vast harvest from the fall hunt was tackled particularly diligently.

The Netsilingmiut would turn up readily and punctually for the communal meals with our Inuit, but they were never far from our houses either, although there were no snacks for them there. They would come from the surrounding camps partly to visit and to satisfy their curiosity and partly to bring articles for sale which we would need when we began travelling again. The chest full of trade goods was in my care and it had a special attraction for them. I found trading and observing how they spent their time to be a pleasant occupation. In summer we had informed the Netsilingmiut that in the fall we would buy all their excess blubber. They had taken careful note of this request and had been catching seals diligently throughout the summer. The blubber was cut into pieces, stuffed into undressed sealskins, and the latter were then stowed under rocks. Eight such containers already lay full in our depots and I went with Netsilik Joe to the mainland to buy a ninth one.

As is often the case in civilized countries too, the Inuit often partake of a small meal after a sale has been made. This can have its interesting, if perhaps slightly less than palate-tickling aspects, as I shall now relate.

The master of the house spreads out a hide and lays on it a piece of half-frozen caribou meat which may vary in weight from 10 to 30 lbs depending on the number of guests; he cuts a piece off and pushes it toward the person sitting next to him. The meat now goes the rounds, with everyone eating from it, until only the bare bone is left. The women take their communal meal only in the company of their own sex. But there is a difference; in the case of the women their mouths have to deal with eating and talking at the same time, whereas in the case of the men a solemn silence prevails during the meal. The meat is accompanied by an *aluut* (a muskox-horn cup) filled with seal oil and this latter has to be emptied to the dregs. Conversation begins only once the meal is over. Even when one is not sufficiently conversant with the language to understand everything, the cold, monotonous character of the northern resident, entirely suited to the land of his residence, seems to be reflected in his conversation. He expresses his thoughts rapidly; but question and answer follow each other only slowly and the uncommonly deep voice which is peculiar to the Inuit of the Netsilingmiut even in youth gives the entire conversation a striking, serious tone.

Things were more lively when Melms and I were trading with the Netsilingmiut. They would bring every possible item to us for sale; among other things some interesting relics came to light. Thus, for example, we obtained part of a large ice saw made of sheet steel no less than one-third of an inch thick, and the upper part of a boat's mast. Always enquiring as to the place of discovery, we thus assembled items from every one of the locations which we had come to know as associated with the deaths of Franklin and his men.

Since we always examined the items thoroughly in order to be sure they were genuine, the Inuit paid close attention and, with time, they discovered that the Queen's broad arrow, which was stamped on every single part of a British warship, played a role in these purchases.

One day the high priest of the tribe, a cunning individual, came to us and offered us a knife made of copper with a beautifully worked bone handle. The copper bore a broad arrow, but it was scratched into it rather than stamped and the old *angakuq* (the term for his priestly office) was not a little amazed when he was shown the door. This was the only case where we could complain of an attempt at deception on the part of the natives. It was characteristic that it was the *angakuq* who tried to cheat us.

According to their accounts the *angakuq* had been involved in finding the first relics of the Franklin expedition by the Inuit and one day he had found a beautifully ornamented powder horn. He took his find home and began to examine the unfamiliar object more closely near the lamp. It is easy to guess what happened. A crash such as he had never heard before and the roof of the house flew into the air. But the shaman's face was so badly burned that he could see nothing for a whole month and, as his countrymen confirmed, to the present day he was 'not quite right in his mind.'

No matter how often we turned him out of our hut he always came back again and finally we had to tolerate his innocent importunity, especially since he readily carried out every task punctually and conscientiously for the payment of a small coffee spoon and some needles and since, despite his childishness, among the Netsilingmiut he was still a person of great influence due to the dignity of his office.

As mentioned earlier, the very numerous Netsilik tribe is in a position to procure sufficient food from its hunting grounds in summer and fall in order to live comfortably through the winter when, apart from fishing through the ice, no particular means of hunting is possible. Their supplies of caribou meat, dried salmon, and significant reserves of blubber mean that they do not require to make any special effort through the winter, and so it was no wonder that we had to put up with them all day long at our camp. There was only one way of getting rid of them, and this we used when we wanted to be alone. Melms or I only needed to take our rifles or a pistol and pretend to clean them. The catastrophe with the *angakuq* had shown them the force of gunpowder, and everything associated with it was a source of awe to them. They admired the power and effect of our rifles, but we could not induce any of them even to try a trial shot. If I was accompanied by some Inuit, and while carrying a rifle over my shoulder with the muzzle facing forward, happened to hold it so that the barrel pointed toward one of my neighbours, they would immediately ask me to carry it differently, even when I had taken great pains to ensure that the rifle was not loaded.

Pastimes are a necessity even for the Inuit, and the Netsilingmiut, even mature adults, always carry a loop of caribou sinew with which, by means of various twistings and knottings (similar to our cat's cradles) they produce a variety of intricate figures.[3] By giving their imagination free rein, they name these after various animals. The illustrations on p 126, with the various names applied to them, provide a pictorial representation of this game. The people compete with each other in terms of the speed with which they can execute these string figures, and derive fun and entertainment from this innocent pastime.

Our visits to Lieutenant Schwatka's ice house provided no great change since he and Gilder were suffering from the same evil as ourselves, ie, mental and physical inactivity. Schwatka had already checked the accuracy of all the examples provided in his navigation books, and for a long period Gilder had been studying in an old *Herald* calendar the progress of American securities since 1877. A terrible storm, which for three days threatened to bury us in the masses of snow which it swept along, brought a certain amount of variety. We had to shovel the entrance clear every half hour, and in order to reach the next hut, about thirty feet away, one had to possess an accurate

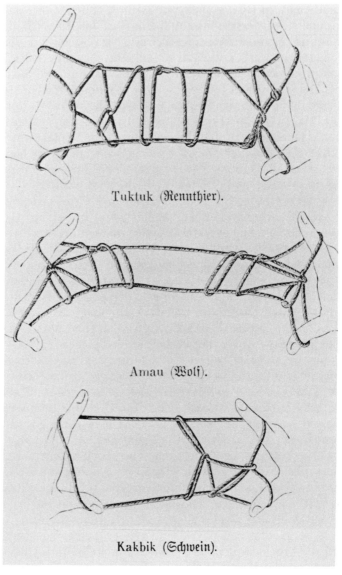

Tuktuk (Rennthier).

Amau (Wolf).

Kakbik (Schwein).

Inuit string games: *tuktuk* (caribou), *amau* (wolf), and *Kakbik* (pig)

sense of direction since one could see absolutely nothing, and it took one's entire strength just to stand upright against the wind. But these snowstorms also had their good aspects, since had it not been for one of them we would never have succeeded in acquiring an Eskimo skull for the American National Museum in the interests of science.

During our searches on the northwest coast we had happened to find an Inuit skull, but our sledge driver was strongly opposed to including it in our load. Only after protracted persuasion did he relent, but this skull always bore the blame when any misadventure struck our sledge driver or ourselves. He would transport the skeleton of Lieutenant Irving without hesitation but not the skull of an Inuk; his religious beliefs forbade it. If he missed a seal while hunting; if he did not spot any caribou; or if the weather was bad – then the skull was to blame. When the ice broke up the skull we were transporting was mainly responsible; hence, finally, realizing that this skull would give us a lot more grief before we got it home, Lieutenant Schwatka gave in to Tulugaq's repeated requests to offload the skull, and the latter was finally left behind.

We therefore had to try to acquire a skull and keep it in such a way that our Inuit knew nothing about it. The opportunity presented itself one day when Melms and I, wandering around aimlessly in the vicinity of our camp site, ran across an Inuit grave. There were no bones in it apart from a well-preserved skull; in front of it, as is the case with all native grave sites, lay a few articles which the individual had used when alive. Just as we were examining our find more closely our importunate friend, the shaman, appeared and made it very clear that we could not touch the skull, which was that of a native and so did not derive from the dead Qallunait (whites). But when we led him to understand, feeling him out as it were, that we would like to own it and asked him what he wanted for it, the old man bristled; he gladly offered the articles lying nearby but would not sell the skull to us. We were not very pleased at the result, partly too we were annoyed by our own excessive uprightness but – we had to have the skull. We left the site along with the shaman – but we had imprinted it in our memories in terms of distance paced and direction so that we could find it at any hour, even in darkness and fog.

Fourteen days passed without special incident and the skull remained under the rocks, but each time that Melms or I came within half a mile of it, the vigilant *angakuq* was on our heels. He was observed equally closely by us in case he perhaps moved the skull to another location, without us knowing when and where he moved it. We could not carry out our plan at night since our tracks would have betrayed us. Not until it began storming and snowing heavily one day did Melms succeed in fetching the skull by a circuitous route; having carried it for about three miles under his skin coat against his bare torso he succeeded in stowing it safely in our snow hut. The falling snow had immediately covered his tracks and the entire incident remained unknown both to the *angakuq* and to our natives, who would now be transporting the skull on one of our sledges day after day.

During the last days of October, Tulugaq, accompanied by a woman, finally took a dog team and travelled to Terror Bay to fetch the items we had left there.[4] He covered the distance there and back, a distance of some 110 miles, in four days and killed three bears en route. They had reacted in precisely their normal fashion on spotting the pack of dogs racing after them at full gallop. Their first objective was a nearby area of open water but they had scarcely reached it when Tulugaq shot and killed them, one after the other, with five well-aimed shots. The most unpleasant task for the two Inuit was probably that of hauling the animals out of the water with the help of the dogs. Judging by the state of their hides they had died in the water, and they must have weighed 800–1000 lbs each. But for Tulugaq nothing was impossible – except transporting the skull of an Inuk.

TABLE 2
Temperature conditions, 1 April–31 October 1879

Month	Month	Average for first half	Second half	Temperature (°C) max.	min.
April	–14	–19	–10	0	–35
May	–8	–9	–7	6	–18
June	0	–2	2	15	–10
July*					
August*					
September	–6	–3	–9	6	–20
October	–17	–12	–22	–4	–39

*Due to the loss of our thermometer on King William's Land, we had to discontinue recording temperatures during these two months.

From King William's Land to the Dangerous Rapids on the Great Fish River, 1 November–12 December 1879

Further division of the party. Departure of the party. Schwatka's
party. Sherman Gulf. The second party prepares to depart. Our
departure. Starvation Cove. The last of the victims. Review of our
search. A farewell meal with the Netsilingmiut. Montreal Island.
A night on the smooth sea ice. The island of Ominakzuak. The
delta of the Great Fish River. Lady Daly Lake. A historic cairn.
A terrible journey. The Utkuhikhalingmiut. Productive fishing.
The Dangerous Rapids. The party is reunited.

The long-awaited occasion of our departure for Hudson's Bay had
arrived and the party again divided into two detachments, travelling in
different directions. Lieutenant Schwatka, accompanied by Gilder,
Tulugaq, Eskimo Joe, and their respective families, were to travel
westward around Adelaide Peninsula with only one sledge and were to
survey a deep inlet which existed there according to the natives'
reports, but which was not marked on the maps. Meanwhile the
remainder of the party was to head directly for the Great Fish River
with three sledges, visit Starvation Cove, erect a monument and
deposit a document there, and wait for the other party at the 'Dangerous Rapids' on the aforesaid river, so that both groups could be
reunited.

On the morning of 1 November, accompanied by several Netsilingmiut, Melms and I walked over to Lieutenant Schwatka's permanent
camp in order to be present at his departure. For greater ease of transporting his large reserves of meat he had borrowed one of our sledges
for the first day, and had given Tulugaq and Joe a free hand in
distributing the loads. The 300 lbs of caribou fat certainly represented
the most valuable part of the load in the view of the natives; then came
the caribou, which were loaded as whole carcasses, that is, minus only
feet and heads. It took until around noon before everything was loaded

on the two sledges. Piled man-high, a picture of surplus, they posed the question of how the party would be able to move at all on later days' marches. To our great regret one item had to be left behind. This was a magnificent set of antlers; with their large shovel-shaped ends and the wide front blades for digging snow, and standing some 5–6 feet high, they would have been a real prize for the collections of our many hunting friends. But we lacked the means of transport for taking them with us.

Our thermometer was reading –33⁰C and the sun was already at its zenith when the well-fed dogs started off and we parted from our travelling companions with a warm handshake and warm wishes that we would meet again soon.

But the sledges had scarcely begun moving when the Netsilingmiut surged into the ice house and began rummaging through it. Antlers, old hides, pieces of meat such as heads which we had not taken with us because they were too full of bone, as well as trivial items which had become hidden in the snow during our month-long sojourn – all these still represented usable and useful articles for them. In the simple, unpretentious life of the Inuit thrift is often reflected in the smallest detail. For example, if a match is found it is guarded very carefully and even, as mentioned earlier, split in two, in order to avoid the tedious chore of making fire by rubbing pieces of wood together.

That Lieutenant Schwatka was able to set out today was in large part due to the agile, energetic Tulugaq. With all his superb qualities, once he had set to work one could not hold him up as a model of the Inuit, but rather one must hold him up as an exception among them, with regard to willpower and perseverance. Unfortunately, Melms and I did not have a Tulugaq with us but a slow and purposeless band who, among other things, could not grasp why we had to make the trip to Hudson Bay in the depths of winter. I fully realized that I would experience many hours of vexation before I could hand over Netsilik Joe and his crew, which was even accompanied by his brother-in-law, to the lieutenant's command at the prearranged rendez-vous point, yet I immediately began to make preparations for our own departure. The meat supplies for my party still lay scattered around the country in *tuktuksuit* and while the Inuit were slowly assembling them we will follow the lieutenant on his way south.

The first day's march was a very short one. Having covered three miles he stopped on the ice of Simpson Strait and stayed there till next morning, still using the borrowed sledge to haul his extensive supplies across the strait to the coast of Adelaide Peninsula. There the whole caribou carcasses were cut up, the dogs fed once again, the more compact mass of meat now loaded onto one sledge, and leaving a large surplus behind the party started out again. From Smith's Point, which like Grant Point to the south runs out into the sea as a low, level point, the party could cast a glance at the two islands lying about five miles away, near which one of the Franklin expedition ships sank. This occurred three miles west of these islands according to Ikinilik-petulak and other Inuit. The party continued its march southward, partly on the land, partly on the sea ice, and at Camp No. 83 reached a large Inuit encampment. They belonged to the Ugjulimmiut and Netsi-lingmiut and all gave reports concerning the ship which had once been found, which coincided with earlier reports. It could not be determined with any certainty whether the boat which was once found in Wilmot Bay and a piece of which we had purchased as a relic had come ashore with men in it or whether it had drifted there after the ship. But the Inuit repeatedly asserted that during the winter following the spring when they had been at the ship and thought they had seen tracks of men, they had also found footprints on shore near the boat. They never encountered any whites themselves. Their statement that the ship had many sails spread may be erroneous; at best the sails may have been loosened from the yards by storms, leaving them hanging in rags.

They established the existence of a large bottle-shaped gulf which extended southwest for a distance of about forty-five miles. As a result Adelaide Peninsula is connected to the continent by only a relatively narrow isthmus. Lieutenant Schwatka named it Sherman Gulf; the party travelled its full length and mapped it as far as the advanced season permitted. Although it offers little of interest to the geographer with its rocky coast and its rounded, rocky islands, yet it is noteworthy in that it makes it possible for the peninsula to sustain such a relatively numerous human population. As already mentioned, the beautiful moss meadows and the very considerable coastal develop-ment attract numerous caribou which all summer long find the salt-rich grazings they need in abundance along the coast. Only with the first snowfall do the herds begin to gather and to move south.

The gulf, which they would have crossed on the ice in the spring, is now open water, too wide for them to swim, and hence the caribou must either choose the eastern route across the isthmus or the channel to the west, which is barely three miles wide, connecting the gulf to the sea. Both sites are kept under close observation by the natives and represent for them extremely important locations in that here they can obtain not only the necessary food for the fall but could also accumulate their winter supplies. Without the latter, given the paucity of other sources of wildlife, they could not survive the long winter, or could support themselves only very meagrely and tediously. Even an Inuk appreciates how good it is to be able to stay at home during winter storms, since essential supplies have already been taken care of during the better seasons of the year.

Near the end of the gulf our travellers found a fairly large lake, which received a significant inflowing river. A connection between this lake and the gulf was not established, although it may exist. Surveying unfamiliar areas in winter is a very difficult and time-consuming task, especially with flat landscapes, and given our simple equipment we could not engage in very precise work in any case. The party followed the river until its course swung away in a direction unfavourable to their line of march.

Continuing in a south-southeast direction, Lieutenant Schwatka reached Back's River, but without having crossed a range of hills marked on the map as Chattery Mounts, or without even having seen it. On 6 December he reached the upper part of the 'Dangerous Rapids' where we were to meet him later.

I shall now return to our party. By means of continuous persuasion and constant urging, on 7 November I managed to get my people to make a short day's march with two sledge loads of meat and supplies of oil. On the morning of the 8th we too broke camp, crossed Simpson Strait, and made our first camp in snow houses some eleven miles farther on. But how difficult this departure was for the natives. We had to leave behind a lot of meat which, according to their ideas, was among the best parts of the caribou, that is, it was nothing but legs and heads.

The trip really proceeded fairly well but we had such terrible loads that we invariably had to relay one part ahead one day, then follow next day with bag and baggage. Hence in order to advance ten miles our dogs had to cover thirty miles, and even though I let them feed well every second day our loads decreased only very insignificantly. We could not expect to see caribou north of 67⁰ since we were mainly travelling on the sea ice, and even if we had, the best hunters were with the other party. In the event of a food shortage I would have had to reproach myself with being the person responsible.

On the second day's march we encountered another Netsilik encampment and on the third, travelling partly across short stretches of land, partly over freshwater ice, and in places even on sea ice across the numerous embayments of the coast, we reached the vicinity of the spot where we had encountered the first Netsilik encampment on 31 May. Today, too, a significant proportion of the Netsilingmiut were again resident in the neighbourhood and since they had already had warning of our approach they sent all their dogs to meet us when we were still five miles out.

Around 2:00P.M. we marched into their camp site and even found our snow houses already built, a courtesy which cannot be overestimated when one is travelling in winter. We found nothing but familiar faces and even the shaman had made a special effort to visit us once again. This was the last encampment we would pass. Our guides belonging to the Netsilingmiut wanted to spend a few days here; this request was granted while we, most importantly, visited Starvation Cove.

This is a small embayment of an arm of the sea which runs deep into the land at 68°9'N, 96°20'W. Its coastal configuration is so flat that were it not for some rocks protruding from the snow one would scarcely have any inkling of the presence of land in winter. Truly, the view alone is sufficient to put the visitor into a mood which matches the historic significance of the site. Mother Nature could probably not produce a more desolate spot on this wide Earth than that where the last survivors of the Franklin expedition found their end. Accompanied by an eyewitness of those sad events which I have already described in an earlier chapter, we soon reached the spot. I had the location pointed out precisely where the boat had been found and where and how the skeletons had been lying around. We then gathered together the relics found in summer, buried them, and erected a monument over them in the shape of a cross, using the rocks we found round about. We also deposited a document in the sand ten feet to the north, which described briefly the significance of the monument as well as the earlier factual progress of our party. As far as one can place any faith in the Inuit's reports, the most significant importance of the site lies in the fact that this was where the lead box of papers and writings was once found. Some informants also asserted that the box also contained a piece of iron with magnetic properties. It is possible that the Franklin expedition may have conducted interesting observations concerning the Magnetic Pole, which was then at Cape Felix, in their immediate vicinity, and that these observations led them to hold the instrument in high esteem. Among the relics that we brought back there is also a vertical needle, and in the interests of the success of our search we might have wished that we had found the relevant papers and writings. But there was no trace of them to be seen, although we visited the site three times, in spring, summer, and winter. Even from the Inuit we could extract only the assurance that the papers had all been destroyed. With the elimination of the documents (since it may well have been them which the survivors preserved to the best of their abilities as long as they, or at least one of them, nourished some hope of seeing home again) geography was robbed of an inestimable treasure. The day was already quite advanced and the moon was high in the sky by the time we finished building our monument. The long shadows, the desolate landscape, the deep lonely silence which not even a breath of wind interrupted did not fail to make a powerful impression on us, and when we finally started for home we gazed one last time at the distant coast of King William's Land, visible in the distance which, with its now snow-covered grave mounds, lonely and abandoned, represents the last resting place of those who perished there.

Next day a boy took us to a hill about five miles south and somewhat east of Starvation Cove and showed us the remains of clothing which seemed to indicate that the man who had died here had been exerting his last strength trying to continue the march which his earlier companions had been no longer capable of, but had ended his life here.

On abandoning the ships, Back River had been the prime objective of the retreating crews under the command of Captain Crozier, since it appeared to offer them a favourable route to the British trading posts to the south. And within sight of that first goal, at the limit of our search, we found the grave of the last of the dead men. We did our duty by erecting a small monument but even then, at the conclusion of almost six months of searching when we had to declare our search finally ended the question still obtruded itself: 'What have we achieved with regard to clarifying the Franklin disaster?'

If we compare the achievements of Dr Rae and Captain McClintock in 1854 and 1859 with the successes of our search, the latter at first sight appear miniscule. But only at first sight. Rae brought back the first news of the missing men and McClintock the first authentic document back to England, and yet after the lapse of twenty or twenty-five years after their expeditions and thirty-one years after that still not entirely explained disaster, we can still place the modest achievements of our small party worthily and with full justification alongside those of the abovementioned English searchers.

The territory we had covered was no longer unexplored; whites as well as Inuit had scoured it previously and by removing the relics which were mainly lying in open view had extensively eliminated the clues for us. Hence our search had to be a very thorough one, and the discovery of McClintock's own handwritten note at Irving Bay provided the most satisfying proof of this. I shall have to leave to the reader's own judgment the question of whether the Schwatka party succeeded, in terms of the great objective of the Franklin search expeditions in general, in bringing new facts to light. But I believe that in answering that question the following points must be kept in mind.

1. The Schwatka expedition has proved by its thorough examination in summer of the western and southern coasts of King William's Land and Adelaide Peninsula that the deposition of detailed documents in a manner that was inviolate to the natives never occurred.

2. By burying 15–30 persons (the number cannot be determined exactly) it fulfilled the humane aims of the expedition.

3. It brought to an indubitable conclusion the sequence of search expeditions as a result of its findings of a negative nature, that is, by proving that time, climatic conditions, and the natives have eliminated any hope of finding sufficient clues for any further searches.

But when one then takes into consideration the means and method of executing its task, its extremely modest funds, the absence of any provisions depots, and its long trip to the search area from a distant base on Hudson Bay, the Schwatka expedition must certainly be placed among the most prominent of the nineteen various search attempts. It certainly acquitted itself worthily.

With the feeling that in view of the circumstances we had completely fulfilled our duty we now turned to the march back to Hudson Bay. Since this trip probably stands alone in the history of arctic travel it will be described in the greatest possible detail.

15 November had been irrevocably set as the last day of our sojourn among the Netsilingmiut. It was to be simultaneously a reconciliation and a farewell celebration. For a long time now the Netsilingmiut and the Aivilingmiut (the majority of our companions belonged to this latter group) had been involved in a feud whose origin was to be sought in long-past generations and was proliferated by the vendettas which still commonly occur among the Inuit. It was this feud which always kept our Eskimo Joe in a certain state of fear when he was in the vicinity of the Netsilingmiut. Even when he departed with Schwatka's detachment he had particularly impressed on us that we should pay very close attention to his father-in-law. By means of close interrogation I got to the root of the matter and immediately had a warning passed via Netsilik Joe to his countrymen that they must not start any hostilities. After lengthy discussions it was also decided that a mutual reconciliation of the interested parties should take place at a communal gathering and I found myself present at this occasion in Netsilik

Joe's large snow house. The individuals, all men, came armed with knives and the transaction began, like all others, with a meal of caribou meat and seal blubber as described earlier. The meal was followed by a long conversation and only after about two hours had elapsed did they all put their knives away and the two hostiley disposed individuals touched each other's chests and uttered the word 'Ilaga.' (My relatives.) Both groups departed, apparently satisfied, and a communal entertainment or *qilautik* was organized for the evening.

This type of entertainment derives its name from the sole musical instrument of the Inuit. A hairless, tanned caribou hide is stretched wet over a large hoop about four feet in diameter with a handle fastened to it, and is then dried over a blubber lamp. This is the *qilautik*. The inhabitants of this village seemed to hold these celebrations quite often since they had built a special, large, and unusually high snow house for holding them. When the shaman gave the signal everybody – men, women, and children – appeared at the site of the celebration. They all appeared to be especially smartly dressed; both men and women wore fringes of bear skin, the former around their necks, the latter hanging down from their heads. Every man who had ever killed an animal wore a symbol of it on a belt of sealskin worn over the shoulder. On these belts were crows', geese, and ducks' feet, the caudal fins from large salmon, seal, caribou, and wolf teeth; and the numerous large bears' teeth indicated how often this tribe had occasion to battle these predators. The shaman's appearance was the most striking. He was entirely clothed in a bear skin cut into narrow strips; his head and hands were free but the remainder was richly and wildly ornamented. All were armed as usual and every one of them, not excluding the women, held their knives in their hands throughout the entire entertainment. The women formed a circle as large as the house permitted while the men formed a second circle around the women; the shaman then entered the circle with a certain dignity. He gave a short speech to the assembled group which naturally we non-Inuit could not understand, then the instrument, the *qilautik*, was handed to him. Without touching it otherwise he handed it immediately to a man of his choice. Thereby his official function was ended and the preliminaries to the performance were over.

The man selected took his place in the circle, took the *qilautik* by its handle in his left hand and a short drumstick in his right, and struck a few gentle strokes on the rim, but not on the skin of the instrument. An elderly woman, acting as a precentor to some extent, began a melody, initially in a low voice but one which became progressively

A Netsilik drum dance

louder, and was gradually joined by all the women. As the song, if one could so designate this ear-jarring singing – began, the *qilautik* player also began his accompaniment; according to whether he struck the rim closer to or farther from the handle the instrument produced higher or lower notes. From a slow tempo the music and singing, overpowering each other, moved to a faster tempo and the player from time to time uttered a barbaric-sounding shout as he turned slowly in the circle.

Ten or fifteen minutes passed like this, perhaps even longer, until the man became tired and passed the instrument to a second player. The same music and the same singing were repeated but on the faces of the participants, especially the women, there was a solemn look which at least betrayed the fact that the people were happy. The cold, uniform folk-character was reflected here again. Finally the performance came to an end, at least as far as the *qilautiq* was concerned, and to the relief of our ear-drums. The women now dispersed to their own houses, while the men and boys began as a group to indulge in a sort of gymnastic competition. These performances were impressive especially in terms of strength and the 10–14-year-olds who on this occasion indulged in a wrestling match revealed how early they acquire the physical adroitness and suppleness which will later become the prime prerequisites for use of the bow and arrow. The entire entertainment lasted until late into the night.

As we loaded our sledges next morning in order to continue our journey, the resident Netsilingmiut stood around to bid farewell. The major proportion of them accompanied us to a small island in Barrow Gulf where today we chose the same camp site as we used on 30 May. From there Ogle Peninsula, some nine miles in width, was the last piece of land we had to cross in order to reach the great gulf-shaped mouth of the Great Fish River; even given the level terrain this was a difficult crossing. The snow was still not present in suitable amount or density as was considered desirable for crossing it with sledges. The season was still not advanced enough for this.

To all the difficulties which the heavy loads and the difficult going placed in our way was added the lethargic slowness of the Inuit. The relaying of supplies ahead each time was only of any purpose if they were advanced a full day's march in the direction of our line of travel, and in order to achieve this either Melms or I had to go along each time. Before we left the mainland on the 24th the individual Netsilik families buried some old articles of clothing under large rocks quite close to the coast. This is one of their religious customs, a duty imposed on them by their belief in a resurrection, which they must always perform before they leave, for any period of time, the area of their birth and the boundaries of their hunting grounds. This area would also correspond to the burial place of their ancestors. On the evening of the 24th we camped on Montreal Island, already quite familiar to us. In the granite rocks of this island we greeted for the first time after long months a higher land formation, more pleasing to the eye, and though the blackish-brown rock with its snow-covered rocky hills offered a simple picture, it was a pleasant change after the monotonous siltstone deposits of the coasts we had recently been travelling.[1]

The west end of Montreal Island lies only a short distance from the coast of the mainland and in the event that Lieutenant Schwatka followed Sherman Gulf, which we believed to be aligned from west to east, for its full length, he would have to reach the Back River, as he crossed the isthmus, at some point on Elliot Bay, ie, in our vicinity. I spent one day searching for his tracks in this direction but found none,[2] and on the morning of the 26th continued my march southward. The ice appeared to be level and I discontinued relaying loads; instead this time we set off with everything at once. The day's march proceeded well; it was a fine day and the surrounding panorama of the landscape was magnificent. The extremely clear air made objects even 10–15 miles away appear much closer and the eastern shore of the great river mouth appeared in beautiful nuances of a variegated mix of colours produced by the rich alternation of granite and snow. I had set a south-southeasterly course in order to reach Gage Point, marked on the British Admiralty chart, before nightfall if possible. But the sun had long since set and the distant view had become very limited, yet still there was no sign of the point for which we were aiming, nor was any trace to be seen of the eastern shore of the river mouth.

Even the natives displayed no special desire to camp on the smooth sea ice, which barely offered enough snow for building houses; but as always in similar cases the energy which they revealed today had a good reason. We made a halt on a small snowdrift and it was not until next morning when we were standing ready to set off in the deep dark of night at 6:00 A.M. instead of 9:00 A.M., and were attempting to get our bearings from the stars, did I learn the reason for this haste which till then had been incomprehensible to me. Years before Netsilik Joe had suddenly lost his mother in this area, on the west bank of the river. As far as we could determine from his account she had had a heart attack, had died quickly, and lay buried nearby. There is a superstition among the Inuit, with reference to their dead, that it is not advisable to spend a long time on salt water ice near the burial site of relatives; hence the haste. Hence, too, the early start, about which, of course, nobody was more pleased than myself. Although I did everything possible to keep the tiresome party moving forward, they made every possible effort to use the slightest opportunity for loitering and so on the whole progress was very slow. This was annoying in that I did not want to make the lieutenant wait too long at 'Dangerous Rapids.' Gage Point appears not to exist since even today, 27 November, we were unable to find it, and in the late afternoon had to alter course to the southeast in order to reach an island to camp. Moreover, the going had become bad; the original ice crust had been broken up again by a southeasterly storm shortly after its formation in the fall and the individual floes lay thrown together in such a fashion that we took three hours to cover three miles and did not reach our campsite until 9:00 P.M. Just as we reached the high, rocky island in the bright moonlight we spotted two caribou, but due to our surprise at seeing these animals here on the salt water ice in the middle of the river we did not get a shot at them. Some cracks in the ice invited us to check the salinity of the water. At full ebb the water was drinkable if necessary but at high tide it was very salty. It was 12 midnight by the time we had finished the huts, which we had to build by a steep rock face halfway up the island due to lack of snow, and since no great progress could be expected the following day I declared it a day for resting and feeding the dogs.

A November noon on this relatively high, rocky island (called Umanakjuak in Inuktitut) is among the top few natural beauties which the North has to offer the traveller. I had climbed to the highest point with paper and pencil and was gazing around over the wide river valley with its mountainous western shore; the latter reaches its most charming coastal landscape in Victoria Foreland, which drops sheer toward the sea. A myriad of small islands was revealed on the bluey shimmering ice surface while to the west a dark line indicated the left shore of the river. The large embayment of Elliot Bay is marked on the map with dotted lines, ie, as being only vaguely specified, but in reality it appears to greatly exceed these boundaries in both depth and width, since as far as the eye could see to the west the horizon was simply that of the level ice surface.

The air was still and the sky clear with a bright light blue colour; but

A November noon on the Back River

the centrepiece of the entire wintry scene was the noon sun which was reaching its highest altitude for the day in the southern sky. Rising scarcely more than its apparent diameter above the horizon, it made the heights lying beneath it stand out in sharp blackness against the otherwise bright landscape which was seamed with long shadows; and the parhelion which is its constant companion on cold winter days on the hazy horizon appeared as a magnificent rainbow-coloured display in two incomplete segments of a circle on either side of it.

Despite a temperature of -41^0C I took great pains to get the beautiful impact of this entire scene on paper with a few lines and supplementary notes. Naturally, drawing involves some difficulties in such a temperature, not to mention many interruptions while one sticks one's hands in one's gloves for a minute or two at a time; but finally the artist manages to execute his design.

Not until the 29th did we reach the long-sought Gage Point, which lies much farther south than is indicated on the map, and from there we had our first glimpse of the dark ridges of hills which border the actual course of the Back River.

At Gage Point the siltstone formation gave way completely to granite. On the 30th, farther south, we passed a sandy island from which we deduced, without investigating it closely, that it represented an alluvial accumulation in the wide, salt water part of the river mouth delta. The island is very flat and scantily covered with moss; it splits the river into two arms of which the more easterly is the main mouth. Although it can be of little significance to the northern inhabitants in terms of availability of food resources, it has its own name in Inuktitut; it is called Siugakalu (the sandy land) after *siugak* (sand). Of greater importance are the so-called *amujets* just in front of, that is, upstream of this delta island. These are a large number of rock reefs, over which the water probably roars in summer, but which partially protrude above the surface in the winter months, resulting in the formation of basins, separated from the water outside until the melting snow from the interior causes an increase in the river's discharge. Fish are trapped in these lagoons and are easy to catch.[3] The salmon is a predatory fish and will take any bait offered to it.

We reached this spot on 1 December and used this and the following day to provide some variety in our menu. Nalijau, who belonged to the Utkuhikhalingmiut and had accompanied us all the way from the Hayes River, had lived in this region earlier and knew the river terrain very well. Our snow houses were scarcely finished before the Inuit began to cut holes in the ice, five in number and about 3–4 feet apart. Large numbers of salmon are trapped in these *amujets* every year by the rapid onset of freeze-up. Over the course of the following day we caught fifty-nine fish, each 2½–3 feet long. They are caught with ordinary fish hooks and lines, with pieces of salmon being used for bait.

A spot so abundantly blessed with *itha* (food) had never been encountered before, at least not in winter, especially by our Aiviling-miut and naturally they would have preferred to stay right there.

As with regard to all types of food the Inuit naturally have various peculiar customs with regard to fish. The most striking was that the fish they had caught could not be brought into the house via the usual entrance but only via a specially made opening, so that they did not enter the hut by the same opening as the seal blubber. They were removed from the hut via the same special route when the sledges were being loaded. Similarly no fish could be eaten in a cooked state on the spot where caught but could only be enjoyed raw; only when one is a day's march away from the fishing site is it permitted to cook the fish over the flame of the blubber lamp. These superstitions had many unpleasant aspects for us whites, since we saw ourselves fully obliged to live in Inuit fashion while accompanied by Inuit, and hence obliged to respect their superstitions. Occasionally I took the trouble to ask about the reasons for all these wise precautions. The reply was a very strange one. These in fact were not the customs of our Inuit but those of the Utkuhikhalingmiut, and as long as we were travelling through their hunting grounds, we were obliged to follow their customary law. 'When in Rome do as the Romans do,' says an English proverb, and its moral seems to apply equally everywhere, even among the Inuit.

To follow the river channel as we proceeded farther would certainly have been the best, if not the shortest route, but Nalijau insisted that if we headed south overland we would reach a large lake which offered an equally good travel route as the river itself. I therefore chose this land route, especially since I thought the alleged lake might be Franklin Lake itself, that is, a major widening of the Back River. It was certainly not a shorter route but we got to know a fine, large lake about 12–14 square miles in area which with its shores surrounded by steep, rocky, precipitous cone-shaped hills, presented a beautiful picture. I named the lake Madam Daly Lake after the wife of the President of the American Geographical Society. It is also further of interest in that a shallow ridge extends like a dam across its entire width from east to west; it becomes evident in winter when the whole ice surface splits, leaving a wide lead. The lead runs almost in a straight line across the entire lake; only on the basis of Nalijau's local knowledge was I able to locate this unique yet simple feature on the ground.

At noon on 6 December, with a temperature of -43⁰C and with a very stiff south wind blowing, we reached the river again at the point where it abandons its easterly course and swings north.

On 7 December we got under way early and passed a cairn which Lieutenant Back had erected, as observed by the Inuit, when he surveyed the river. It consisted of four large rocks placed on top of each other in a column, but when we searched the cracks between them we found no documents. About four miles east of there we were met by Inuit who belonged to the same group which we had met the previous spring on the Hayes River. Their appearance was better this time and a brief conversation soon convinced us that this year they had set aside significant quantities of fish, as indeed we had been hoping out of our own interests. Once we had reached their snow house our first enquiries were naturally about our other party but nobody had seen or heard anything of whites in the vicinity.

We camped and our snow houses were almost finished when two boys who had been upriver all day to fetch some fish which had been cached there returned to camp, bringing the news that they had seen whites some distance to the west. The latter had bought many fish from them and had ordered another load in case they had a surplus.

As I learned later, Schwatka's detachment, which had arrived a day before us, had already almost completely exhausted their reserves of provisions and had been wandering around the region searching for us or some natives, of whose presence they had heard. Instead of people they had found some large cairns in which fish were stored and they had taken some of them to feed their dogs, intending to reimburse the owners later. The following morning, ie, the 7th, they went out again but had gone only a short distance from their snow house when they were called back by Tulugaq's wife, who pointed out two boys, hauling a sledge with the help of two dogs. The boys had realized that somebody had broken into their fish cache and by following the tracks of the strange sledge, had reached Schwatka's house. The mutual surprise was considerable, but Tulugaq soon explained the state of affairs to the newcomers and reimbursed them for the fish which had been taken.

When I learned that Schwatka was nearby I had a sledge quickly unloaded, took a native as a guide and a boy as a dog driver, and left my party in order to look for the lieutenant. Incidentally, although it was 4:00 P.M. it was a dark night when I set off to begin a three-hour trip which was to be quite unforgettable. It is now as interesting a memory for me as it was an unpleasant experience at the time.

Our dogs were tired and there was a frost crust on the snow which increased the friction of the runners, rather like sand scattered on the snow, and slowed our progress noticeably. We had travelled scarcely a mile from our starting point when I suggested that we send the sledges back and that my guide and I proceed on foot; but the latter demurred and informed me, via the boy, that we would need the sledge later. This argument sounded absurd to me, admittedly, but it seemed even more absurd when all three of us had to harness ourselves to the sledge, which we had taken with us as our means of transport, in order to help the dogs pull.

In the meantime we had left the level ice; the going became rough, the calm had ended, and we became aware of the rushing of water. A few minutes later we were standing between a high rock wall on the left and some wildly roaring rapids on our right, the two lying only about 12–15 feet apart. The water roared in foaming waves; from time to time one could detect the speed of the water by a piece of ice as it was carried past and I was fully inclined to adopt the name 'Dangerous Rapids' and to examine the situation by daylight next morning from a point situated farther away. But this point was just the start of a labyrinth of open places which we passed during the next hour and which were all of the same character. We then came to better stretches but I was watching my guide, who was directing our course through the dark night, with some anxiety. Now and then he would halt the sledge while he went a few paces ahead with a stick, looked around, listened with his ear to the ice and determined in the most cautious manner how safe the route ahead was. We would advance a few paces and then he would stop again; finally he decided not to go any farther on foot. The snow cover on the ice had disappeared completely; there was only bare ice beneath us. I saw a dark spot about three paces ahead of me and mistook it for a stone, but I had scarcely started to move toward it when the boy held me back by the sleeve. He took his stick and with a light blow right beside the sledge he poked a hole through the ice. The ice was barely 2½ inches thick and I now realized the situation. We had to cross the rapids at a point which had frozen over only very recently and where the ice was very thin. I wondered how we would tackle this but the answer only became clear to me once we had reached the other side. We all sat on the sledge, the dogs were urged forward, and as if they knew what it was all about they ran as fast as they possibly could; once it was moving across the smooth ice the sledge slid rapidly behind them. This continued for about ten minutes without halt or interruption; a halt would have meant that we would have disappeared, or at least broken through. We could see nothing, but the water roared beneath the ice cover, barely two inches thick, all the more fearsomely for that and the Inuk's wildly echoing shouts sounded like a chorus and music against the horrendous roaring of the dangerously camouflaged, wet, cold element beneath us.

We were all highly delighted when we left the mirror-smooth surface and again had snow-covered ice beneath us. If anybody wants to take a really wild sledge trip I can recommend he take a trip such as this; he would not even need to take a blanket since I can guarantee that despite the temperature of –45⁰C I found myself sweating.

Meantime 7 o'clock had passed; it was a dark night with neither moon nor stars and there could be no thought of getting any sights. I wanted to extract from the Inuit how far away the lieutenant's snow house lay and since I was familiar with their expression 'Qanituqkulu' (very near) with regard to their limited concept of absolute distance, I asked them whether it was less or more than the distance which we had covered during the day between our two camp sites. I received the reply that it was not as far as our last day's march, that is, not more than a maximum of seven miles. But when it seemed to me that it was a rather long seven miles I asked the driver how far we still were from the lieutenant's snow house and received the reply 'Qanituqkulu.' Next I enquired which was farther, to the lieutenant's house or back to the Inuit's camp, and received an affirmative for the former alternative. Dissatisifed at the outcome of my question I was wishing that I had postponed my nocturnal expedition to the following day, when the dogs began running and hauled us ashore over rough ice and rocks and stopped beside a cairn which had been thrown up. This was the spot where the fish had been stored and from where the lieutenant's party had taken their dog food. Spotting the cairn, the dogs thought they would be able to find a meal here. Only with some difficulty were we able to get the sledge back on the ice again, and after about another hour we swung into a small embayment in the shore. A dim light glimmered through the darkness; it shone through the ice window of the snow house we sought. A few moments later and I was standing inside the house, to the general surprise of all the occupants.

We quickly exchanged our respective experience; next day after a well-deserved night's rest I received orders to return, buy as many fish as I could, have my dogs well fed, and return to the main party on the 10th. Hence I stayed for two days with the Utkuhikhalingmiut busy buying fish. The nine families of this group live almost exclusively on fish. The alternate name for the Back River, namely the Great Fish River, is certainly fully justified. Apart from salmon, *kapisilik* are particularly abundant in the river; this is a species which resembles the salmon in shape, position of the fins, and in its head, but has large scales and does not exceed eighteen inches in length.

At the height of summer, when the water reaches its maximum level, it fills a large number of rock basins and pools; a large number of side channels and islands are formed and it is in these side channels that the Inuit catch large quantities of fish using nets. When the water drops back to its normal level in the fall fish are equally abundant in the rock pools.[4] They are beheaded, quickly gutted, piled tightly in great heaps, and covered with rocks as a food reserve for the winter. The heads and guts are boiled to produce a type of oil which has a perceptible, somewhat sweet smell and provides the natives with the rare convenience of illumination during the long nights.

On the morning of the 10th I left the Inuit camp with my three sledges in order to move to the lieutenant's camp site. The Inuit had indeed been right when they told me on the 7th that this distance was no greater than that between our last two campsites; it was actually no farther than seven miles, but then in the darkness we had had to make long detours for reasons of safety. We had to stop at the 'Dangerous Rapids' (*Itumnakzuk* in Inuktitut)[5] in order to load the fish we had bought when we had passed here earlier. I now had an opportunity to examine more closely the spots which we had passed at night previously. Among the imposing phenomena of the various rivers of the world the rapids of the Back River in winter occupy a prominent place. Certainly one cannot call them grandiose, and beautiful even less, but for wildness and turbulence they are matchless. The high river banks on either side suddenly squeeze close together and the otherwise uniform ice cover is, as it were, truncated. Two feet away from the edge one is still standing on ice of normal thickness but only a short distance away the water is boiling and foaming along in waves 3–4 feet high at a speed of 6–8 miles per hour. Along both banks narrow ice shelves extend. Where the river emerges from the gorge the force of the water ceases and the ice begins again. What strength the water must possess here if, as is reported by old people living in the immediate vicinity of the rapids, the maximum arctic cold – at the pole of cold itself, I might add – is incapable of forming an ice cover over the open spots.

The 'Dangerous Rapids,' consisting of three major sections, are about

The Dangerous Rapids

eight miles long, but the large open sections are far from being the most dangerous. As already mentioned, one encounters large areas of ice where there are openings only 1–2 feet square which sometimes are barely visible; the ice around these never becomes strong enough that one can travel across it safely. These are very shallow spots and if any ice crust forms at all it reaches only minimal thickness.

At 2:00 P.M. on 10 December we reached Lieutenant Schwatka's camp with our sledges and I was delighted to hand over to his command again the detachment entrusted to my leadership. I had been detached since 6 August and was really pleased that in the future I would be spared the responsibility for constantly having to urge the Inuit along.

CHAPTER TEN

On the Back River,
12–31 December 1879

The Back River. Surveying. Dead reckoning. The accuracy of
arctic maps. A fine example of parental love. The rapids.
Christmas Day. The silence of the arctic night. A sad situation.
A final decision.

The Back, Mackenzie, and Coppermine rivers are the three great
arteries that drain the northernmost part of the American continent to
the Arctic Ocean, having their sources in the vast lakes region of the
interior. The first of the abovementioned rivers flows out of Sussex
Lake at about 64°N, 109°W from Greenwich, and feeding a large
number of large and small lakes along the way follows an occasionally
northeasterly and occasionally easterly course. Lieutenant Back of the
Royal Navy travelled its entire length during an expedition in 1833–5
and mapped it. Particularly its lower course between 66° and 67°N, that
is, the stretch which our party had selected for its return route,
deserves mention both in geographical and touristic terms.

Although our main task was not a scientific one, our party aimed
always at placing particular value on accurate determinations of
position with regard to the areas we traversed. To solve this problem
we took astronomical observations when possible and otherwise
represented our route graphically by accurate field calculations, or by
so-called dead reckoning. Dead reckoning is simply a detailed, graphic
representation of direction and distance. The two journals kept separately on this topic by Lieutenant Schwatka and the writer, corrected on
the basis of astronomical observations, served as the basis for drafting
new ones and correcting the old ones. Only if it had been possible to
determine the compass deviation from true north every day could we
have used this method for determining our line of march (due to the
proximity of the North Magnetic Pole). But there was neither sufficient
time nor opportunity for this daily task and hence moon and stars, in

conjunction with our chronometers, provided the only means for determining the direction of travel as accurately as possible. The distance covered was estimated on the basis of practice from rest-stop to rest-stop. By measuring off a mile and repeatedly pacing it off, those making the calculations had determined the time required to cover a mile at various speeds; thereafter, without taking into account the varying speed of the sledge they could proceed on their way, constantly mindful of their task, along a straight line of march wherever possible. At each rest-stop they would plot the distance they had obtained by comparison with the time required, on squared paper which they carried for the purpose. While the procedure is quite simple, it is the only way to make a calculation appropriate to the conditions and to the purpose. But when we could see neither sun nor stars it became even more difficult for us to determine the direction; since we were familiar with the wind directions we were left with simply using the snow drifts as the basis of our operation. The prevailing storms which influence the deposition of the snow are either northwesterly or southeasterly at these latitudes, and if all other means fail the snow drift alignment is the best available clue for determining direction while on the march. It is also the custom of the Inuit to use this method when he literally has to feel his way back home when surprised by a blizzard. But the snowdrifts are only reliable when the land is fairly level and offers no obstacle to the wind direction. This method of direction determination is not applicable in a river valley; here, in the event that visibility is clear for a sufficient distance, an observation from one sledge of those travelling a certain distance ahead and behind remains the ultimate device for plotting one's route.

The three sledges then form the delimiting points of a triangle and at turns, if one is located at the apex, that is, on the centre sledge, it becomes possible to determine the size of the angle corresponding to the bend in the river. This three-sledge technique was used a few times on the Back River, but more often on the Hayes River.

Naturally one cannot rely on the precise accuracy of the abovementioned survey techniques, but one does not need to rely wholly on them; if one can check them from time to time by means of exact determinations of longitude and latitude the result, with some practice of course, can be very satisfactory. Even if they are quite portable, the instruments one takes with one become unreliable in part due to climatic conditions, in part due to sledge travel, and the simpler one's survey procedure – and the less detail one attempts – the better and the safer will one meet the requirements for geographical knowledge of the North.

The lower course of the Back River revealed some differences as represented by its namer, as compared with our survey. The part of the river lying north of the 'Dangerous Rapids' is correct, with only minor deviations which may be ascribed to irregular gains or losses of the chronometer influenced by weather conditions. South of the rapids, however, a significant error had to be corrected. The course as plotted on the British Admiralty charts shows it as taking a general northeasterly direction between the specified parallels of 66^0 and 67^0. But as far as our party followed the river channel (to $66^05'N$) it forms an angle whose sides run north-northeast then north-northwest, so that at the point where we left the river the difference between the actual and the previously plotted courses was about thirty miles.

This reference to our practical techniques and to the identification of this error is certainly not intended as praise of our own maps or as criticism of the British ones. Its purpose is, simply, on the one hand to present to the reader the difficulties with which the surveyor has to contend in the Arctic, and on the other to provide him with proof of how easily even very significant errors may creep in.

With regard to plotting individual islands and the rapids in the river, Lieutenant Back was wholly successful in achieving great accuracy. Only the fact that we found everything else plotted correctly on the map eliminated the doubt we had been nurturing that perhaps on our southward march we had strayed onto an unknown tributary instead of following the main river. The Back River receives only one tributary, the Herman along the stretch under consideration, and it was followed upstream for only ten miles by our hunters. A few hundred metres above its mouth there are major rapids and it is rapids such as these which certainly make the Back River one of the most interesting rivers on earth.

In the midst of the monotony otherwise peculiar to the Arctic landscape, especially in winter, it offers the traveller the most varied scenery and the most imposing impressions. We will now return to the party itself in order to get to know some of these scenes.

We had set 11 December as the date for completing all necessary preparations for the continuation of our march. Our presence was very acceptable to the Utkuhikhalingmiut and they did not stray far from our camp; they had some fish, fish oil and, of particularly great significance, some fine dogs for sale, and we gladly paid good prices for them. But the most important reason for their continued presence was to urge the lieutenant not to take Nalijau with us to Hudson Bay as he was planning.[1]

This had originally been the wish of Nalijau himself. He was a very willing, brave, and diligent Inuk, who in a very short time had learned to use the rifle he had been given, and had already killed many caribou with it. Our natives' stories about whites had roused in him the desire to see a ship, etc. for himself. He would gladly have gone with us with his wife and child, but unless he left his child behind with the Utkuhikhalingmiut he would be breaking a very strong Inuit tradition.

His little girl, about 5–6 years old, was the future bride of an already quite mature boy of the tribe. Afraid that if Nalijau went to Hudson Bay he would never return, the latter had asked that he leave his daughter behind as a pledge.

It was a painful situation for Nalijau and his wife! On the one hand they would have a better, more carefree, easier life without their beloved child; on the other, an existence under the most wretched conditions but with their child. I observed the couple as they struggled all day with their decision, restless, excited, and still undecided. Toward evening Nalijau came in to the lieutenant's snow house, sat down near him, and announced that he would be staying. The parents' love for their child had waged a hard struggle against the prospects of a better life and, to the credit of Inuit in general, let it be said, they had resolved it to general satisfaction. We gladly permitted Nalijau to stay and provided him with abundant ammunition and his wife with other gifts as compensation for the services they had rendered us. But Nalijau's decision had a decided disadvantage for us. He knew a route whereby one could cross the divide between the Back River and Hudson's Bay and after an overland march of only four days reach the sources of a river which discharged into Chesterfield Inlet.[2] But if we did not succeed in finding this critical route ourselves we had to be prepared to trek about 200 miles overland. At any rate we and Tulugaq, who otherwise was very knowledgeable of the terrain, collected the most accurate possible information as to the spot where we had to leave the Back River. On the morning of 12 December we left our campsite with four sledges; at noon the previous day we had recorded our lowest temperature yet, –54^{0}C. Despite the majestic appearance with which they were endowed by their long-haired harnesses made from muskox hide, our four new dogs were tired after only a short march and refused to go any farther. This caused us a great deal of vexation, yet on each of the first two days we advanced nine miles and

even killed two caribou on the second day. Tulugaq hit and killed them
both with one shot; this was the eighth time he had succeeded in
making this masterly shot. But in general the river did not offer us the
advantages we had expected. The area immediately adjacent to it was
poor in game and even as a travel route it was not as useful as we had
hoped. On one stretch of some sixty-six miles we passed ten open
rapids which not only obliged us to make detours but even twice
forced us to leave the river valley and to make our way with great
difficulty and effort over the mountainous river banks.

From a distance a dense cloud of frost-smoke revealed the presence of
open water and the longer the ice-free stretch the darker and more
billowing the appearance of the columns of clouds against the partly
snow-covered hillsides beyond them. If the rapids were only very short
and if no particular air movement was perceptible, the clouds of vapour
would assume the shape of columnar smoke formations which rose
almost vertically upward until they were above the summits of the
hills and then lost themselves in the cloud formations. But observation
of the various individual rapids possessed less pleasant aspects than
simply passing them. The immediate vicinity below the rapids was
usually an area of uneven, shattered ice thrown wildly together; but
the vapours emanating from the open water would be deposited for
miles around as rime on the snow surface, slowing our progress just
like sand. Moreover, the snow cover would be quite unequally distributed and over entire stretches the ice would lie bare to the sky,
scraping the icing completely from our sledge runners. It was these and
many other unpleasantnesses which allowed our party to make only
short days' marches; certainly the river did not fulfil the fine hopes
which Lieutenant Schwatka had had in choosing the river route.

An enumeration of our daily sufferings and achievements would
only be boring in its monotony and hence I shall select a single day to
describe our life during our travels in greater detail and to present to
the reader the bright and dark sides of a cold winter's day on the Back
River. Let this day then be 25 December, Christmas Day. Near one of
the rapids we can recognize our party, stopped for its noon rest: four
sledges to which woolly dogs are harnessed and surrounded by figures
bundled in furs. They form the sole sign of life in this strange
landscape. The snow beneath their feet covers the monotonous ice
surface of the entire river channel; it is piled in massive banks against
the steep walls of the river bank, fills every smallest crevice in the
massive granite blocks, crowns the giant granite shapes of the surrounding area, and obscures the distant view of the horizon along

which dark cloud formations tower. Only to the south is the monotony interrupted. The circular rainbow-coloured ring which the astronomers call parhelios and the English call sundogs, the invariable accompaniment of the sun in cold regions, is visible in its upper half. In its centre a shining spot rises above the hill ridge, travels rapidly west, and disappears just as quickly again behind the hills. This was the noon sun rising and setting simultaneously; the day has ended and the darkness which will soon be gathering warns the travellers to continue their march. The moon has not even set; he is lord of day and night equally and under his guidance our group is in the habit of using part of the dark period for travelling too. With loud howls the dogs lean into their harness; the people associated with each sledge also lean into their traces and in an instant only the guiding shouts of the dog drivers can be heard. And so the hard work continues for another 1½ hours across the partly snow-free, partly abominably rough ice, until the stars are glimmering to each other and the now cloudless sky unfolds in a majesty visible only in the Far North. The narrow river channel has widened and we are standing on a lake surrounded by various hill forms; the abundant accumulation of snow along its right shore invites us to pitch our Christmas camp here. The sledges are brought to a halt and the construction of the snow houses is started in the manner already described. On the spot where eternal silence had reigned only half an hour before, lively activity now begins. Everybody has his contribution to make; while the men set snow block upon snow block, the women pile the outsides with snow to a thickness of three feet in order to make the houses warmer. Some distance away the whites chop and chisel the usual water hole, and everybody does something in order to keep warm. Even the children burrow in the snow with knives and small shovels; only the dogs lie inactive, huddled close together and apparently asleep. But soon they introduce some variation into the scene. Today is feeding day and the rapid unloading of the sledges is of special interest to them. The large lump of frozen fish which has just been unlashed and which a grown-up lad takes from the sledge in order to chop it into so-called 'mouthfuls' (in fact quite suitable portions), using a pickaxe, has not escaped the notice of our largest and strongest dog, Ublubliaq, (Star, in Inuktitut). First he raises his head, then stands up, and in an instant the entire unruly pack of dogs has followed his example; without any apparent effort dogs, sledges, and everything on them are racing in a wild chase to the point where the fish supplies are located.

The Inuk, without any attempt at opposition, leaves it to the dogs to undertake the chopping-up of the fish themselves. The scene which now follows is of short duration but wholly typifies the Inuit dog as being the nearest relative of the wolf.

Once the spot is finally cleared the sledges are driven back to their original positions and peace is restored. In the meantime the snow houses are completed and the men start moving the supplies into a small outhouse while the women start arranging the interior for receiving its occupants, heating and lighting it in the normal manner. In view of the Christmas celebration the lamp will not be used for cooking tonight. Since we left King William's Land we have been saving thirty-five caribou tongues for this occasion and we have also brought two giant salmon (each four feet long and eleven inches in diameter) from the Utkuhikhalingmiut.

In order to cook all this we have been collecting heather for days, digging it out from under the snow. Today, as a special dispensation, we will allow ourselves the privilege of using the cooking kettle belonging to the Franklin expedition, which we had found. Cooking like this, at night, under God's open sky at a temperature of -55^0C (the average temperature for 25 December was -54^0C) is not very enjoyable. Since, moreover, the treatment of the various foods under these circumstances had to be quite special, I feel obliged, in the interests of my dear reader, to discuss this subject in detail.

The meat is cut up as usual with a carpenter's saw, while the fish and tongues are cut up with an axe (to save time and fuel). The kettle is filled with water and brought to a boil and one piece is dropped in after another until the cook is convinced that every smallest corner in the kettle is being utilized. One never overcooks food in the North; on the contrary it is always undercooked. Once the kettle is full, the culinary art has achieved its goal; maintenance of the fire and a strong hand armed with a good stick (which must be oak) now remain the important factors. It would be a boring business to stoke the fire for 1½-2 hours without a break, but the dogs standing around in a circle ensure that nobody is bored. The cook is kept fully occupied in ensuring that he is not surprised by an attack mounted with all kinds of deviousness. Ublubliaq knows very well how to overturn the entire fire, and in executing such a manoeuvre he always finds powerful support from his companions. Spicing the soup does not take much effort since the pepper is still where it grows, and we have had no salt for a month. A sharp appetite helps us to survive all such shortages and everything in the large snow house is already prepared for the great feast, which will be eaten communally. The diners finish their work faster than the cook does, then everybody goes his separate way.

Sunk in thought I had been pacing up and down in front of the snow houses. Thereby I gradually and accidentally moved around a nearby hill and sat down on a large rock. From there the snow houses were visible and I stared up at the sky which, strewn with stars and with the moon visible, riveted my attention. Its light seemed pale and I got the impression that even it was shining with only half its normal magnificence in this barren spot. Around me the rocks, the shadows, the bluish snow surface, and the deep grave-like silence all had a profound impact on my mood. Not a breath of wind, not a bird call, not a sound of any kind could be heard and an oppressive feeling lay on me like a mountain. The silence had become tangible, perceptible; it settled on the rock on which I sat; it settled on the river, on the ridges, and everywhere. It had ceased to represent the negative significance of the non-presence of noise and, as the polar traveller Dr I.I. Hayes had so strikingly commented, it had emerged as a positive force. It reflects the majestic scale and magnificence of this region; it embraces its desolation and loneliness; in the fullest meaning of the words it is the 'terrible silence of the polar night.'

I felt alone and abandoned; as I stood up my first footstep on the hard snow rang out like an echo; I could hear something again. It sounded like life and the ghost was routed.

The faint glow emanating from the snow settlement appeared very welcome to me and the monotonous women's songs, the normally unpleasant shrieks of the children, and the hideous snoring of the Inuit were now beloved sounds to me. The simple wretched snow house was a dear home to me again, and after I had passed through the little doorway on hands and knees I recognized the value of human company.

Now came the final task of the day, getting undressed. After one's clothes have been carefully beaten while they are still on one's body, one divests oneself of the outer fur layer and lays it on the caribou-skin sleeping bag in such a way that the latter does not come in contact with the snow wall. One's fur boots come next and then one's fur stockings. The former are placed in such a fashion that they do not thaw out and the latter so that they do not freeze where they lie beneath the first fur layer at the head end of the sleeping bag. No further explanation is necessary since once the last artificial layer, in the form of one's fur shirt is off, one is already in one's sleeping bag, with one's various items of clothing forming a pillow, lying in the sequence in which they will be donned again.

A sleeping bag such as this is without doubt the best and only warm bed in these regions. But since one crawls in quite naked and the sleeping bag has been lying on top of the sledge all day the initial sensation is not a pleasant one. 'Ikkii' shouts the Inuk, pulls his knees up to his chin and pulls the covers up to his ears. Body heat and warm breath soon take care of warming up the sleeping bag in a few minutes. Then one sticks one's head out again, lights one's pipe, and enjoys extracting comfort and pleasure from one's sleeping bag and pipe.

The individuals, arranged like herring in a barrel with their heads all to one side, look very cheerful. When there is a full house, ie, when there are enough people that when one turns over the whole row has to do the same, the housewife closes the door with a block of snow and extinguishes the lamp. All further conversation is abandoned and each of us searches for a better Christmas celebration in his dreams.

But the realization of our fine dreams and our return to the pleasures of civilization still lie far in the future. The reality of the present does not promise a very rosy picture. On Christmas Day our dogs had consumed the last reserves of fish and even for the men there was very little meat left on the sledges. The dogs were thin and were becoming weak from the daily work, and both they and we lacked that essential source of nourishment to stand such bitter, persistent cold, namely fat. The wide snowfields of the river showed not even the slightest trace of animal life; not a single wolf was sighted, which might have indicated the proximity of caribou. Muskoxen, on whose presence we had confidently counted, could not be found; the hunters we sent out to search for game returned without success and with anxious faces.

On the 28th we travelled one day's march, ie, seven miles, farther south and stopped for one day again to hunt, but again without success. Only when Netsilik Joe came back on the 30th with two caribou after a thirty-six-hour hunt did we learn that the left bank of the river revealed signs of caribou. However, these tracks indicated that larger numbers of caribou could only be found farther into the interior.

We were still about twenty miles from the point where we expected to leave the Back River and so we would need at least another three days to cover this distance. But then there was still the question whether we would succeed in finding the crossing of which Nalijau had told us. Here at the close of the year the prospects were far from bright for our party, involving as they did the lives of twenty-one people and forty-two dogs. Only reluctantly abandoning the original route, on the evening of 30 December Lieutenant Schwatka decided to leave the river for our further line of march the following day and to begin the overland march in a southeasterly direction.

CHAPTER ELEVEN

The Overland March from 31 December 1879 until 27 February 1880

We leave the Back River. Loss of some dogs. The sun's first New Year's greeting. Low temperatures. Their effect on men and animals. Inuit stratagems. External signs of extreme cold. Good qualitites of Inuit dogs. A noon rest. Cold work. The tongue as a warming apparatus. Complicated smoking. Cold night quarters. A dangerous situation. Alcohol. Wolves' impertinence. The Inuit's murderous devices. An exhausting trek. Accurate distance calculations. A surprise.

It had long been a puzzle to the natives as to why we were following the river in a south-southwesterly direction when Pitsiulak (Depot Island), their main abode in Hudson Bay, lay southeast of us. Today, on the last day of the year, as we headed off in this latter direction they all seemed to be happier. Altogether the mood along our entire column of march was better as we left the river at 9 in the morning and slowly headed up the heights along the river. Our route lay over an even, undulating hilly area, and we continued almost without rest until evening, when we made a halt on a small pond.[1] But today proved to us how necessary it was to reach a game-rich area soon. Two of our dogs collapsed and were immediately unharnessed and left lying. Our favourite dog, Miqijuk (he is little), which we had bought in Hudson Strait as a pup, and which since then had accompanied us on all our trips and excursions, today collapsed and died.

On New Year's Day we stayed at our camp site to hunt; both Tulugaq and Netsilik Joe headed out, intending to stay out the following day too, in the event that they did not spot any caribou today. For those of us who stayed behind New Year's Day held a joyful, even if quite insignificant surprise. Not exactly in the best humour, we were sitting together in our snow houses, gloomy and silent, when around noon the first sun's ray penetrated through the ice window into the interior and aroused a feeling of grateful joy even among the Inuit. 'Namakpuk mana siqiniq qaigit' (Now everything is fine; the sun has come back)[2] was the general exclamation. For the first time in a long time the full disc of the sun had risen above the horizon and for the Inuit this signified the start of a new year, the beginning of a longer day and with it the arrival of better, warmer weather. The sunless days are hated by the Inuit too, and with total justification, I must admit. Even if there are some hours of daylight, the entire landscape still bears a peculiar stamp which is difficult to describe; one might express it as lacking a life-giving source. The nuances of the clear sky which, however, could still not be termed blue, indicate by some faint bluish-reddish strips the spot where the sun still exists beneath the horizon, shining on better areas, and from this spot, which moves then disappears with the advance and ending of the day, a shading which becomes steadily darker, a peculiar grey, rises toward the zenith. Today the scene was different. No matter how low, the sun was visible; there could be no doubt about it. This pale red, unusually large disc must be the sun since it emitted rays and produced shadows which we admired with pleasure for the first time in a long time, on the wide snow surfaces, which were now freed from their previous gloomy, pale blue shading. Both we and the Inuit left our houses to regale ourselves with the full view of our New Year's gift – but it did not last long. As if it had already done too much good the sun rushed along the horizon (one could easily observe its rapid progress) sank, and was gone again. A slight evening glow followed and then the day was over. With a certain contentment we then glanced at the northern horizon but there we could see no sign that the sun had brought its first greeting. The dark night sky had long since spread its wings over the regions from which we had come. At Cape Felix we had experienced a long endless day, but we had escaped from a perpetual night.

In the evening Netsilik Joe came back with a caribou and reported that he had seen masses of caribou tracks, but at the same time also an entire pack of wolves. Our other hunter, who did not return until late the following evening, confirmed these reports, but he had been more fortunate. He had to fetch his kill, which numbered four animals, with a sledge the following day. Thus only one day's march from the Back River the difference with regard to abundance of game was already striking. The reason that the river bank areas themselves were not densely populated may be sought in the fact that the mosses required to support the animals are absent there or, perhaps, that the caribou are much safer from attacks by wolves in an open landscape.

However, from the traveller's point of view the river offers the advantage that the wind is not so noticeable there. At the temperature which now prevailed even the slightest breath of air became sensitively perceptible.

On 3 January 1880 our thermometer reached its lowest reading. The three observations at 8:00 A.M., 12 noon, and 6:00 P.M. gave readings of -56^0, -55^0, and -57^0, hence a daily mean of -56^0, one of the lowest temperatures ever observed. Otherwise the day was fine, clear, and completely calm and Melms covered a day's march of eleven miles with his sledge.

On such days the execution of meteorological observations was not a particularly pleasant task and yet the greatest care had to be taken. Our Fahrenheit alcohol thermometers turned out to be very fine instruments; at these low temperatures if one laid them on the snow blocks on the outside of an occupied snow house as against on the ground they recorded a difference of about $1-1\frac{1}{2}^0C$. Under normal circumstances the temperature was at its lowest around 10:00 A.M., ie, shortly before daylight became perceptible and reached its highest level around 1 o'clock.

The impact of cold on people made itself felt from about -45^0C since even with the warmest clothing one could not stand still during a stop outdoors for longer than a maximum of five minutes and if otherwise unoccupied one had to at least attempt to retain the influence of one's bodily heat by walking up and down.

In calm weather the cold as it makes itself felt in these regions is not dangerous for people as long as they have an adequate quantity of food, are in a position to consume a sufficient quantity of fats, and know how to observe closely the little tricks which the Inuit adopt under low temperature conditions.

All three of these conditions have the purpose of maintaining bodily heat or even increasing it if at all possible without producing perspiration. Fats, whether they be the blubber normally used in this country, caribou fat, salmon oil, or the fat from the birds which are caught in large quantities for this purpose in summer, are used by every arctic traveller. They are a necessity and with time they will overcome any disgust which whites, due to their greater gastronomical refinement, initially feel toward them. Similarly, the loss of our dogs was less due to an inadequate amount of food than to a total lack of the necessary fat content in their meat.

With regard to the third stipulation the keenest observation of every movement of the Inuit represents a profitable lesson in combatting the impact of low temperatures on people. If an Inuk has nothing to do with his hands he will pull his arms out of his sleeves and cross them on his chest. He always walks with his fists clenched in such a way that the thumb lies next to the palm of the hand. And if there is a wind blowing and he has to walk into it, either directly or at an angle, he will always hold his head turned to one side. In this manner the hood, which is pulled over the head and projects on the windward side, forms a shelter from the wind, just as the Austrian polar travellers were in the habit of adding to their attire.[3] But in a situation where the wind is blowing directly into one's face, careful mutual co-operation is essential since cessation of the burning, stinging pain in the chilled area signifies the start of frost-bite. This makes itself visible as a waxy yellow patch standing out sharply against the normal colour of the face, but it can be easily eliminated by placing a warm hand on it. We had to thank the vigilance of the Inuit women in particular for the fact that no significant frost-bite occurred on our long winter march. They seemed to derive special pleasure in being able to practise the technique of laying on their hands in this healing fashion. Each of us had a particularly susceptible spot. In Gilder's case it was his nose, in Schwatka's his nostrils and eyelids, in Melms' his cheeks, and in my case my knuckles, if I was not particularly careful to cover them completely with my gloves. The effect of the cold on the party's appearance, just as on its surroundings, had many aspects.

Every reader will be able to remember cold days when the human breath was visible in the form of a vapour or even a light fog. On our coldest days this 'Ha,' as it is popularly called, became a cloud of smoke which, like the frost smoke from the 'Dangerous Rapids,' accompanied every living thing. It emanates from men's mouths and from the dogs' respiratory organs; it betrays the caribou and makes their presence in large numbers visible for miles. A sledge in motion looks at some distance as if it is enveloped in fog, and a fleeing caribou herd resembles a railway train, since their hot breath is revealed so clearly against the bitterly cold air. Furthermore, wherever a warm object comes in contact with a naturally cold one steam will rise; even the spot on the ground from which one has just raised one's foot will produce steam. Anyone who is travelling is quite a sight; their beards, their hair, every item of clothing near their heads becomes white. A tobacco chewer is to be most pitied since all the tobacco juice gathers first in brown plugs, but later in the form of a mass of ice on his beard. In the evening he has to use a hammer or an axe to free himself from his day's load. Once a water hole has been opened and cleared of all the

Travelling in extreme cold

ice, within five minutes it becomes covered over with an ice crust on which one can no longer make an impression with a finger; a light blow is necessary to break through it. Occasionally I tried using a native drinking cup for this purpose but the muskox horn which formed its raw material was not strong enough and the cup broke instead of the ice. I received a sermon from the owner, my old housekeeper, not for the damage, but just for the idea; it would have done a mother-in-law proud. In order to thaw out our meat which was frozen rock-hard, we hung it about two feet down in the water hole; the difference in temperature was so great that within an hour it would be soft and palatable. Transmission of sound waves is also noticeably different at low temperatures. One can hear a sledge at a distance of three miles as it glides with a squealing noise over the smooth snow surface. But the most noteworthy aspect is the strikingly clear atmosphere. A hill visible on the horizon fifteen miles away reveals its outline just as clearly and sharply as if it were only two miles away.

In the interest of improving our chances at hunting we did not always travel together, but divided ourselves into two and quite often even into three parties. Thereby we gained the advantage that the group following behind could always use the first party's house if it had already abandoned it. We were rarely farther apart than one day's march but often reassembled after only three to four days.

The terrain, which rose in monotonous snowfields from the Back River, possessed a more rocky, hilly, more rugged appearance as we proceeded farther into the interior, and became less and less endowed with ponds and lakes until on the 15th we finally crossed the divide between the Back River and Hudson Bay. Caribou now became more frequent and muskox tracks also appeared, yet despite the better feeding scarcely a day's march passed which did not cost us a dog. Although our supplies of blubber were almost exhausted, in the hope of keeping the dogs alive we had already fed them the contents of an entire sealskin but without any particular success. It was particularly the animals which we had bought in part from the Netsilimiut and in particular from the Utkuhikhalingmiut and which at first had looked strong and impressive, which were among the first to collapse. They were accustomed to being fed only seal meat and fish, and caribou meat was too lean a meat for them. Also, the constant work may also have contributed to their rapid collapse.

I have already had many opportunities to talk about Inuit dogs, but their devotion to man did not display itself to greatest advantage until their final days. They are particularly patient and tame toward the children, who, among the Inuit too, like to play with the dogs and who similarly often maltreat them. I have never seen a case, and have heard of only one instance where a child or an adult was bitten. But if this does occur, according to Inuit tradition the dog has to be killed immediately. One cannot spot in advance a dog's degree of exhaustion. Our dogs would run with the team, pulling well and strongly right up to the moment when they collapsed powerless.

In the first few cases we tried to rescue them; we even loaded them on the sledge in a few cases but in vain; they were lost to us. Subsequently we simply removed the harness and left them lying; fifteen minutes later we would hear a pack of wolves quarrelling over the animal we had left lying.

With the more frequent appearance of caribou the wolves also made themselves more noticeable and increasingly disturbed our dogs but no regrettable attacks occurred. They must have been finding enough food in this game-rich area, since when Tulugaq left caribou he had killed out in the open and did not retrieve them with the sledge until the following day, he would find an abundance of wolf tracks around his cache but the wolves would not have touched the meat itself.

Our continuing march involved very slow progress, at times over a stony plateau, at times over terrain evenly blanketed in snow. On the latter the short snow ridges were an obstacle and in order to conserve our traction power we dismantled one sledge in order to use the runners to join two of the others together in tandem. In this way we put together a sledge about twenty-four feet long; with a double team it travelled more easily over the many irregularities than the short ones. But the days when the dogs provided our sole traction power were over. By the 17th eight dogs had died and we were all obliged to assist in hauling. The agile, easily mobile marching column which we had come to know the previous spring had changed its appearance. Instead of a single leader, who previously had formed the vanguard of the sledge party, today we would have three or four people walking ahead of the team, each of them leaning with all his strength into a harness. In addition, all the rest of the people attached to each sledge, not excluding the dog drivers, would be hauling on lines fastened to the sides of the sledges. Instead of the twelve, fifteen or nineteen miles which we had been able to cover daily on the march to King William's Land, today ten miles represented a good day's travel. We needed to stop for a rest more frequently than in the previous spring, when we had been able to travel for ninety minutes without a break. Especially around noon the party presented a typical scene of nomadic life in winter. By now the sun had risen about 6–7⁰ above the horizon and the temperature difference between locations in the direct sun and those in the shade was about 10⁰. At low temperatures a difference of 10⁰ is particularly significant, especially since we had become accustomed to calling any temperature above –40⁰C warm weather. No wonder that everyone sat in the sun. The old woman who by her own admission had never made such a long and difficult march in her fifty-five years is speaking the truth when she comments 'Siqirniq ukuujuq' (The sun is warm).[4] Only to the dogs and those making our travel calculations does the sun bring no comfort. The former lie together in a dense tangle in order to keep each other warm; their degree of emaciation is becoming daily more noticeable, and with it they have lost all their wildness and energy.

For Lieutenant Schwatka and myself recording the distance and direction of our march since our last rest stop has particularly unpleasant aspects. First of all each time we start and stop it is essential to check our watches no matter how short the distance covered. In the case of us arctic wanderers these are not so readily to hand as when one makes a habit of carrying them in one's vest pocket. In order to carry them where they are totally serviceable, the watches have to be completely free of even the smallest amount of oil and are then carried in a small pouch made of caribou hide, hung around one's neck against one's bare body. But if one wants to look at the watch, it is necessary to take the pouch out, pull the watch out, stow it away again as quickly as possible, and hide the pouch beneath one's skin clothing again. Naturally this entire operation has to be effected with bare hands, and the same applies to plotting our march on the map. In terms of an operation such as this the sun still has no alleviating strength and would not acquire any until we had reached the coast of Hudson Bay.

While we were occupied with entering the relevant data Tulugaq would have taken a piece of meat from his sledge. Admittedly from its shape and hardness it would not look like meat to the layman, and even less so after Tulugaq had attacked it with an axe and ice chisel in order to break it into pieces. Once this was done everybody would sit around on the snow to take a frugal meal; anybody who had not learned, or had not noticed the advantage of first breathing on the meat before sticking it in his mouth, would have to learn by experience. The adhesion of firmly frozen objects has unpleasant but also sometimes positive aspects. An Inuk is familiar with these positive aspects and knows how to use them. In order to cut frozen meat or some other hard object with his knife one must first warm the knife blade so that it does not break or rebound. There is probably no stranger, more peculiar experience than to observe this warming procedure. He touches the first one or two inches of the knife blade nearest the point with his tongue, which naturally immediately sticks to the metal. He then leaves it in this position until the relative temperatures allow the two objects to separate without immediate removal of the skin. In every case bodily heat has to fulfil the function of a warming apparatus and in order to select only one example from the numerous demonstrations occurring daily, let us select the smoker for a change.

The party's abundant supply of smoking tobacco allowed its members the enjoyment of a pipe throughout the entire trip, with the exception of the last few days. The preparation of a pipe for smoking in this cold weather was a fairly troublesome and time-consuming operation. Only clay pipes with the bowl and stem in one piece were usable. The pipe itself had first to be thawed out before every smoke and even once it was filled it was sometimes a real art to light it. We took the greatest care in keeping our matches dry but despite this they too had acquired a low temperature and this had first to be raised in order for the wood to catch light from the burning sulphur.

For this purpose the match was rubbed between the palms of the hands until its temperature had been raised, and since the phosphorus became moist again during this operation the Inuk would rub the appropriate end in his hair until that part too was dry. Combustion itself would be achieved on the point of a knife or on a little stone carried for the purpose by the women, who alone are fortunate enough to possess pockets. In a similar fashion we had to learn to help each other in all kinds of minor operations.

Let us return after this digression to our real theme, our party's progress. The region was quite varied and with it the presence of our major food source, the caribou, also varied. The Quoich River ran generally transversely to our overland march; as the map indicates it flows in a mainly southerly direction to Chesterfield Inlet. Although its course had been plotted on the map by Dr Rae in individual details, we had justifiable doubts as to the accuracy of the information. When one engages in overly precise surveys, especially on winter marches, one makes the greatest mistakes, and both our observations in the spring, as well as the plotting of our line of march by means of the dead reckoning already discussed, led us to the realization that the existing British Admiralty charts revealed an error of at least 12–18 miles in the representation of the coast and of river courses. Hence we wanted to determine exactly when and where we crossed the abovementioned river and to establish its precise geographical position. But especially on level terrain and in winter, following a river is a difficult task since connection between the pools which arctic rivers display in vast numbers, in general ceases completely at that time of year, and thereby an apparent interruption of the river course is introduced. On 18 January we experienced an example of how easily one can miss these connections. We had reached a large lake which we had recognized for quite some time, over a distance of about nine miles, as being part of the river from following its interconnected components. We pushed rapidly ahead, following it southward but then, around 2 o'clock, high hills formed a barrier which, despite a search of more than 1½ hours, offered no sign of a passage. In the course of our march along the lake itself farther north we had left a small opening to the west unexplored, since we thought that, judging by the fine river banks, the course of the stream remained southerly. This lack of attention now left us no alternative but to climb the hills. These wild granite cones with their points, gullies, and clefts, their little hill lakes and ponds, represented a westerly continuation of the Hazard Hills, of which we had earlier touched the easterly outliers, and even though it was via a rather tortuous route we maintained a southerly direction as we crossed them.

Toward evening of that same day we crossed the tracks of six muskoxen which could not be more than two days old; immediately this observation aroused the interest of all the Inuit. From a nearby hill they thought they could spot the present location of the animals from a regular column of steam rising about eight miles away. Lieutenant Schwatka agreed to their request to use the morning for a muskox hunt. Accompanied by the Inuit, he and Gilder set out in pursuit of the animals next morning with all the available dogs, but after they had followed their tracks for about thirty miles the onset of darkness forced them to abandon the hunt. An Inuk who had turned back earlier due to a sore foot suddenly ran across the herd they were pursuing while on his way back, some four miles from camp. But he had no dogs with him with which to bring the easily scared animals to bay, and hence the entire day was wasted for us and the hunt was a total failure. In very severe winter weather even the Inuit very rarely continue a hunt to the point that they have to build a small snow house for the dark night hours and spend a short period asleep.

Another incident gave Melms the opportunity to spend such a night in a snow house. We had forgotten our last box of powder, which had been drifted over in a severe snowstorm at an earlier camp site, and my companions drew lots to retrieve it, accompanied by an Inuk. Shortly after midnight the two men left our camp site to walk back; they had to walk for two days before they reached their goal and its forgotten treasure.

Without any light and constantly prepared for a possible attack by wolves, at a temperature of $-46^{\circ}C$ they stretched out without sleeping bags in one of our abandoned snow houses and alternately tried to sleep as well as they could. Their bodies were adequately well protected. They pulled their hands out of their sleeves and kept them warm on their bare torsos, but their feet, which had been sweating from the long march, would not permit them any sleep. To this was added a lack of drinking water, since they had no means of drilling a water hole through the ice which was at least six feet thick. Snow and ice only aggravated their longing for a good drink. After an absence of almost thirty-six hours they caught up with us with the recovered powder, but Melms never again had any desire to repeat such a night.

I find it appropriate to mention here that taking alcohol is advisable on arctic expeditions, only if its use is limited to the rarest cases of absolute necessity. Alcoholic drinks such as schnapps certainly warm one quickly but they also make one sleepy, and that first rest might easily be the cause of the person concerned freezing to death. During its entire actual journey the Schwatka party did not carry any alcoholic drinks yet despite, or perhaps because of this it survived the greatest hardships and the most intense cold. But if one wanted to take alcohol along, high-grade alcohol in sealed cans will suffice; it should be under the sole and special control of the party leader and he can distribute it, mixed with water, in exceptional cases. For the modest requirements of arctic life alcohol completely fulfils the purpose for which it is intended and is quite sufficient in small quantities and is easily transportable.

For the whole month of January we had atrocious weather, which delayed our progress for days. It was also unfavourable for hunting caribou. In spring, with its deep snowdrifts, we could expect to creep up unnoticed on game in the soft snow but now we did not have this advantage. Creeping up inaudibly in this pure air was out of the question since despite the snowdrifts sounds carried a long distance and scared our quarry. All the many caribou which we now killed were shot at long range, whereas normally the Inuit do not fire from any range greater than a maximum of 100 paces.

It was now a rare occurrence if we were all travelling together;

usually Lieutenant Schwatka went ahead with his sledge and the other two sledges followed, either together or separately, depending on circumstances.

Since the first sledge had the least people but by far the best hunters, the lieutenant often left meat for us as we followed behind, in his abandoned houses. But he had to cease this service when, in early February, we reached an area where wolves occurred in large numbers. They became daily more numerous and slunk around the immediate area even in daylight. It would often happen that as we came within sight of the snow house left by the first party in the evening, a wolf would suddenly appear at its door, look at us in surprise, and only very slowly and reluctantly would abandon his comfortable spot as we approached. But this insolence was only the start of the unpleasantness which the wolves had in store for us on our homeward journey as they constantly became more numerous.

In Arctic America three species of wolves may be distinguished. The smallest, blackish-brown in colour, is a species very similar to our Central European wolf. The true arctic wolf is the largest, whitish-grey in colour and occurring only singly, whereas the third species, medium-sized and light reddish-brown in colour, exceeds the others in its predatory behaviour. This last species always occurs in packs and, according to the Inuit, even attacks man. Our Eskimo Joe told us of a very instructive encounter with them from his own experience. While he was at Repulse Bay with the arctic traveller Charles F. Hall he was attacked by about eight wolves at the height of summer. Since he was armed only with a muzzle-loader he could think of no other means of escape but to retreat hip-deep into the waters of a nearby pond. More than an hour passed and Joe was still standing in the water while the wolves still kept watch on him from the shore. Finally, when he felt the joke had lasted long enough he shot one, loaded his rifle again (one can just imagine the awkward manipulations involved) and killed a second member of the pack. The others now threw themselves on their dead companions and devoured them. While they were satisfying their hunger Joe seized the opportunity to make his getaway by wading through the water for some time.

Tulugaq landed in a much more serious situation during our march. He was attacked by a pack of about thirty wolves and only the fact that there was a high rock nearby saved the life of our best hunter. He leaped onto it and with his magazine rifle began providing food for the wolves from their own midst. Stories of this type began to seem uncanny as the wolves daily became more numerous and more insolent; they no longer had any respect for our signal rockets, which we had used with so much success in the spring. The lieutenant lit one, and later even two together, but the wolves appeared to be entertained by the light with its changing colours and did not retreat. We could not shoot them since our ammunition was running low; the dogs were so exhausted that we could not expect any protection from them, so we lived in a constant state of tension.

On 9 February Tulugaq had shot several caribou and was feeding the dogs late in the evening. He had cut the meat into large pieces and had thrown it to his dogs in front of his snow house and was standing by when he suddenly thought he spotted a large dog trying to steal the meat from a smaller one. He kicked the supposed dog but when the latter snapped at him he realized his error; a closer look confirmed that some wolves had mingled with the dogs in order to share their meal with them. Tulugaq fetched his rifle and killed the visitors on the spot.

Melms and I were a day's march behind with the other two sledges, and there we had an even sadder experience. A pack of wolves had been accompanying us all day and since, as already noted, we could not waste any ammunition on them we had to satisfy ourselves with using our rifles only in cases of very great crisis. The next night was a very restless one for us, since we could constantly hear our dogs barking with fear and had to go out every minute to protect them. On this occasion Netsilik Joe experienced a battle with one of the predators and he had only his agility and the fact that he was holding a rifle in his hand at the time to thank for the fact that he escaped without injury. But despite our vigilance that same night the wolves launched an attack in which four of our dogs were torn apart. This was too much for the otherwise good-natured Inuit, who were not easily riled; they now set in operation their indigenous machines of death.

Next evening a special type of snow house was built for the remainder of the dogs and the team was locked up there overnight. Netsilik Joe then smeared caribou blood on the blades of two very sharp knives and buried them in the snow with the blades upward, in such a way that only the blood remained visible. It was not long before the wolves arrived and began licking the knives; they lacerated their tongues badly, then continued to lick up their own blood, which they mistook for the caribou blood, until the animals bled to death. In this way three wolves fell victim to this device; admittedly it sounds like a hunter's tall tale, but it was indeed fact. But another trap was also being set for the wolves.

Netsilik Joe had cut strips from a piece of baleen which he had been carrying for a long time; they were about two feet long. He fastened little triangular blades about ¼ inch across to their ends and filed them sharp. The strips were then rolled up tightly, tied together in this spiral-shaped coil with a piece of caribou sinew, and hidden in meat which was then frozen rock-hard. Three or four such pieces of meat were scattered around in the immediate vicinity of the camp and were very quickly devoured by the wolves. The speed with which the animals swallowed the entire bait allowed this strange device to reach their stomachs unconsumed. After it had all thawed out and the sinew was loosened by the warmth the whalebone would suddenly spring apart inside the wolf and result in a fearsome death. These are indeed gruesome methods which the Inuit employ, but they offered the only chance of keeping the few dogs we had left. The wolves appeared less often but unfortunately the caribou also became rarer and we had to accelerate our rate of march in order to reach the coast. On several occasions our food situation looked very bleak; once we expressed great joy when one of our hunters went out to look for caribou and found the remains of an animal which the wolves had killed and left lying. By the second half of the month our situation was particularly gloomy. With a great deal of effort we slowly hauled our sledges southward across the hilly terrain, which was devoid of any variation. In the evenings, exhausted, we would build our snow houses, but the comfort and cheerfulness which we had found in them a month earlier were no longer present. Our supplies of blubber had shrunk to a minimum and we could no longer wait in bed until the woman handed each of us his piece of cooked meat and hot soup for his evening meal. With great difficulty we dug moss out from under the snow in order to cook the few mouthfuls of food. But the hardships, the diet, and especially the lack of fat had left their mark on us in other ways too, and this made it desirable that we soon reach a spot where there was a greater degree of comfort. Our snow houses were no longer witness to the cheerful life of several months before; instead everyone lay down, mute and silent in his sleeping bag. The monotonous 'Aya, aya,' of the women, sung to a monotonous melody which could drive one almost crazy and which completely matched the situation, accentuated the unpleasantness which the cold and darkness had already created in such a gross fashion inside our quarters. When we left King William's Land our sledges had been laden with hundreds of pounds of seal blubber; today we could pour our entire supply into a litre jug, yet apart from the bag which we fed to the dogs we have not used any wastefully.

Under these circumstances, after prolonged searching and waiting, we finally reached the Quoich River,[5] and crossed it since we had decided not to follow it south but to maintain our southeasterly direction across country. However, we did resolve to take an observation of the sun's noon altitude next day if possible in order to locate the river more precisely. On 20 February the sun's altitude as it crossed the meridian was $14^0 29' 30''$ and hence our latitude was $64^0 21'$N.

Since the end of November we had not been able to check our dead reckoning with observations, yet after a march of 300 miles our calculations revealed an error of only 1½–2½ miles. This infinitesimally small error proves clearly what practice in estimating distance can achieve.

25 February brought us a very pleasant surprise. We had not travelled that day and Tulugaq and Eskimo Joe had gone hunting; they returned without any caribou certainly, but they had met an Inuk whom they knew well.

Next morning despite a terrible storm and a temperature of -52^0C we broke camp, and after a march of about two hours we finally reached the houses of men again. Asedlak (the Inuk seen the day before) had himself left the ships wintering at Marble Island shortly after our party had left there in March 1879 and had come with his family to this region, where he had found caribou in abundance and also a good camp site. He had lived here for almost a full year with his wife and two children, cut off from every other human being. Yet his appearance and that of his family proved that he was in excellent condition by our standards, as far as one can apply such a concept to the Inuit. Asedlak was of great interest to us in many respects. He still had abundant supplies and this allowed us to provision ourselves well for the few days' marches which we still had to cover to reach the Hudson Bay coast. His intention to remain here for a few more weeks allowed us to put into practice a plan which we had long cherished, namely to leave behind the heaviest portion of our loads and to cover the final lap quickly and easily, later fetching the items we had cached.

Our fine Asedlak, an Inuk of the Qairnirmiut band, living south of Chesterfield Inlet, declared that he was prepared to give us every possible assistance in both areas in return for a rifle with an appropriate amount of ammunition, and hence we made our final preparations to cover the last lap of our journey by forced marches.

CHAPTER TWELVE

The Final Stretch to Marble Island, 28 February–23 March 1880

The final marches. A birth. On the Connery River again.
Meeting with the Aivilingmiut. Our reception. A sad scene.
A terrible disappointment. An Inuit diet. Starvation. A death.
Funeral ceremonies of the Inuit. Dreary days. Salvation.
Arrival at Marble Island.

According to Asedlak we could reach the Hudson Bay coast with light sledges in two days; encouraged by this information we began the continuation of our journey on 28 February 1880, with an air temperature of –55°C. All the baggage we could leave behind was stored in a snow house over which water was then poured so that an ice crust formed over the entire thing in a few moments. This would present an impenetrable obstacle to the wolves even if the Inuk, who had undertaken to watch our things, were to leave the spot before we subsequently retrieved them. Asedlak had sold us six caribou; twenty-six dogs had fallen victim to the cold and the wolves between the Back River and here, but we now fed the sixteen survivors and loaded the remainder of the meat on two sledges. We had to dismantle the third sledge for fuel. We then set off bound for our long-cherished goal, hauling in the traces ourselves; our course lay east-southeast, partly over gentle hills, partly over large lakes.

There was little hope that we would reach our goal in two days, although the Inuit at times will cover up to fifty miles in a day in forced marches. Our traction power was too limited to progress at this sort of rate. The region presented no special attractions to our eyes; the snowy hills strewn with large and small granite boulders, the valleys liberally scattered with small water bodies and magnificent lakes, these had become commonplace to us. We were looking only to the southeast, to see whether we could spot that dark blackish-blue strip known as the water sky, which alerts the traveller in the regions of snow and ice to the presence of open water, and would warn us of the proximity of Hudson Bay.

On the afternoon of 2 March we found a large pond with an outflow which looked very similar to the Connery River we had left in April 1879, and we followed its course for a long time, indeed until our usual rest hour, looking for indications which might confirm this suspicion. But we could not find any reliable clue to confirm it.

But an important event was to occur. While occupied with building the snow houses the Inuit suddenly abandoned their work and began with all haste to build a small, separate snow house. It was very quickly finished and soon after she had entered the house Netsilik Joe's wife gave birth to a son; she had walked twenty miles that day hauling a sledge. We expected that our progress would be delayed by this event but next morning she was wrapped in skins and placed on the sledge, and we covered a further seventeen miles.

On the morning of the 3rd we passed through a ravine, through which the already wide river forced its way. Its great variety, with its striking granite formations and its rich alternation of rock, snow, and ice, was to form the final scene of the regions still unfamiliar to us. A few paces farther and we definitely recognized the river as the Connery again, and joyfully greeted the rough coastal pressure ice, caused by the alternation of low and high tide. In the evening we built our 53rd snow house camp since we had left King William's Land on almost the same site as on 1 April 1879 on our outward march; it was also the last one of our trip.

Next morning nobody needed to wake the Inuit and to haul them out of their sleeping skins. With the first rays of the rising sun we emerged from the mouth of the Connery River, which had provided us with a welcome route for the past forty-two miles, onto the open ice of Hudson Bay. During the eleven months and four days which we had been absent from Hudson Bay we had covered a distance of 2820 miles (705 German miles or 5287.5 km). We had achieved our task in an exhaustive fashion considering the time factor and circumstances. We had supported ourselves and our dogs solely by hunting the game of the area we had crossed, notorious as being a barren desert of snow, without losing a man. Indeed, we had survived the dangers of the long journey without illness and had defied the discomforts of a severe arctic winter in the open. And now we were near our goal, near, we assumed, the long-cherished food supplies of civilization and, most appealing of all to us, near the homes of men. Almost three months had elapsed, during which, limited to our own company, we had encoun-

tered only the desirable caribou or the hated wolf; now the raven which circled croaking over our heads was a welcome sight. Not for nothing does the Inuk wandering in the barrens greet him with a cheerful 'Tulugaq, tulugaq!' (Raven!); and his statement that where a raven is to be seen there are also people in the vicinity is certainly true. Ahead of us lay the water sky we had been seeking for so long and from behind the last headland Depot Island finally emerged; near it lay Camp Daly, the spot where for eight long months (from August 1878 to April 1879) we had carried out our course of training for our trip. Even the dogs recognized that the goal of their long journey was near and without any encouragement from the whip they raced lustily across the smooth ice surface.

There were important questions which would be answered in the course of the next two hours. Were there any ships in Hudson Bay which would take us back to the bosom of civilization next summer? Had any news from home arrived with those ships? And had arrangements been made in America that we would receive the long anticipated additions to the supplies we had left behind for the period remaining until our departure? Finally, had the Inuit cared properly for the depot left in their charge? These were all questions which were of keen interest to us, as one, then two, and finally several human figures became visible on the ice horizon and were later joined by an entire dog team. There could be no doubt as to the identity of the figures who now approached us from all directions. Our earlier nearest neighbours during our winter sojourn here, the Aivilingmiut, had been keeping a look-out in the direction in which we could be expected to return, and all that was needed was for us to give the signal we had prearranged the year before in order to make known on both sides the joyful news of our return. Tulugaq, our most courageous and experienced hunter, excitedly tied an old blanket to a stick and waved it from his sledge as a recognition signal and in order to avoid any possibility of error we fired a few volleys from our breech-loading rifles. The two parties came closer and closer together; already one could distinguish the familiar physiognomies of individual Inuit in their fur coverings. A short time later handshake followed upon handshake and we were being congratulated on our safe return. These were simply Inuit greeting us but for eyewitnesses of this scene this first meeting with these fine natives will remain unforgettable. In his sincerity and heartiness an Inuk is not satisfied with a firm handshake, which feels so rough to more tender hands; no, he lays his hand on his friend's chest and with his 'Maniktumi' (approximately 'Welcome')[1] he seems to be trying to

reassure himself that the great joy at this meeting is not perhaps just
an idle dream.

But the poet's dictum 'Life's unmixed joy is not part of any earthly
scheme,' was to find confirmation even here. Only too soon the loud
greetings of 'Saimu!' fell silent and in place of them there began a loud
lamentation which was pitiful to hear. With the return of the
aforementioned Tulugaq it was the duty of those greeting him to
inform him of the death of his mother, which had occurred in his
absence. Whether it was the pain of this loss which caused Tulugaq
and his wife to fall unconscious on the sledge, then give vent to their
feelings in long, protracted, loud cries of lamentation, or whether there
were other causes for this scene, has remained unclear to me, but in
later months I repeatedly had occasion to make similar observations in
various instances of death. It was not a bitter weeping and half-
suppressed sobbing, representing a fairly strong expression of inner
pain, but a wailing which assaulted the bereaved person's own organs
of speech and the hearing organs of the bystanders to the utmost, and
its very short duration leads me to the conviction that there we were
encountering a custom similar to that which oriental peoples commonly exhibit in their mourning ceremonies. After the wailing had
lasted fifteen to twenty minutes Tulugaq stood up, took his whip in
his hand, and his entire external appearance revealed him once again as
just the man we had known for months, our energetic, willing, and
always cheerful companion.

But we whites were also faced with a terrible disappointment.
Repeatedly and especially during earlier months we had looked
forward to a small feast which we would organize for the whole party
on the day we reached our goal, on the basis of the food supplies we had
left behind. But to our great shock these food supplies had not been left
behind for us. When we had first landed in 1878 we had taken as much
of our supplies ashore with us as we needed immediately and had
asked the captain of the ship which had brought us from New York to
our first arctic residence to leave the remainder of our provisions at
Depot Island when he returned to America in August 1879. Without
detailing further the irresponsible behaviour of the captain in question, who had left nothing for us, not even a few lines by way of
explanation, I shall note here only that our position was less than
enviable since now, having safely completed our journey and reached
our goal we still had to undergo some difficult hours which certainly
none of us had expected.

Since we had only the meat supplies which lay on our sledges and were scarcely adequate for one day, what better could we do than accept the invitation of our Inuit friends and place our faith in the hope that they could look after the new arrivals. If not starving, we were certainly not well nourished, but once we had recovered from our eleven months of restless wandering, had regained our strength, and rested, we could search out the whaling bark *George and Mary* wintering at Marble Island some thirty German miles farther south. From her we could expect immediate assistance and transport to America.

The first few days passed quite well. After being greeted by the female population of this relatively large settlement we crawled into various snow houses and were very well received. There is a great difference between coming into a snow house which is just newly built or has been occupied for only a few days and one in which people have already spent weeks or months. The longer occupied hut certainly does not offer any advantages with regard to cleanliness, but after some months one is accustomed to the appearance of such a household and the temperature prevailing is the predominant criterion in the choice between a cold, new hut and a warm, old one.

The interior of a hut in which people have been living and cooking for some time has been warmed several times to above the freezing point and the snow blocks nearest to the lamps and in the upper ceiling have developed an icy glaze as a result of melting of the snow, absorption of the resultant water into that part which is still firm, and by regelation of the entire mass. This glaze is then coloured blackish by the smoke. Whenever the temperature again rises to some point above zero the water collects on small edges and projecting points and begins to drip, drop by drop, on the skins which serve as bedding. This *kuttuktuq* (dripping) is greatly disliked by northern residents and in order to eliminate it, at least for a time, they have a tested means which, however simple, demonstrates how quickly even a person uneducated in physics can, without knowing it, make the laws of nature his beneficial servant just through instinct or his powers of observation. The housewife always has a piece of snow ready to hand for this purpose and at the first drop she cuts off a cube-shaped piece, breathes on one surface, and applies it to the spot from where the drip came. A moment is sufficient for the cold snow to draw so much warmth from the little accumulation of water that it freezes, and thereby the little cube of snow sticks to the ceiling.

By means of this repeatedly applied operation, as well as by occasional renovations to the ceiling itself, with blocks of snow being cut out and replaced, the interior acquires the appearance of a small, stalactite-hung cave, and if one considers the peculiar lighting from two or three brightly burning lamps, the motley confusion of the primitive household and its residents, the little ones resembling the gnomes in one of our fairy-tales as they leap around their mother, bundled in their furs. Could anyone criticize us if today in such surroundings, among people whom we had been looking forward to seeing again for months, we entirely overlooked the dark side of the *iglu* (snow house) and engaged in cheerful conversation, considering ourselves fortunate in that this time we could sleep undisturbed, instead of having to think of breaking camp, hitting the trail, and sledge-hauling early next morning?

Throughout the camp great activity reigned until late into the night as our companions made the switch from their diet of caribou to eating walrus meat, although in making this change they had to wash themselves first. This was therefore a sort of exceptional holiday for them.

There was no end to the exchanging of stories. The small group of old men, the patriarchal heads of the band, who gathered round their old friend Eskimo Joe, known far and wide as an interpreter on arctic searches (he had accompanied the whites on two polar voyages and three Franklin search expeditions), were absolutely amazed that it was possible to find one's way in this abnormally severe winter, through the midst of a vast, unknown country and to reach the salt water of Hudson Bay again precisely where we had left it on our outward journey. Next day one of those frightful storms was howling outside, such as sweep for days across the wide ice surfaces of the North, and we could congratulate ourselves on having taken such good advantage of the final few days before the onset of the equinoctial storms, and on having reached our goal. In each hut arrangements were made to cook for some of the new arrivals; under the circumstances we were hosted in the best possible way. Arrangements were even made that our dogs were well fed. And yet we could not conceal from ourselves the fact that the settlement's meat supplies were at a desperately low ebb.

And indeed the very next day the invitations became fewer; on the third day was only one meal and on the fourth day an unknown food was placed before us as an emergency makeshift. This was called *issik* (walrus flipper)[2] and it really was not so bad. A lover of pig's feet would find it a significant improvement with regard to taste. We found not only the meat a delicacy, but also the broth resulting from cooking it was much stronger and much more nutritious than that from caribou meat. Thus while this dish had some advantages in terms of quality, in terms of quantity there was only the disadvantage that the *issik* was too small for such a large number of people. Today we left our meal hungry since we knew that there was nothing more to eat, and that we would get nothing more until the wind swung into the south or east and allowed the men to hunt walrus.

Our encampment was not on land but on the sea ice about one German mile from the coast. The Inuit had selected this spot so that they could reach the floe edge more easily and quickly. Hudson Bay never entirely freezes; only along the coast, depending on the conditions and land forms is there a belt of fast ice all winter long, reaching up to two miles in width. The remainder of the ice drifts with the winds; if they blow from north and west the edge of the fast ice is washed by open water; but if they blow from the opposite directions the drift ice, on which the walrus usually congregate, would be located immediately adjacent to the fast ice. Our northwesterly equinoctial storm had first to blow itself out and give way to a more favourable wind before we could hope for a walrus hunt. Admittedly the Inuit did their best to hunt seals, but their efforts were unsuccessful and the situation in the encampment assumed a serious nature.

After the *issik* our food was walrus hide, which normally is only fed to the dogs; next day even this was entirely consumed and for the next five days we endured a fasting period, which one could call a period of starvation in the fullest sense of the word. Day after day the Inuit came to us and asked whether we were very hungry, and consoled us with 'Witschaho seliko aiviq' (We will kill a walrus soon), but even they, who were only too familiar with persistent storms, were not in a particularly good mood. Little was said in the houses, and even that in a low tone, while the crying of the children for food was the most painful aspect of the situation apart from one's own discomfort. The Inuk's well-nourished look disappears very quickly when he is deprived of food, especially when he cannot satisfy his stomach by drinking lots of water, as he likes to do in similar situations. In spring not only is there no walrus meat but the supplies of blubber are also exhausted, and since out on the sea ice water can be obtained only by melting snow over a blubber lamp, this emergency measure is also eliminated.

For the first few days we could still find a piece of sealskin here and there, and we even found a seal's skull from which ten or twelve of us ate the brains, but even these sources soon dried up. In order to reduce the pangs of hunger we stayed in our sleeping bags. The Inuit men

daily made repeated efforts to catch seals but in vain. The wailing of
the children really pained them and at one point one of them remembered that he had killed a walrus out on the ice some time before. This
good man went out in a really violent storm one morning and came
back in the evening with the blood-soaked snow from the spot where
he had cut up his kill. This blood-soaked snow was melted for the
children; the water was brought to a boil and among the most grateful
celebrations this admittedly very meagre meal brought some satisfaction at least for some time. Everyone had been so pained to see the
suffering and the feelings of the mothers when they could offer their
children nothing in response to their wailing requests. As regards my
own person I shall permit myself to dwell here on the quiet reflection
which occupied me through those long hours.

The reader who finds Dr Tanner's forty-day hunger cure credible may
perhaps be surprised that after such a short number of days we began
to feel a certain weakness, but permit me to draw attention to the fact
that there is a great difference between reaching this situation from a
well-nourished condition and from a condition such as ours. We had
been marching for months; although our food had been sufficient,
particularly over the past few weeks, we had not had so much food that
we had been able to accumulate a surplus of fat. Finally, and this may
be the critical aspect, we had been living exclusively on a meat diet,
with absolutely no bread. If one reflects further that in winter the
caribou itself is thin, and that for the past three months we had had to
dispense even with salt, one can perhaps find our situation understandable.

On the third day Lieutenant Schwatka, as expedition commander,
finally decided to set off on a trip with the best dogs and two Inuit to
the wintering harbour mentioned earlier and to send back supplies for
us.[3] We three whites left behind passed the time as well as we could.
Although we had been longing for some reading material for a long
time, now that we possessed some, even although it was neither very
scientific nor very highbrow, we could find no interest in it. Hence I lay
in the snow house and stared all day at the pages of my *Leibarzt der
Kaiserin*, yet even today I do not know whether it is a thriller or a
romance, let alone who the author is. My stomach felt horribly empty
and I was really afraid to move.

It is remarkable the changes to which one's wishes are subject. On
King William's Land for two months we had had nothing else to do but
eat well; there I would have gladly given five whole caribou, complete
with hide and hair, for a small novel, however bad. But during the
March days I am describing, that is, only about five months later,

during our starvation period, or fasting period, I don't know what would have been of greater importance to me, the German classics in their entirety, or ten pounds of meat.

But to fill our cup of suffering to the brim the reaper also appeared among the residents of our encampment. One has to be aware of the terrible superstitions of the Inuit in order to appreciate the importance of such an event. In the struggle for life the husband becomes a stranger to the wife; the mother to the child; the child to the parents; in the face of death kinship ceases to exist, and in the fear of death love for one's neighbour and every human assistance ceases. The Inuk who dies a natural death dies alone.

And so it was today. Kudliak, a young woman, had been ill for a long time, and by the rattle in her throat one evening intimated that she would not be among the living for very much longer. Immediately the occupants of the hut in which she lay took their entire possessions and went looking for another sleeping place. The hut was closed up and the dying woman was left to herself and to heaven. Next morning she was a corpse. Only now were the feelings of the Inuit aroused; the sad news was whispered from hut to hut but nobody would have dared to try to see the dead woman since that would have been a violation of custom. A man and a woman, in this case her husband and her aunt, had the duty of looking after the burial. Two hours after they had heard of the death the corpse was sewn up in all her clothes and some skins and was placed on a sledge which the two people themselves pulled to the nearest headland. Dogs cannot be used for this purpose; the reason for this probably lies in the Inuit's belief that the dogs might visit the graves, built of rocks above ground, when they were hungry. The sledge left the encampment without any ceremony and the people did not even leave their huts to dignify the simple burial procession with a last glance.

No matter how simple the burial itself a death brings with it a number of customs which, particularly in our present situation, were very unpleasant. If the *angakuq* (a sort of high priest) is present, he imposes a so-called taboo on the nearest relatives of the dead person, that is, a period of a week to a month depending how close or distant the relationship was, which those involved must spend in their present accommodation, whether it be a tent or a snow house. By Inuit reckoning there are thirteen months in a year, and the period from new moon to new moon is called *taqiq*, as also is the moon itself. On this occasion the *angakuq* was not present and they satisfied themselves with recognizing three days (since this was the third death to occur this year), during which nothing could be done. By strict law the men should not go hunting or eat in company, while the dogs should not be harnessed to the sledges or even be fed on the ground. The greatest care also had to be taken that nothing was dropped, not even scraps of caribou clothing.

But under the prevailing circumstances the Inuit went out early in the morning, when the wind finally changed, to hunt walrus. Those of us left behind in the snow houses sat in great tension. It looked totally comfortless inside. The lamps sat empty; the kettles had been standing in a corner for two days now and everyone brooded over his far from cheerful thoughts, whether he be white or Inuk. The past few days had made themselves visible on our faces and the beautiful eyes of the children lay deeper in their sockets than ever before. Would today bring us something to eat? Would the men spot some walrus? Would they still have enough strength to catch them? And finally would the starved dogs be strong enough to haul the kill back to the encampment without a sledge (since the sledges could not be taken along under any circumstances)? These were the questions we put to ourselves and tried to answer, when the barking of dogs rang from the ice. In an instant the women and children leaped up as if from a dream and dashed out of the houses.

There was no longer any doubt as to the solution of our problem. The barking dogs were hauling something; the men were urging the dogs on, waving their arms, and loudly shouting incomprehensible words. But even if they were incomprehensible they could not fail to elicit a reply and shouts of 'Alianai' (the Inuit's shout of joy) rang out a hundred times from every throat. I have heard utterings of joy from many nations but of all of these 'Hoch! Vivat! Eljen! or At'-zije!' none sounded so fine, so sincere, and unanimous as the 'Alianai!' of this crowd, which was so delighted at now being able to satisfy its hunger. It is quite understandable that it did not take long to carry the walrus, which was already cut up, into the house; equally understandable is the fact that the lamps were set up, the kettles hanging above them, and that cooking began immediately. But we could best realize how weakened our stomachs were from the fact that we could all eat only slowly and for limited periods. Those who ploughed in too hurriedly were even overtaken by a sort of fainting spell.

With satisfied stomachs we slept better, but next day the taboos associated with death were observed in the strictest manner. The dogs were fed, because the Inuit were concerned about their survival, but not on the ground as they usually were. Instead they were fed on the low elevation on which the camp was placed and each one had to be fed from a separate dish.

On the evening of the third day after Kudliak's death the two undertakers were taken to a separate snow house and there they had to spend the night alone. At sunrise they went to the dead woman's grave and until they returned everyone had to remain fasting in the camp. It would have been interesting to know what they did at the grave site but the Inuit are enormously taciturn when it comes to divulging their religious customs, and it is extremely difficult to eavesdrop on them.

After the two people had returned the inner circumference of each snow house was imprinted by the man of the house with an object which I do not feel it proper to name here, and which for the entire period of mourning was fastened above the entrance.[4] The man of the house and all the occupants by order of age, right down to the youngest child capable of speaking, then turned to various directions inside the house and uttered the word 'Tavva,' that is, enough. The entire ceremony came to an end with the washing of hands and faces.

Only then did we gather for a communal meal and anyone who wants to observe eating should watch the Inuit. Admittedly we did significant damage to our share, too. That same day a sledge appeared bringing mail from the ship wintering at Marble Island; apart from hardtack, pork, and molasses it also brought a letter from Lieutenant Schwatka with orders to come to Marble Island. Lieutenant Schwatka had covered the last seventy-five miles to his goal non-stop and without food, on foot, and accompanied by an Inuk, in twenty-three hours.[5]

Three days later we too were heartily welcomed aboard the ship and were being looked after by the whalemen with every possible comfort. For a long time the ship's cook remained our best friend. Thus ended our first significant fasting period among the Inuit and also the last lap of our main journey.

TABLE 3
Temperatures (ºC) from 1 November 1879 until 31 March 1880

Month		Average for			
	Month	1st half	2nd	Max.	Min.
November 1879	−31	−27	−35	−17	−55
December 1879	−45	−43	−47	−36	−56
January 1880	−47	−49	−44	−30	−57
February 1880	−43	−46	−39	−23	−55
March 1880	−32	−39	−25	−11	−50

The Last Months in Hudson Bay, April–August 1880

The transition to a civilized life-style. The impact of a higher
range of temperature. Snowburn. Our last snow house. Melms
and his expedition retrieve the items we had left behind. A
continuation of winter. Weather conditions. Our tent camp. The
transition to summer. Inuit techniques of catching seals and
whales. Whale skin as a delicacy. Inuit capacities for observation
and educational abilities. Departure from the Inuit. Tulugaq.
The voyage home.

It would be pointless to try to draw parallels between the life of our
own party on the journey which we had just finished and that on board
the ship among the comforts of civilization. Even if it cost us no
particular difficulties to live as civilized people again, our long accus-
tomedness to privation and abstinence often made itself noticeable.
The same stomach complaints and minor problems which had manifested themselves during the slow transition from a civilized diet to an
exclusively meat diet now repeated themselves, this time all the more
striking since in the case of the earlier transition the enjoyment of
canned vegetables had not played a role. At first we had no desire at all
for baked goods, especially freshly baked bread; they appeared to
possess no food value for our stomachs, which were apparently bottomless, to judge by the quantities of food we consumed daily. Nor could
we understand why anybody would want to drink tea or coffee.

Fourteen days passed before we noticed a change in our appearance
and a certain feeling of well-being made itself felt. We had probably
never been ill, but simply looked a little emaciated and when, after a
period of almost six months the repeated use of water, soap, and face
cloth allowed our true facial colour to surface again, our weather-
tanned faces reflected a health which was indicative of the benefits of
the rough but unchanging northern climate. Even the discarding of

clothing made exclusively from skins initially had some negative aspects, but our greatest enemy was and remained that artificial producer of heat – the stove. According to our modest concepts a temperature of –7-10⁰C would be called normal while 1-2⁰ above zero was warm; and now we had to spend the entire day in temperatures of about 16⁰C! The constant influence of such heat, as this temperature literally represented for us, was quite unaccustomed and with the slightest carelessness it could be quite injurious. During our sojourn of almost two years we had never known what coughs, sniffles, catarrh, or even a normal cold was. But scarcely had we encountered artificially produced heat when we felt the need of so-called better, warmer clothing as soon as we stepped outside into the great wide outdoors. It is not the cold which so often hampers arctic travellers in the execution of their plans but purely and simply the circumstances that they spend the entire winter in overheated ships' cabins and are physically incapable of standing the great change when they make the switch to the raw spring climate outdoors. The Caucasian is accustomed to the considerable and rapid changes in our climate, but this is of no benefit to him when exposed to the northern climate; conversely they represent the main reason why the Inuk does not feel at home and cannot become acclimatized in the temperate zone.

It has often been clearly and adequately proven in the past that the Caucasian with a firm will and a prescribed goal can withstand the climatic rigours of the North; but how easily this hardening becomes lost due to the negative results of the stove is best demonstrated by our return trip to Depot Island, where we still had to spend three months before we were able to start our return voyage to the United States. The bark *George and Mary* was present in Hudson Bay in order to kill whales, and remained in her winter quarters at Marble Island until the end of May. But thereafter she had to cruise after whales until 1 August and only then, on that fixed date, could she leave the Bay. Apart from the fact that a three-month stint on board a vessel of only 105 tons burden would certainly have been tedious, the prospect of a pleasant summer sojourn made it appear desirable that just as during our acclimatization period we should settle at a point on the coast readily accessible by ship, and maintain our own household, as one might say.

On 1 May we left the ship in a group, in order to travel the route we had already often travelled, from Marble Island to Depot Island, once again.[1] Our mode of travel was significantly different from that previously. This time we were in no hurry and, since we had a sufficient number of well-fed dogs in our team, we could ride for the greater part of the way. But very soon experience taught us that at this season the only right time to travel is night-time. The weather was exceptionally fine and the sun's warm rays had a deleterious effect on the pampered skin of our faces. After the second day of travelling our foreheads, cheeks, and noses were strikingly red and even when only slightly exposed to the direct rays of the sun a severe, stinging pain became noticeable. Yet the previously unknown power of the sun and of the blinding snow revealed itself only next morning when we woke and felt a striking tautness of the skin on our faces and an incredibly rapid swelling. At first nobody wanted to show his face to the others and when, finally, all three of us got up (Melms was not with our party at the time) we could not contain our laughter. Only the right side of Lieutenant Schwatka's face was swollen: with the help of a mirror I found that I had a significant enlargement on both sides; and in Gilder's case the swelling process had proceeded so far that he could scarcely open his eyes wide enough to look closely at the caricatures of his two companions as they stared at him in amazement.

This condition is known to our mountain and glacier climbers at home as snow-blindness or snowburn. The cause probably lies in the combined effects of the burning sun's rays and the simultaneous cooling effects of the ice and snow. Inside the snow house it poses no problem, but when one exposes the swollen, severely reddened parts of one's face to the sun the pain is enough to drive one crazy; whenever the Inuit stopped the sledges to procure a seal basking on the ice we would happily lie flat in the shadow of the sledge in order to alleviate the pain by the touch of the snow on our faces. Travelling by day by now had come to an end; we travelled only at night but even this had its dubious aspects. Although the sun could no longer torture our faces it expended its entire force on our snow houses.

What circumstances motivated our Inuit to build such a strikingly large snow house on 6 May, in contrast to their normal custom, I do not know, but we were to learn the impractical aspects of a snowbuilt dome of large dimensions. It was the early hours of the afternoon and we were all lying in the deepest, most peaceful slumbers when an audible and unfortunately very sensible impact wrenched us from our dreams. Anybody who has experienced the pressure of an avalanche would be the most likely to be able to imagine our situation; a considerable weight of snow blocks pinned us from head to toe, while the water-soaked chunks of snow produced an unexpected cooling effect on the naked forms inside the sleeping bags. The entire great dome above us had disintegrated and had literally buried us poor, unsuspecting mother's children. As we worked our heads, with some difficulty through the snow blocks lying on top of us the author of the entire disaster, the sun, greeted us mockingly and produced further pain on our faces as it shone through our roofless home. The male members of the accompanying group of Inuit stood about 100 paces away; laughing loudly they came over to dig out first ourselves and then our clothes. Thus ended our final sojourn in a snow house for the winter season of 1879–80 and hence the final snow house on our long journey. While this type of accommodation always provided us with an acceptable home throughout the long duration of the expedition, the parting feature of the catastrophe just described cast a cloud over snow houses which we remembered for many years. From now on we used a tent which we hurriedly sewed together from an old sail borrowed from the ship, but even in May the snow house would have been preferable as regards other aspects of comfort. The temperature fluctuation during the day was striking; for example, Table 4 will provide the various thermometer readings by two-hourly intervals for 7 May 1880.

TABLE 4

	12	2	4	6	8	10	12	2	4	6	8	10	12
				A.M.						P.M.			
Temp. in shade (^{0}C)	−17	−20	−15	−10	−7	−3	1	4	3	1	0	−3	−7
Temp. in sun	–	–	–	−8	−3	4	9	10	7	5	2	–	–

We found our Aivilingmiut at the same spot where we had left them in mid-May. The task of retrieving the items left behind at Asedlak's encampment had fallen on Melms and he had executed this task to the total satisfaction of everyone. His journey, as he reported it, had been an extremely difficult one, since as soon as the sun begins to make its effect felt on the colossal masses of snow in the interior, there is scarcely any snow left on the hill tops, while the gullies and highways are transformed into bottomless morasses where progress becomes all but impossible. If we compare our experiences, in terms of climatic conditions, in the spring of 1880 with those of the spring of 1879 beyond the divide between Hudson Bay and the Arctic Ocean we find no striking differences with regard to the temperature itself despite a difference of almost four degrees of latitude; yet proximity to the coast makes a sojourn in the south significantly more pleasant than in the northern areas with regard to weather conditions, and especially with regard to the prevailing winds. The immediate vicinity of the pole of cold is characterized by a constant northwest wind which hinders the snow from melting, while around Hudson Bay, where there is open water throughout the winter, the prevailing winds are from precisely the opposite direction, that is, southeasterly. The fact that open water, just as do ice and snow, exerts a significant influence on temperature conditions of various land areas is demonstrated by a comparison between Marble Island, which is only nine miles from the mainland, and Camp Daly, located near the coast, only a short distance to the north. The month of January 1879, during which we had the opportunity to record temperature observations at both simultaneously, displayed a mean difference of 5.5°C, to the advantage of Marble Island. It is surrounded by fairly ice-free water all winter, while the waters of Hudson Bay along the coast at Camp Daly are covered with close, motionless ice 5–6 miles in width from December to May. To this ice and snow cover can also be ascribed the fact that in late spring and summer the southeast wind, which thus blows across drifting ice floes still clogging Hudson Bay, is relatively cooler than the northwest wind which warms the snow-free land areas. But in fall and winter precisely the opposite occurs.

Every year when spring is already quite well advanced a certain relapse in the weather conditions makes itself felt. Whereas when we first arrived at the Inuit encampment its occupants found themselves obliged to protect their snow houses from the direct influence of the sun with curtains of skins, only a few days later, after we had successfully moved to Depot Island, we had ample reason to regret that we had abandoned the snow houses so quickly. For in the month of May and even in early June there followed some wretched weather and our already dilapidated tent provided no adequate protection either against the renewed cold or against the gales and the persistent, protracted snowstorms. For almost four full weeks new snow piled up on the granite rocks of Depot Island, which towered barrenly from the surrounding ice masses and on whose highest point, about seventy-five feet above sea level, stood our tent. On 23 May the thermometer dropped to –19°C and made our stay in our supposed summer residence very unpleasant, while the snowstorms often lasted for three days without relenting in intensity in the slightest. Then, after an interruption of some hours, they would begin anew from another direction. But just as suddenly as this relapse had arrived, just as suddenly it disappeared without any perceptible transition. The storms ceased, the sky cleared of the snow masses which had been flying around, the clouds disappeared, and the magnificent June sun shone on us with all its mildness and all its strength and began the work of eliminating the snow and ice. The white rows of the mainland hills which bounded the horizon to the west became daily more distinct as the rocks steadily emerged. The snow masses disappeared with daily visible progress, leaving behind white lines only where the topography on the one hand, and the deep snow banks on the other, resulted in the melting proceeding more slowly. The uniformly coloured surface of the ice surrounding the island first displayed faint greenish patches, then small pools of water on the surface of the ice. In the rough coastal ice, made rugged by the alternating water levels of low and high tide, deep cracks and wide rents revealed the destructive influence which the present temperatures were exerting on even the most colossal ice blocks. Piece after piece broke away from the ice fields which only shortly before had stretched miles out to sea, and drifted out into the open sea. The slightest wave movement often produced miles-long cracks, and as the tide ebbed it took the floes thus separated with it. The open water daily came closer to the island and soon was washing the rocks of the island itself on the seaward side. Only the ice bridge between the island and the mainland remained intact; finally it became passable only with the greatest caution, then a few days later, on 4 July, it too broke up. But on the island itself the transition to summer revealed itself as being extremely beautiful and interesting. The moss-grown level surfaces, the innumerable pools of water, the modest little flowers rapidly shooting up, all this had such an impressive and surprising impact on us that we thought we had instantly been transposed to a magic realm on this little island, which was scarcely two square miles in area and actually quite monotonous. The cheerful activity of many species of birds now reigned from early morning until late into the night, where earlier scarcely a sound was to be heard. Having arrived instantaneously overnight, the birds would select the island itself or the surrounding waters for their sojourn. The name Pitsiulak which the Inuit gave to the island refers to a species of bird which occurs in large numbers, a small species of duck which they call *pitsiulak*.[2]

Depot Island in itself would not have represented a suitable spot for such a long sojourn if special circumstances had not made it advisable to live on a somewhat restricted area on the one hand, and to choose an island to the mainland on the other. It gave us a better chance of spotting the ships we expected in summer as they ran into the Bay.

The island became a lively place as a result of our encampment. Our

tent became a point of attraction for all the Inuit, not just those living
in the vicinity but also those who had established their camps farther
away from us during the past winter. Even the Qairnirmiut who lived
south of Chesterfield Inlet visited us regularly and brought us numbers
of furs for sale. Fairly large parties of Aivilingmiut even came from the
northern part of Hudson Bay, specifically from Wager Bay. They had
heard of us and now pitched their tents near ours until an impressive
encampment had sprung up on the island, probably numbering 300
souls, men, women, and children.

The walrus and seal occurring in large numbers on the ice floes
floating nearby formed the main source of food at this season. The
Inuit had managed to acquire some fairly old boats in return for
numerous services rendered to the whalers who frequented the area.[3]
These were no longer suitable for whaling but they always lay ready
along the shore; as soon as game was sighted they were manned by the
male population and launched. A very vigilant look-out, always armed
with our party's good telescope, was stationed on the highest point of
the island; he could attract the attention of the entire population when
a group of walrus came into view. The hunters would then approach
the walrus in the boats which were lying ready and in their numerous
kayaks; the walrus would be lying sleeping indolently and carelessly on
an ice floe enjoying the beneficial influence of the warm rays of the
sun. There would often be large numbers of them; when possible the
Inuit would approach from various directions, then open a violent fire
on them. They would first choose as their targets the animals lying
nearest the water, thereby depriving the animals in the centre of an
escape route. But if one of the first animals was only slightly wounded
and still had enough strength to dash into the water, alarming the
other animals, then watch out! As soon as it was in the water the entire
herd would refuse to abandon their wounded comrade, and the boats,
especially the kayaks, would find themselves obliged to flee as quickly
as possible. In general the walrus is a very ungainly animal, but when it
is aroused, pursued, and forced onto the defensive it becomes very
dangerous. Once the hunters had succeeded in killing one or several
animals they were hauled onto the ice, if they were killed in the water,
and cut up. Among the Inuit there exists a custom that everyone who
takes part in a hunt, or indeed is simply present, possesses a right to a
share of the kill. The sharing itself is very interesting to watch because
of the scrupulousness with which it is executed. Since for the
Aivilingmiut walrus meat possesses the same important significance
as winter food as caribou has for the Qairnirmiut or fish for those

living in the vicinity of Adelaide Peninsula, all the parts intended for later consumption are purposefully buried immediately after the animal is killed. For this special purpose all the bones are carefully cut out, the blubber which covers the entire animal in a layer 1–3 inches thick, is removed, the meat is then packed in the thick hide as tightly as possible, and the whole thing is tied together with sealskin lines. This mass is then buried under rocks and is left lying until it is needed in winter. The blubber is cached separately in sealskins in the manner already described. Walrus meat is undoubtedly the best food source for the Inuit and it is also recommended that arctic travellers take with them carefully prepared and well-packed supplies of this food with them as being the most abundant and the most practical.

Walrus meat is the most nutritious of any animal species occurring in the North; its abundant blubber forms a totally adequate material for lighting, heating, and cooking, and its hide (*kau* in Inuktitut) represents an excellent dogfood which is uniquely sustaining for long trips. From the experience of the Schwatka expedition, a medium-sized walrus is equal in food value to ten caribou and the fact that walrus occur wherever there is open water makes it the sole and best possible means of provisioning for polar journeys for a self-sustaining expedition such as ours. Only the liver of the walrus is inedible in certain cases; this is always the case with large male animals in particular. Our own experience, and cases I have seen myself, suggest that one should first examine the liver carefully since it is often traversed by white, slimy veins which are the surest sign that it is inedible. The Inuit, who consider the liver a very desirable item of food, are very familiar with this peculiarity and they assert that the liver causes symptoms of poisoning in the human system because the walrus has been eating seals; this occurs normally only in the case of large walrus. They maintain that the liver of the polar bear is completely inedible for the same reason and do not even feed it to their dogs.

In 1873 I myself witnessed how a party of eighteen Caucasians who were not familiar with this fact suddenly fell seriously ill after eating a large walrus liver. A similar instance also occurred during our sojourn with the ships wintering at Marble Island.

With the disappearance of the ice the number of walrus visible from Depot Island also diminished significantly; thereafer they were harpooned when the sea was calm, just like the various species of seals. In this situation the Inuit make use of what they call a *puuk*, that is, a carefully skinned-out sealskin, which is cut only around the head as the animal is removed from it, and which is then turned into a large bladder. A tube made of horn is inserted in one end and through it the whole thing is inflated; the air is prevented from escaping again by a cork. This *puuk* is attached to the harpoon line so that when an animal, be it a seal, an *ugjuk*, a walrus, or a whale, is struck but not fatally wounded, one can tell from the bladder which always floats above it the position of the animal when it sinks; it also prevents it from sinking too deeply. Their weapons otherwise are quite simple, but this ingenious and very practical device provides the Inuit with their only opportunity of catching a whale from time to time. It is surrounded by as many kayaks as possible, and struck by as many harpoons as possible, to which bladders such as these are attached. They finally make it impossible for the whale to dive deeply. Once it has been tired out in this fashion, which may take hours, it is finally killed; its end marks the start of a great feast for the Inuit involved. Such a gigantic animal meets the food requirements for a large encampment for a whole month; its blubber meets the oil requirements for a month; and its baleen (whalebone) represents a gladly accepted trade article as far as the whalers are concerned, given its present market price. The black skin of the whale (*mattak*, meaning 'black' in Inuktitut) is a delicacy for the Inuit; there is scarcely a single meat dish in our civilized cuisine which can match the skin of a young whale. Sometimes it reaches a thickness of 1½–2 inches and is completely black, whereas that of an older animal is tougher and also lighter with increasing age; it may even become quite white in places.

A major *mattak* feast occurred on Depot Island when one fine day the bark *George and Mary*, which had just emerged from her winter quarters at Marble Island, suddenly appeared over the horizon with her trypots smoking.[4] The whalers use wood only for initially firing up the trypots for boiling out the oil; for keeping the fire going thereafter they use the cracklings, and this was the source of the black smoke which we saw rising from the chimney. We were dependent on Captain Michael F. Baker of this ship, and on his surplus supplies, for our provisioning for the remainder of our stay in Hudson Bay as well as for the period of our return journey. I feel greatly obliged to record our thankful recognition of his goodness and attention as well as the generosity of the ship's owner, Mr Jonas Bourne, with which they took care of the needs of our party, cut off as it was from its own source of assistance.

We also received newspapers from the ship, and since we had been totally cut off from the bustling activity of the great world since June 1878 everything they contained was news to us. The dates of the papers extended up to May 1879. Naturally these newspapers were studied through and through in our tent. We all wished that Hudson Strait would soon become free of ice, in order to permit the entrance into Hudson Bay of the ships which had sailed from the United States this year. We rarely left Depot Island, and apart from a fine, wide view of the island itself our camp had little of interest to offer. The Inuit to whom frequent reference has been made in the preceding pages remained our permanent neighbours here, too. We got along well with them; they were frequent visitors to our tent and we spent many hours of our three-month stay in their sealskin dwellings. During the daylight hours each of us found some occupation. Schwatka reworked and completed his journal, which he had kept only in the form of key phrases during the cold weather. Gilder wrote his report for the *New York Herald*; I had adapted an old chest as a table and I worked on it partly on my paintings, partly on my maps. Even on these occasions I very rarely enjoyed being alone. The Inuit took an only too lively interest in my work; from early morning to late at night they would crowd round my rather unstable, primitive working desk. Men, women, and children all displayed the same curiosity on this occasion, indeed an interest and a sharpness of observation which one would scarcely have attributed to such an otherwise uncultivated people. The men preferred to observe my maps and the women and children the pictures, naturally, and it was amazing how long the latter in particular could occupy themselves with a simple book. If the number of children standing around me became so great that they became a nuisance then I would give them a book and tell them to sit with it in a corner. I would then be left undisturbed for two or even three hours and when I finally looked to see what the children were finding so interesting in it, I realized that they had set themselves the task of searching for a letter which particularly appealed to them on one page, on all the other pages.

I have had occasion earlier to stress the acute powers of observation of the Inuit and cannot omit to mention here that this also applies to objects which would not appear to be of any interest to them. This reveals itself not only in conversation but, significantly, even when they are alone and are looking for a pleasant pastime. Books and pencils have a special appeal for them and a volume of a serialized edition of Lessing's works, which I always kept near me for this purpose for casual Inuit use, was invariably in the hands of my visitors. The people would sit down quietly beside me on my bed and would hold the book just so in front of them, even if it were upside down, and would look at it with a serious, eager play of expressions as if they were deeply involved in study. The children watched my pencils becoming smaller with even greater attention. Since my supplies of drawing materials were very definitely running low I had to work very thriftily with them, and only when a pencil had become so short that it was unusable even in a crayon holder could I afford to give it away. As soon as I started using a new one the children would lay claims to its final remnant and would come daily to determine by how much it had grown shorter in a day, and displayed great, almost inexpressible joy when I kept my promise and finally gave them the little piece of pencil and a piece of paper. Then the fun would really begin; letters from the book' and even individual illustrations would be copied. In short, the best possible use was made of my gifts. One has to ascribe all these observations mainly to a certain innate curiosity on the part of the Inuit, but it is precisely this curiosity which has proven its value in the civilizing of uncultured peoples, as being the main prerequisite for the success of the true, humane missionary work of this century. An overview of the life of the individual Inuk from cradle to grave, his family life and also the social relations of the band, provides the proof that given their limited view on religion, etc., these basic ideas exist which, among uncultured peoples, if indeed we can count them in this conceptually wide-embracing category, they possess as being one of their highest and most complete attributes. As the last chapter of this book I shall sketch in the major features of the religion, customs, and traditions of the Inuit, but here I shall say only that a missionary among the Inuit of North America (and they alone will be the subject of the relevant chapter) will first and foremost have to take the attitude of a teacher and spiritual instructor before he can dare to censure in the slightest the religious views of this good-hearted, but equally stubborn people.

Here education must displace suspicion through true insight, and only when the Inuk is convinced that it is beneficial to him will the missionary be able to count, on the one hand, on acquiring interesting details for the cultural history of mankind from the traditions of this northern people, yet, on the other, derive from the same source useful guides to the ultimate clarification of the mysteries of the North which have remained locked away for so long and so obstinately.

Apart from the Inuit and the view, Depot Island had nothing of interest to offer. By the end of July our sojourn had even become somewhat tedious. The main reason for this lay in the fact that water was becoming scarce. On 26 July, when the bark *George and Mary* sent a boat ashore with the message that we should hold ourselves ready for departure, we began packing our belongings with great pleasure.

Old items of clothing, tools, cooking dishes, etc. had all been promised some months earlier and when at 4:00 P.M. on 1 August the long-awaited three mastheads appeared on the horizon, the entire crowd gathered around our tent in order to receive the items which had now become superfluous to us. They helped us dismantle our last arctic home, and transported us and our things in their own boats out to the ship. *George and Mary* lay about three miles off the island and it was around 10:30 P.M. when we got aboard with our bag and baggage, and went to the quarters allocated to us.

The island itself was now devoid of people since the entire band, from old men down to the smallest child, had accompanied us. We had become very fond of the Inuit and vice versa, and our parting on the morning of 2 August, as the ship's crew weighed anchor and a light breeze filled the sails for our homeward voyage, was a difficult one. Depot Island had already become a small, barely visible spot, yet the four old whaleboats and the numerous kayaks still lay alongside the ship, and the deck was filled with sad groups who departed only very reluctantly. Tulugaq, our faithful, diligent, and brave guide, shook hands with us in farewell, with tears in his eyes. For a full year we had been indebted to this man for the fact that the execution of our plans had proceeded so well. We could thank only his skill and indefatigability as a hunter for the fact that we had not been exposed to more severe tests, with regard to the matter of living or dying. We would gladly have taken him with us to the United States, but the experience of Eskimo Joe scared him from going,[5] and like the latter he stayed in his home country where he had been born and which offered him and his family totally sufficient abundance, by his standards, to satisfy their living needs.

To the best of our ability we had rewarded our Inuit for the services they had rendered; apart from our collections we had given away everything, even our own firearms. They slowly clambered down into their boats and cast off from our ship; a long 'Tavvauvitit' was their final parting shout.[6]

At 5:00 P.M. on 22 September we trod our home soil again for the first time, in New Bedford, Massachusetts. In recognition of our services we received adequate compensation on the part of the educated world for the privations we had undergone. The lively hustle and bustle of the people of the Union on the occasion of the presidential election carried me and my companions along with it and soon put us back on the rails of civilized life. But above all the impressions, the experiences of my more than two year sojourn in the North will remain with me as beautiful memories for the rest of my life.

TABLE 5
Temperature conditions (⁰C), 1 April–31 July 1880

Month			Mean for		
	Month	1st half	2nd	Max.	Min.
April	−15	−22	−8	−5	−37
May	2	1	3	13	−19
June	9	7	11	18	−2
July	12	11	13	26*	5

*This strikingly high temperature reading was an exceptional instance of very short duration (barely half an hour), with dead calm and a midday sun.

CHAPTER FOURTEEN

The Inuit of the American North

The Inuit as a nomadic people. Religion. Relationship of bands to
each other. Vendettas. Blood feuds. Insignia (distinguishing
features) of the different bands. Hair-styles. Tattoos. Language.
Words. Sentence formation. Designation of colours. The *angakuq* as
a doctor and soothsayer. Antidote for snow-blindness. A peculiar
cure. A strangely acquired bald head. *Nulluga*. A communal meal.
Life of the Inuit from cradle to grave. Birth. Marriage customs.
Old age. Conclusion.

The demarcation line of the treeline across the American continent
also coincides with the boundary which separates the inhabitants of
the American North into two groups. All the groups of people living
north of this line are Inuit; all those south of it are Indians. A fairly
significant difference, visible in the physical make-up of the people,
may be observed only between bands living at great distances from
each other; even the Netsilingmiut, with their reddish skin tone, are
reminiscent of Indians, while the cast of their eyes and other facial
features belong incontestably to the Mongolian race. With regard to
the bands living south and west of northern Hudson Bay, in contrast to
those living north and east of it, there is even an easily detectable
transition to the Indian in terms of language, physical features, and
character, and although the ancestors of the Inuit may have come from
the east as belonging to the Finnish race, the influence of the peoples
living to the south of them cannot be denied. As a result the Indians
play a role in the oral traditions of the Inuit, since there exists in
Inuktitut a particular expression for the Indians.

The short discussion on the religion, customs, and habits of the Inuit
contained in the following final pages is intended to fill the gaps which
have emerged in these areas in the course of the book. But in this
regard the author will confine himself exclusively to the bands with

whom the expedition made contact, namely the Ugjulimmiut, the Utkuhikhalingmiut, the Aivilingmiut, the Netsilingmiut, and the Qairnirmiut.

There are no grounds for identifying the Inuit as a nomadic people, in that on the basis of rules which are continued from generation to generation they restrict themselves to a certain area and may cross the boundaries of that area only with the approval of their neighbours. They migrate with the varying seasons and with the varying animal resources, but only within their own hunting grounds.

In terms of their religion they possess the concept of a single deity, of whom they make small idols. One also encounters the idea of a future life in an eternal summer, as well as a belief in heaven and hell, that is, in a good and a bad place. These basic concepts are accompanied by an array of superstitious views which are reflected both in interband relationships and within the social life of individual bands. They also permeate family relationships even to the smallest details. Superstition, as a sort of maxim among the various bands, varies with the local conditions of individual hunting grounds, and the preceding pages provide sufficient specific examples that I do not feel that it is necessary to relate any more. Let us therefore proceed directly to the mutual relationships between bands. As far as it is possible to learn from them about their traditions, feuds between individual bands appear to have occurred frequently earlier, but nowadays a dispute between them is more a matter of the perpetuation of a vendetta than a holy duty. Even when entire bands cannot see eye-to-eye only a certain number of selected persons from either side will pursue the argument. The following description will serve as an example. Two members of the Qairnirmiut had stayed with the Aivilingmiut for a summer, and during a communal target-shooting contest one of the guests was slightly wounded. All the Qairnirmiut took the part of their kinsman and a deputation recovered the wounded man; they held the Aivilingmiut responsible for the incident and demanded compensation for the injury. With every justification this demand was refused; thereupon the claimants selected three men, as did the Aivilingmiut. These six men would pursue the vendetta in the event that the claim was not settled. While the two bands as a whole continued to live in peace each of these six men could cross the boundaries of their adjacent hunting grounds only at the risk of being killed by one of his opponents. To protect our neighbours, the Aivilingmiut, Lieutenant Schwatka interposed himself and settled the matter in a peaceful fashion. But trivial incidents such as these are often grounds for long feuds which then continue as blood vendettas for generations. Our Inuk Ikuma provided an example of how far the duty to prosecute a feud was taken; in the middle of a very severe winter he made a journey of 400 miles to carry out his duty of killing a Netsilik who had murdered his uncle.

To distinguish one band from another the men wear their hair cut in a variety of ways, while the women identify themselves by various styles of tattoos. For example, the Aivilingmiut wear their hair long, hanging down over their temples but cut short, just above the eyebrows, across the forehead. The Netsilingmiut wear their hair cut quite short, while the Qairnirmiut have quite long hair, although the top of the skull is almost completely shaved to form a large tonsure.

The variations in tattoos consist of fairly minor deviations in the length and number of lines on the nose, cheeks, and chin.

Variations in clothing are not a sure indication of band connection, but variations do occur here, too. For example, the Netsilingmiut wear tails like those on a frock-coat, while the Qairnirmiut, who take this design so far that they have to tie up the hanging part to prevent it from trailing on the ground, ornament their clothing in a manner which at times is quite tasteful, using the white belly skins of female caribou.

There are minor variations in language in terms of individual words between the various bands, but in general the language is common to them all. Although the language is marked by an extremely limited number of words,[1] it is rich in vowels. In order to demonstrate both the poverty and the sound of the language I shall now list a number of words as examples for the interested reader:

ataata: father
anaana: mother
aninga: his older brother
naja: his sister
nulijanga: wife
eisiki: man[2]
kuni: woman[3]
irnik: son
panik: daughter
miki: child (also small)[4]
qingmiq: dog
mitiq: duck
aiviq: walrus
arviq: whale

ublaaq: morning
qingaq: nose
nuja: hair
tikiq: index finger (also thimble)
pisuktuq: to walk
arpaktuq: to run
taakuni: night (also dark)
qausuq: twilight
aput: snow
mako: rain (maktu: to rain)[5]
tarksituq: fog
takusaajuq: visible
piksiktuk: invisible[6]
ikuma: fire

ungasiktuq: far
quanikpuq: it is near
kanitukkulu: very near
ublak: sky[7]
nuna: land
tariuq: salt (also sea)

kokepuktu: to talk[8]
mamakpuk: to taste or smell good
(pimakpuk, among the Netsiling-miut)
piujuk: good
atgai: no (nauk, among the Qairnir-miut)

In order to express an idea by joining several concepts together, words are not strung together; instead syllables are attached to root words which indicate a certain direction of activity. Thus, for example, the syllable *mut* indicates some sort of beginning, eg, tuktukmut: to go caribou hunting; snikpumut: to go to sleep, etc.). The syllable *nami* implies accompanying somebody else. Tuktuknami thus means to accompany somebody on a caribou hunt. The syllable *langa* means 'provide me with'; *imiq* means water; imiqlanga: give me water.

The syllable *suak* or *nuak* implies a magnification; thus, for example, *tasiq* means a pond or lake; tasiksuak: a large lake. Kuuq: a river; kuuksuaq: a large river. *Lug* implies a reduction in size; thus, for example, qaqqaq: a mountain; qaqqaqlug: a hill.

The syllable *kuni* implies intensification of a condition. Thus kaaktuq: hungry; kaaktuq kuni: very hungry. Mamiana: regrettable; mamiana kuni: very regrettable. Quiena:[9] well, healthy; quiena kuni: very well.

The poverty of the language in terms of words[10] may be seen from the fact that it possesses only one colour, namely black, or rather dark, that is, mattaq. All other colours are expressed by comparisons. For example, red is expressed as taimatuq au (like blood); blue as taimatuq imiq (like water); colourless as taimatuq sikku (like ice).[11]

The Inuit also handle time of day and seasons in a similar fashion; they live in a carefree fashion from day to day. They do not record their ages and have no worries. If they are forced by some circumstance to indicate a time of day the position of the sun suffices for them. If they have to give a fairly precise identification of a season they refer to March as the time when the seals give birth; April as the time when caribou begin to moult; and August as the time when caribou skins are most suitable for light clothing.

As band members they derive real pleasure from their communal life. They are extremely sociable, and as often as their food resources permit they assemble in the largest possible numbers in quite large encampments. Their partriarchal organization came to the foremost clearly here. The oldest men are the unelected, unappointed, yet readily obeyed councillors, and wherever they go, and whatever they start doing, the rest follow like a flock of sheep following a bell-wether. If there is one other single authority who can exercise a certain authoritative influence, it is the high priest or *angakuq*, of whom we have already become acquainted with an example among the Netsiling-miut. We have already encountered an *angakuq* in his role as dignitary at celebrations; we have also already mentioned his dictatorial input as prescriber of the period of mourning (*tarbu*); it only remains to mention his activity as doctor and soothsayer.

If somebody falls ill he sends for the *angakuq* himself, or for an old woman substituting for him; the person in question then asks the nearest relatives about the condition of the sick man as well about the presumed cause and location of the illness. The means whereby the doctor tries to achieve a cure may vary, but I have to admit, reluctantly, that although the Inuit are generally happy to allow whites into their tents, on these occasions whites are always requested to come back *witschaho* (later). As a result whites do not have the opportunity of attending such ceremonies in the interests of satisfying the reader's curiosity. Only once did I manage to watch an attempted cure performed on Eskimo Joe on Adelaide Peninsula. With the onset of his illness a rock weighing 5–6 lbs had been placed beneath his pillow; it was removed by an old woman three times per day and its weight checked, while every possible prayer formula was intoned. With regard to soothsaying (prophesying) the *angakuq* achieved a great deal both in the form of the promises made and in their delivery. But I have never seen them use any of the plants as remedies as the Indians do, although the resources are admittedly meagre. Only in the case of snow-blindness and other eye afflictions do the Inuit use a physical antidote; they cut away part of the skin from near the eye of an arctic hare, then place small pieces of it in the corners of their own eyes. I have never seen an antidote used from which one might expect any real assistance. The most common method of curing in the case of minor illnesses is the soothsaying already mentioned, and the communal singing of *aya-aya* by all the women of the encampment, as already described. This is enough to make a healthy person ill; how it affects the patient I have never had the desire to experience. If an illness is serious the patient is left unattended, but if he is near death he is left entirely to his fate. It is truly miraculous that Inuit can recover from wounds which in our society would be entrusted only to skilled doctors. For example, there is an old man living among the Aiviling-

miut, with a large bald patch, something which is extremely rare
among the Inuit. However, this was not due to age, but was caused by a
large bear which wrestled with the old man, threw him to the ground,
and scalped him with its long claws. For months his life hung by a
thread but today, without the assistance of any medications, he is
completely recovered and spry, and since then has wrought his revenge
on many another bear.

As regards the social life of the Inuit this is everywhere characterized by their games and modest entertainments, their communal
meals, the communal use of supplies and other property, and finally by
their close family relationships.

Their games and entertainments include the *qilautik* already discussed on the occasion of our farewell feast on leaving the Netsilingmiut, but also a type of game of chance, the so-called *nulluga*.

The *nulluga* of the Inuit is a piece of bone or walrus ivory through
which a hole is drilled parallel to the long axis. It is suspended freely
from the ceiling by a piece of plaited caribou sinew, and to increase its
stability it is steadied by a stone hung beneath it by a line. The players
stand in a circle around this object, each equipped with a short spear
whose end just fits into the hole in the bone. When the signal 'Atii'
(Begin) is given everyone stabs at the hole; the person who gets his
spear into the hole is the winner and receives a prize, eg, a needle or a
spoon, which one of the players has wagered. Given their modest
means the men often wager large prizes; it is not uncommon that
caribou and muskoxen are wagered which are still running around in
the snowy expanses of the interior.

The communal meals represent one of the most interesting studies.
In the snow house or tent of one of the elders of the band the housewife
cooks a very substantial meal; as soon as it is ready the shout of 'Ujuk!'
(Cooked meat!) announces the news to the entire camp. Every man and
boy heads for the spot, armed with a sharp knife, and takes his place in
the circle or squats on the ground in summer. The man next to the
man-of-the-house then receives a piece of meat, cuts off a large
'mouthful,' and passes it to his neighbour. If the meat is caribou or some
other lean meat it is followed by a piece of freshly cut blubber, and
finally by a vessel containing the juice of the meat. All of these go
around the circle until there is nothing left. The cutting-off of the meat
in question is in itself a feature of Inuit meal etiquette which is well
worth seeing. No matter how large the piece of meat in question the
desired portion is placed in the mouth, held firmly with the teeth, then
the remainder is sliced off with the knife, close to the mouth. It is often

frightening to watch a small boy, barely 5-6 years old, slicing off a piece of meat with a large, keenly honed knife barely a quarter inch from the tip of his nose. It is truly remarkable that accidents are not frequent. The women only partake in a meal separately, never in the company of the men.

Just as with meals, so everything represents communal property, by and large, in terms of the provisions and tools in an Inuit encampment. As long as there is a piece of meat to be found in the camp it belongs to everyone, and in the sharing everyone is taken into consideration, especially childless widows and the sick.

This care of one person for another is best reflected within the family, and in order to select the most interesting aspects from the numerous interesting ones in this regard, special mention will now be made of the life of an Inuk from cradle to grave, including birth, marriage, and old age.

If the band is living in a permanent encampment, four weeks prior to childbirth the pregnant woman is separated from her spouse and taken to a separate dwelling to which nobody has access except women. Here the child sees the light of day in isolation and the breast at which he suckles is also the only means whereby he is sheltered from the severe climate. Not until a month after the birth does the mother return to the side of her husband with the young child; only then does the father see and greet his child for the first time. On entering the company of their fellow men a girl becomes a bride and a boy a bridegroom respectively, that is, according to the sequence of their births (with the sole exception of siblings) children are promised as man and wife well ahead of time. But even at this early age the school of life begins for them, and whether boy or girl, their games represent a faithful prelude for the work which later years will demand of them. The boys start to participate in hunting and other male activities from an early age, and only when they have demonstrated by their skill and the number of animals they have killed that they can support not only a wife and family but also the parents-in-law, are they permitted to enter the state of marriage. It sometimes happens that a boy loses his future spouse due to death or other circumstances. In this case he takes precedence as the first legitimate claimant, to the last young man promised a girl, and the next birth will provide him with a spouse, as long as it is not his sister. It is inevitable that under such circumstances the couple may be of widely separated ages, but generally girls are ready for marriage at the age of thirteen or fifteen. Apart from tattoos, which are the mark of a married woman, there are no marriage ceremonies; only among the Qairnirmiut does the *angakuq* claim his *jus primae noctis*. The number of wives a man can have is limited to two, and a man is even obliged to take his brother's widow as his second legitimate wife. Girls betrothed to boys who die before marriage, as well as widows, are free, and in this situation they are even free to marry into another Inuit band. Even after marriage children remain under the supervision and guidance of their parents, that is, those of the mother, and are obliged to give any part of any game they kill to them. Until he is close to death an old man enjoys great respect and the most attentive care and only when an Inuk is close to the end does he suffer the neglect which was discussed in detail in Chapter 12. However, there exist traditional stories among the Inuit of long-past and forgotten generations, but these are unknown to the scientist; only old graves at particular locations with their moss-covered rocks and rotted bones remind us of the past of a people about whom we know so little thus far, and which perhaps holds the key to great, long-sought discoveries in the area of arctic exploration. May the contents of these pages provide a first, modest step toward a better knowledge and toward the most advantageous utilization of the Inuit for the purposes of geography and science. In taking his leave of his good readers, this is the hope of the writer.

Postscript

Over the years quite an appreciable number of expeditions have visited the area of King William Island since the Schwatka expedition completed its search, many of them looking specifically for relics or documents, despite Klutschak's assertion that such searches would be futile. The first of these expeditions, Amundsen's, had no direct interest in the fate of the Franklin expedition; despite this it is quite surprising how little he managed to collect either in terms of oral accounts or material remains.

During his pioneer voyage aboard *Gjøa*, Amundsen wintered twice (1903–5) at Gjøa Haven on the southeast coast of King William Island (Amundsen, 1908). In terms of oral traditions, it was not until *Gjøa* was about to depart that Amundsen learned something of the Franklin expedition:

It was only now that we were on such good terms with the Eskimo that they really trusted us and imparted their confidence to us. I had often asked them if they knew anything about Franklin's Expedition, but I merely got an evasive answer. At length, however Uchyuneiu, the Ogluli Eskimo, told me what he knew. He was a very brave and intelligent fellow and his account agreed very well with what Schwatka had obtained twenty-five years ago. One of the ships had driven down towards Ogluli and was found by the Eskimo one winter's day when they were seal fishing on the south coast of Cape Crozier, the most westerly point of King William Island. They had then removed all the iron and wood work they could remove, and when spring came and the ice broke up the ship sank. At that time the Eskimo had eaten something from some tins which were like ours, and it had made them very ill; indeed some had actually died. They knew nothing of the other vessel . . . (Amundsen, 1908, Vol 2:6)

The only skeletal remains found were those which had previously been found and buried by Hall near the Peffer River. While on a boat trip west to explore Simpson Strait and establish a depot at Cape Crozier in the summer of 1904 Lieutenant Godfred Hansen and Helmer Hansen

found some skulls and bones of two white men. They were lying scattered over the low foreshore at Point C.F. Hall, and had been placed by this Arctic explorer under a stone cairn. Close by we found the stone on which he had cut the words 'Eternal Honor to the Discoverers of the North-West Passage.' We collected the bones together again and covered them over with stones, on the top of which we placed Hall's stone. (Hansen, 1908:297).

Although Amundsen visited both the area of Starvation Cove and the Todd Islands he found no Franklin relics or remains at either site. However, he visited Starvation Cove in winter. His reflections on the surrounding area are revealing:

It is an irony of fate that this sinister name has been aplied to what is in reality one of the most beautiful and lovely spots on the American north coast. In spring, when the channels are opened, enormous quantities of large, fat salmon are met with. A little later the reindeer arrive in countless hordes and remain here throughout the summer, then in the autumn an unlimited quantity of cod can be caught, and yet here – in this Arctic Eden – those brave travellers died of hunger. The truth probably is that they had arrived there when the low land was covered over with snow; overcome by exertions, worn out with sickness they must have stopped here and seen for miles before them the same disheartening snow-bedecked landscape, where there was no sign indicating the existence of any life, much less riches, where not a living soul met them to cheer them up or give them encouragement and help. Probably there is not another place in the world so abandoned and bare as this in winter. There when summer comes and millions of flowers brighten up the fields; there where all the waters gleam and all the ponds sing and bubble during the short freedom from the yoke of ice; there where the birds swarm and brood with a thousand glad notes and the first buck stretches its head over the ice harbour; there a heap of bleached skeletons mark the spot where the remains of Franklin's brave crowd drew their last breath in the last act of that sad tragedy. (Amundsen, 1908, Vol. 1:254–5)

Some twenty years later, probably as a reflection of the vastly superior linguistic skills at his disposal, Knud Rasmussen was able to gather much more information on the Franklin expedition during his remarkable Fifth Thule Expedition, while travelling by sledge from his winter quarters at Danish Island in Frozen Strait west to Alaska in

1923-4 (Rasmussen, 1927; Mathiassen, 1945). Reaching Pelly Bay in April 1923 they encountered an old Netsilik, Iggiararjuk, who told them the following story:

My father, Mangak, was out with Tergatsaq and Qavdlut hunting seal on the west coast of King William's Land, when they heard shouts, and perceived three white men standing on the shore and beckoning to them. This was in the spring, there was already open water along the shore, and they could not get in to where the others stood until low water. The white men were very thin, with sunken cheeks, and looked ill; they wore the clothes of white men, and had no dogs, but pulled their sledges themselves. They bought some seal meat and blubber, and gave a knife in payment. There was much rejoicing on both sides over the trade; the white men at once boiled the meat with some of the blubber and ate it. Then they came home to my father's tent and stayed the night, returning next day to their own tent, which was small and not made of skins, but of something white as snow. There were already caribou about that season, but the strangers seemed to hunt only birds. The eider duck and ptarmigan were plentiful, but the earth was not yet come to life, and the swans had not arrived. My father and those with him would gladly have helped the white men, but could not understand their speech; they tried to explain by signs, and in this way much was learned. It seemed that they had formerly been many, but were now only few, and their ship was left out on the ice. They pointed towards the south, and it was understood that they proposed to return to their own place overland. Afterwards no more was seen of them, and it was not known what had become of them. (Rasmussen, 1927:172-3)

Subsequently, Rasmussen spent most of the summer at Malerualit on the south coast of King William Island. Here he heard more reports of what had happened to the Franklin Expedition, the most detailed being that of an old man named Qaqortingniq:

Two brothers were out hunting seal to the northwest of Qequertaq (King William's Land). It was in the spring, at the time when the snow melts about the breathing holes of the seal. They caught sight of something, far out on the ice; a great black mass of something, that could not be any animal they knew. They studied it and made out at last that it was a great ship. Running home at once, they told their fellows, and on the following day all went out to see. They saw no men about the ship; it was deserted; and they therefore decided to take from it all they could find for themselves. But none of them had ever before met with white men, and they had no knowledge as to the use of all the things they found.

One man, seeing a boat that hung out over the side of the ship, cried: 'Here is a fine big trough that will do for meat! I will have this!' And he cut the ropes that held it up, and the boat crashed down endways on to the ice and was smashed.

They found guns, also, on the ship, and not knowing what was the right use of these things, they broke away the barrels and used the metal for harpoon heads. So ignorant were they indeed, in the matter of guns and belonging to guns, that on finding some percussion caps, such as were used in those days, they took them for tiny thimbles, and really believed that there were dwarfs among the white folk, little people who could use percussion caps for thimbles.

At first they were afraid to go down into the lower part of the ship, but after a while they grew bolder, and ventured also into the houses underneath. Here they found many dead men, lying in the sleeping places there; all dead. And at last they went down also in a great dark space in the middle of the ship. It was quite dark down there and they could not see. But they soon found tools and set to work and cut a window in the side. But here those foolish ones, knowing nothing of the white men's things, cut a hole in the side of the ship below the water line, so that the water came pouring in, and the ship sank. It sank to the bottom with all the costly things; nearly all that they had found was lost again at once.

But in the same year, later on in the spring, three men were on their way from Qequertak to the southward, going to hunt caribou calves. And they found a boat with the dead bodies of six men. There were knives and guns in the boat, and much food also, so the men must have died of disease. There are many places in our country here where bones of these white men may still be found. I myself have been to Qavdlunarsiorfik [a spit of land on Adelaide Peninsula, nearly opposite the site where Amundsen wintered]; we used to go there to dig for lead and bits of iron. And then there is Kangerfigdluk, quite close here, a little way along the coast to the west.

And that is all I know about your white men who once came to our land, and perished; whom our fathers met but could not help to live. (Rasmussen, 1927:239–40)

Later that summer Rasmussen had an opportunity to visit one of the sites mentioned on Adelaide Peninsula. In late September 1923 the schooner *El Sueno* arrived from the west; on board were a Swede, Peter Norberg, and a Dane, Henry Bjoern, who had come to King William Island to establish a Hudson's Bay Company post. In October, Rasmussen and Norberg sailed across to Adelaide Peninsula, with Qaqortingneq as guide, to Qavdlunarsiorfik, near Starvation Cove (Rasmussen, 1927:241). Here they found scattered bones and bits of cloth and shoe leather. The skeletal remains were gathered together, a cairn was built over them, and the Danish and British flags were hoisted at half mast in tribute (Rasmussen, 1927:241; Mathiassen, 1945:92).

In the late twenties Major L.T. Burwash made three trips to the Canadian Arctic under the auspices of the Northwest Territories and Yukon Branch of the Department of the Interior; his mandate was to collect information on a wide range of topics concerning both the environment and the people of the area (Burwash, 1931:11). During his first visit to King William Island in 1925-6, while based on Tulloch Point and making several trips to the western part of King William Island, he heard from several of the Inuit that a large wrecked ship was known to lie off the northeastern tip of Matty Island (Burwash, 1930:60). On a later visit, at Gjøa Haven in April 1929, two old men, Enukshakak and Nowya, apparently older than sixty years of age, told him that as young men they had discovered a cache of carefully stacked wooden cases on a low, flat island northeast of Matty Island. The cases were filled with tinned goods of various kinds. They had appropriated the wood for their own purposes. They had also found a number of planks, approximately 10" wide, 3" thick and more than 15' long (Burwash, 1930:602; 1931:72). They claimed that the submerged wreck lay about three-quarters of a mile off this island. Burwash would argue that this ship is one of Franklin's vessels which either drifted from the northwest coast of King William Island, or was sailed to the vicinity of Matty Island by part of her crew, who had returned to the ship on perceiving the hopelessness of the overland trek to the south.

On the other hand William Gibson, who was the resident manager at the Hudson's Bay Company Post at Gjøa Haven during the period of Burwash's visit, totally discounts the story of a wrecked ship off Matty Island (Gibson, 1937:69). Gibson believed that the basis of the story is that while negotiating the waters around Matty Island in early September 1903, Amundsen's *Gjøa* ran hard aground on a reef. In a desperate attempt to refloat her Amundsen ordered most of her deck cargo, including lumber and boxes of dog pemmican, to be jettisoned (Amundsen, 1908, Vol. 1:68-74). Conceivably most of the cargo may have floated ashore and may have been salvaged and stacked by some other, unknown Inuit. Or as Gibson suggested (1937:70) this jetsam, 'through faulty interpretation and misunderstanding,' may have given rise to the Matty Island story.

But on his third visit to King William Island, in 1930, Burwash found much more concrete evidence of the fate of the Franklin expedition, as a product of the first aerial search of King William Island. Flying from

Gjøa Haven on 5 September 1930, the pilot landed at Victory Point
(Burwash, 1931:92):

The following morning Mr. [Richard] Finnie and the writer examined the
coastline northward to Victory Point. We were fortunate in locating a cairn
which had not been previously examined, but, upon taking the cairn down,
were rewarded with specimens of blue naval broadcloth only. At a point
opposite this cairn but close on shore we located what had evidently been a
fairly large camp where more broadcloth, the remains of a linen tent, a number
of ropes of various sizes and a small barrel stave, a piece of what appears to be
imported coal, and the rusted remains of what may have been a knife blade,
were found. These have been brought to Ottawa ...

Farther to the south on Lady Jane Franklin Point, evidence of stone
structures, which may have been cairns, caches or tent foundations, were seen
but all of these had been overhauled by earlier parties and were devoid of any
relics of the Franklin party. The distance between Victory Point and Lady Jane
Franklin Point* is approximately five miles, a fairly deep basin separating
them. When examining the area around the head of this bay a cairn was found
which had not, apparently, been examined by those previously visiting this
area. This area was carefully taken down until the ground area covered by its
base was completely exposed. A square of naval uniform cloth had been placed
on the ground and the cairn built over it. The gravel below this cloth was dug
up but nothing was found under it nor did an examination of the ground within
a radius of ten feet of the cairn produce any relic left by the Franklin party.
The uniform cloth found under the cairn had been lying for many years in a
damp and shaded spot so that it had become little more than a mass of pulp,
the only thing about it remaining being its colour. Short fibres could be
identified and occasional small fragments could be separated which showed
the texture of the cloth. After making an examination the cairn was rebuilt on
its former site as it might, at some future date, serve as a datum point for
further investigations.

The cairn was located about 600 feet back from the water's edge and stood on
a low, shingle beach about fifteen feet above sea level. Almost immediately in
front of it, and within thirty feet of the shoreline, a series of quite regular
gravel mounds were found ... While working on these mounds ... some rags of
naval uniform cloth were noticed half buried in the shingle of the beach. These
lay a few feet from one of the mounds examined and, upon a careful
examination of the ridge, or first beach, upon which we were, other evidences

*It seems probable that the writer means Franklin Point, in which case the
'fairly deep basin' would be Collinson Inlet. (W.B.)

of the former presence of white men were secured. These consisted of small cordage, an eleven-foot section of one-inch rope, many scraps of uniform cloth and linen tent cloth, two small oak barrel staves, a small quantity of imported coal (burned on one side), samples of rusty iron which may have been parts of the blade of a long knife, and a strip of linen cloth twelve feet long and ten inches wide which had evidently been the lower part of a tent. These were all carefully collected and have been brought to Ottawa. The relics found at this place were scattered over possibly 300 feet of coastline along the crest of a low shingle ridge, such as would naturally be selected as a camping ground. No other signs of white men were found along the coast north of this campsite, including Victory Point. (Burwash, 1931:93-4)

Later, on 6 September, the party made a landing in Terror Bay and found a grave which may have contained two or more bodies. This was carefully rebuilt (Burwash, 1931:94).

The following June (1931) William Gibson conducted a search of parts of the south coast of King William Island (Gibson, 1937:67; 1932:402), and surrounding areas. On the Todd Islands he found the partial remains of at least four skeletons.

Two of these were found embedded in the soft sand of a low spit running out from the most southerly islet of the group. One was almost intact and lying in an extended, natural position, evidently that of a slight young man. The teeth of both jaws were complete and remarkable in their flawless perfection. These skeletons had been well preserved in the moist sand and patches of the blue naval broadcloth held together and were taken away by us. Digging in the vicinity of the other remains - which were very incomplete - the vivid colour only of the broadcloth was discernible, the fabric having entirely disintegrated. (Gibson, 1937:67)

Returning to King William Island, Gibson and his party spent some time searching for the grave which Schwatka had found in 1879 and Hansen again in 1904, built by Hall in 1869, but they were unsuccessful (Gibson, 1932:405; 1937:67). West of the Peffer River, at the site where Hall had found the remains of Lieutenant Le Vesconte, guided by an Inuit report, Gibson found a femur and some other bones quite close to the beach. He buried these remains and built a cairn.

On a small island about 500 m long by 150 m wide, some 3 km from the head of Doublas Inlet, near its eastern shore, Gibson's party made their most exciting discovery; scattered over the island were seven skulls and a great number of other bones. There was also a scattering of pieces and shavings of oak and also of Norwegian pine (Gibson, 1932:406). Gibson suggested that these may have come from a lifeboat which the Inuit had long since broken up. The remains were interred on the highest part of the island and a large cairn was erected over the grave.

On Tulloch Point the party easily located the large cairn which Hall had built over the remains of one of the Franklin party. It had been partially demolished and a skull and bones had been scattered around. Gibson and his party replaced the remains in the cairn, which they rebuilt. They continued their search westward to Cape Herschel, but no further Franklin remains were seen. However, the walls of Rasmussen's hut at Malerualit were still intact and well-preserved (Gibson, 1932:407).

In September 1936, L.A. Learmonth of the Hudson's Bay Company, starting from Gjøa Haven, made a reconnaissance of part of the northeast coast of Adelaide Peninsula. On a low point known to the Inuit as Tikeraniyou, about 24 km west of Starvation Cove, he found several scattered skulls and other remains, all at or just above high water mark. Associated with them were a George IV half-crown, minted in 1820, and an ivory button (Gibson, 1937:68).

The next search of King William Island was undertaken by Inspector Henry A. Larsen of the Royal Canadian Mounted Police in the summer of 1949 (Cyriax, 1951). Travelling on foot, he searched the coast from Cape Felix to Cape Franklin, and also spent some days on Adelaide Peninsula, where he searched Starvation Cove and area:

At Cape Felix Larsen found the remains of a human skull embedded in moss between some rocks on a ridge about half a mile from the sea. These remains were examined in Ottawa and found to be parts of the skull of a single individual, slightly built, of white race and aged about twenty-five years ... Larsen's discovery is of great interest, for none of the previous searchers had found the bones of members of the Franklin expedition anywhere on King William Island to the north of Crozier's cairn. (Cyriax, 1951:212)

Near Cape Maria Louise, Larsen found pieces of oak and many hardwood chips. At the point where Crozier left his record he found many scattered remains of equipment: a large button, blue cloth, canvas, rope, a piece of cheesecloth with a lead stamp, two pieces of a wooden keg, boat nails and parts of two boots, and two iron brackets for strengthening a sledge or boat. Nearby was a cairn which Larsen dismantled; under it was a fragment of blue cloth and two bone buttons. Cyriax has surmised that this was the cairn rebuilt by Burwash from the remains of the cairn erected by Schwatka at Irving's grave.

From here to Cape Jane Franklin, Larsen collected a variety of relics including fragments of blue cloth, chips of hardwood, canvas, rope, and a cork sole. At Cape Franklin he found the tops of two tins. On the mainland, near Starvation Cove, he found a leather boot sole and the remains of old camps on a low point jutting out from the south end of Point Richardson. In conclusion, Larsen suggested that due to the difficult nature of the country 'the route travelled by the Franklin party cannot have been very thoroughly searched or examined, except perhaps by Eskimos' (Cyriax, 1951:214).

The next recorded visit to northwestern King William Island was that made by Paul F. Cooper in August 1954 (Cooper, 1955). He searched the area from Cape Jane Franklin north to Crozier's camp. At the site of the camp he recorded that 'bits of cloth and rusted metal and hemp can still be picked up, though nothing of any size was found (Cooper, 1955:10). For the information of later visitors Cooper made some explanatory comments re the cairns just immediately north of Crozier's camp:

The present cairn, which marks the grave of Lieutenant Irving, was originally built by Schwatka in 1879. It has twice been taken down and rebuilt, once in 1930 by Burwash, who believed it to be a Franklin cairn, and once again by Larsen in 1949. It stands 625 feet inland from the tip of a small promontory that forms the northern side of a tiny bay.

Some 250 feet NW by W, between this cairn and the end of the promontory, are the ruins of a second cairn, the one in which Crozier left the record found by Hobson on 6 May, 1859. It is now only a circle of stones, so flattened out that, even at a short distance, it can hardly be distinguished from the surrounding rocks. (Cooper, 1955:10).

On the occasion of Canada's centenary in 1967 yet another search for Franklin relics was mounted by the Canadian Armed Forces, in an exercise with the code-name 'Project Franklin' (Wonders, 1968; McKenzie, 1969). Working from a base camp at the Gladman Point DEW-Line station and using helicopters, five land-search parties and an underwater search party were deployed over a wide area.

On the section of coast between Cape Jane Franklin and Cape Felix the two cairns at Cape Jane Franklin were once again dismantled – to reveal that they contained nothing. No cairn or any other evidence was found at Victory Point. At Victory Point four cairns were investigated: two contained messages left by Henry Larsen in 1949; one was built by a party identified as Coleman and Holmberg, who had been here in 1965 on the site of a possible Franklin observation cairn, and the fourth was an Inuit cairn also previously investigated by Coleman and Holmberg in 1965. The sole and heel of a boot with wooden pegs was found. A wooden tripod 2 m high was erected at Cape Felix to commemorate 'Project Franklin.' Farther south a ground search of the north and east shores of Terror Bay revealed nothing, while a search around Starvation Cove similarly turned up no evidence of Franklin survivors.

The most productive part of the operation was that which focused on O'Reilly Island. While nothing was found underwater, searches of the beaches at the north end of the island revealed significant amounts of material including copper sheeting, spice tins, a block, belaying pin, oar, etc. (Wonders, 1968:126). The several pieces of badly crumpled copper sheeting have been submitted to careful expert scrutiny (McKenzie, 1969). Four copper nails still attached were dated as having been made by a process commonly used between 1820 and 1850. Spectrographic analysis of the sheeting revealed it to be remarkably pure, containing neither silver nor arsenic, and it was deduced that it was probably of British origin. From the size of the pieces and the amount of copper concentrated in one place McKenzie felt that it represented a ship's sheathing rather than a patch from a ship's boat.

On the basis of this find McKenzie has presented a very interesting hypothesis with regard to the identity of the ship reported by the Inuit as having sunk off O'Reilly Island. The crucial point is that neither *Erebus* nor *Terror* were copper-sheathed. *Investigator*, on the other hand, was; McKenzie would argue that after she was last visited by Krabbe from *Resolute* in May 1854 (Great Britain, Parliament, 1855:96–8) *Investigator* was carried out of Mercy Bay by the ice, drifted eastward and southeastward with the ice, and finally sank when the ice released her, off O'Reilly Island (McKenzie, 1969:31). It should be noted that Wright (1959:225–8) had earlier suggested the same hypothesis on the basis of the 'two long, heavy sheets of copper, three and four inches wide, with countersunk holes for screw-nails' (Nourse, 1879:418) which Hall had purchased from the Inuit near Booth Point on southeastern King William Island. On the other hand, Learmonth (1969:32–3) completely rejects the idea that *Investigator* might have drifted from Mercy Bay to the area of O'Reilly Island, suggesting that warships of that period contained large amounts of copper sheet and fittings apart from the hull sheathing, and that whaleboats were also copper-sheathed for arctic service.

McKenzie appears to have overlooked the most telling argument against the possibility that the ship which sank off O'Reilly Island was *Investigator*, namely the presence of boats on board. Inuit who visited the ship later told Hall that the ship seen off O'Reilly Island had four boats hanging in davits (Nourse, 1879:257). In his list of provisions and equipment left at Mercy Bay in May 1854, Krabbe states that he left six boats with gear on shore and none on board *Investigator* (Great Britain, Parliament, 1855:100). This eliminates any possibility that the ship seen off O'Reilly Island was *Investigator*.

A further search for Franklin relics was mounted by another military group in the summer of 1973 (Walsh, 1974). Using assault-boats for transport, several parties of men of the First Battalion, the Royal Canadian Regiment, searched an unspecified sector of the coast of King William Island. Corporal David Willard, a member of a party led by Sergeant Ron Eddy, while searching the coast between Gladman Point and Tulloch Point spotted two human leg bones beside a large rock. Closer inspection revealed an almost complete skeleton, associated with which were several shirt buttons and jacket buttons. These latter artifacts have been identified as of European manufacture, mid-nineteenth century. The skeleton and these and other artifacts are now in the Museum of Man in Ottawa.

The most recent field search for remains of the Franklin expedition is the ongoing project conducted by Dr Owen Beattie (Beattie & Savelle, 1983). In July 1981 Beattie discovered skeletal remains on a long, low spit about 2.5 km west of Booth Point on the southeast coast of King William Island. The site had been pointed out to Hall, but he himself had not seen the remains because they were snow-covered at the time of his visit (Nourse, 1879:40-2).

The remains were scattered over quite a wide area, approximately 10–14 m wide, concentrated on a poorly defined tent-ring. Associated with the remains were a shell button and a clay pipe stem. Beattie and Savelle have made the following deductions from the skeletal remains:

The cranial fragments, especially the frontal bones, indicate that the individual was a male, while the patent coronal suture indicates an adult in the third decade of life. Frontal contours and features at the supraorbital tori suggest a Caucasoid individual. Subperiosteal lesions characteristic of scurvy are clearly evident on the femur and tibia shafts. (Beattie & Savelle, 1983:102)

All the bones were found within the tent circle, and Beattie (1983:76) has suggested that this fact, the complete lack of axial and facial material, and the presence of three cut marks on the right femur hint at the possibility of cannibalism.

At Tulloch Point, Beattie's party investigated both the 'grave' found by Schwatka in 1879 and also the structure examined by Gibson in 1931, and which the latter thought to be the same feature as that examined by Schwatka. They are in fact two separate features and Beattie's conclusions were as follows:

Analysis of skeletal remains and artifacts associated with the 'small stone' structure of Schwatka suggest it is an historic (approximately mid-19th century) Netsilik Inuit adult male burial. The material reported by Gibson, on the other hand, is that of an Inuit adult female, and although no diagnostic cultural material was recovered, it too is probably of 19th century origin. (Beattie & Savelle, 1983:104)

Beattie and his party easily located the cairn built by Gibson in 1931 over the remains of seven skeletons which he had found on a small island in Douglas Bay, but all the skeletal remains had been removed.

In 1982 Beattie searched the coast of King William Island from Cape Maria Louise southward round the shores of Erebus Bay, almost to Little Point (Beattie, 1983:68–9). Despite careful searching, none of the previously reported materials was recovered. With regard to Schwatka's procedure of burying all the skeletal remains he found, and of erecting a cairn over them, Beattie commented:

By burying the bones, and then placing probably one or two stones on the grave, Schwatka ensured that later rediscovery would be unlikely. Given the nature of the King William Island coastline, graves such as these would disappear into the landscape. (Beattie, 1983:69)

Thus far, therefore, nobody has been able to disprove Klutschak's statement, namely that 'deposition of detailed documents in a manner that was inviolate to the natives never occurred.' On the other hand, the long list of searches presented above gives the lie to another of Klutschak's statements, namely that Schwatka's search would put an end to the sequence of searches because it had proved that any useful clues on which to base further searches had been eliminated by time, weather, or the Inuit.

But there can be no doubt as to the validity of his statement that the

Schwatka expedition acquitted itself well and that in the light of its achievements and its logistics it must be placed among the most prominent of all the searches for Franklin remains or relics. Quite apart from anything else, the sledge journey made by Schwatka and his party is one of the most impressive in the history of the Arctic: a round trip of 5287.5 km in 11 months and 4 days, during which the party subsisted almost entirely off the land. It becomes even more impressive when one considers the travelling conditions on the winter sledge journey back to Hudson Bay. Travelling across the Keewatin tundra by dogteam in January and February with mean monthly temperatures dropping as low as $-47^{\circ}C$ and absolute minima dropping to $-57^{\circ}C$ is a feat which rarely, if ever, has been matched. And most impressive of all is the fact that the party emerged with its numbers intact and without even a serious case of frost-bite.

The secret, undoubtedly, lay in the party's total adoption of Inuit techniques, clothing, diet, and life-style. It is also, undoubtedly, to this strategy that Klutschak owed his success in his other declared objective, namely to describe the life-style and customs of the Inuit. Although inevitably handicapped to some degree by his mid-Victorian European background, which manifests itself in some condescendingly 'superior' value judgments on Inuit attitudes and behaviour, Klutschak nonetheless makes some very valuable observations on the various Inuit groups with which he came in contact. His remarks on the Utkuhikhalingmiut and the Netsilingmiut of the Adelaide Peninsula are particularly valuable, since no Europeans had previously spent any time among them. We are greatly in Klutschak's debt.

Afterword

My own involvement with the investigation of the third Franklin expedition (and, by extension, the Schwatka search) began in the spring of 1981 when archaeologist James Savelle suggested a collaborative project involving a resurvey of the coast of King William Island. I say a 'resurvey' as the King William Island area has been extensively searched from the early 1850s right through to the present. We anticipated that we would be following closely in the tracks of the two most important searches of the nineteenth century: M'Clintock's of 1859, and Schwatka's of 1879. The primary goal of our project was to relocate the human skeletal remains of the Franklin Expedition crews originally observed and recorded by both searchers, and to discover other materials that they may have missed. It was felt that a modern, detailed analysis of these skeletal remains could provide fundamentally important information on possible health- and behaviour-related problems which may have contributed to the disaster. As I began my background reading for the project I was struck by the sometimes incredible hardships encountered by the dozens of nineteenth-century search expeditions and the perseverance demonstrated by individual searchers: it was a period that produced heroes of near-mythological stature. Perhaps the most captivating chronicles for this period describe the search conducted by Lt Frederick Schwatka. The separate journals of Schwatka and his colleague Gilder (both in English) provided us with some of the best information on the locations of Franklin Expedition sites on King William Island, and more importantly for our research the locations of human skeletons attributable to the expedition. Although I was aware of the German edition of Klutschak's own account, I did not use it as a source of information. However, as our research progressed, and as I read and reread Schwatka and Gilder, I realized that these records were themselves somewhat incomplete. During certain periods of their searches they broke up into separate groups, one being composed of Klutschak and Melms. Certainly, the incomplete coverage of the findings of these two are criticisms of both Schwatka's and Gilder's writings. Therefore, when asked, I jumped at the opportunity to read Bill Barr's English translation of Klutschak's journal. Reading about Klutschak's experiences and descriptions of sites we have visited ourselves has been an enjoyable and valuable experience. Barr's translation is highly readable, preserving Klutschak's personable character and sense of humour while providing another perspective on the successes and ordeals of the Schwatka expedition.

During July 1981 Savelle and I surveyed the south coast of King William Island from Booth Point westward to Cape John Herschel, with a very brief stop in the vicinity of Starvation Cove. Based on their discovery of human skeletal remains, Schwatka's expedition identified the Starvation Cove area as the furthest distance reached by some of the Franklin crews. Near Booth Point we discovered a small camp site from the Franklin expedition, along with the associated fragmentary skeletal remains of a single expedition crewman who died in his early twenties. The analysis of the materials identified bone changes due to scurvy, and probable cut marks on one femur.

During the 1982 field season the search was extended to the northwest coast of King William Island from Cape Maria Louisa south to a few kilometres west of the 'Boat Place' in Erebus Bay, traversing exactly the same land course as Schwatka and his crew in 1879. Along this route are a number of old campsites marked by tent rings and caribou and seal remains, and I am certain some, if not most, were the camp sites used by Schwatka's parties. The descriptions of their camps in Schwatka's, Gilder's, and Klutschak's written accounts correspond closely in location and features to those seen by us in 1982. Unfortunately, the effects of time and vulnerability have taken hold, and it may not be possible to identify these in the future as relating to the Schwatka groups. From the drawings made by Klutschak it would appear that they left ample evidence of their survey: relatively large stone cairns are depicted in many. Thorough searches by us in 1982 failed to establish the exact locations of most of these cairns. It seems certain that visitors to these locations have, over the decades, completely dismantled most, if not all of these markers of Schwatka. For our own searches this was a disaster. Schwatka had carefully interred many skeletal remains under these cairns, and we anticipated their rediscovery during our own survey. This was not to be the case. We were unable to find any of the human remains originally discovered, and subsequently buried, by Schwatka. It is my feeling that they have either been found and scattered or taken away, or (because the stone markers have been removed) the buried remains are now so much a part of the landscape as to avoid detection forever. Whatever the case, the importance of historical documentation is underscored when the physical evidence becomes degraded or destroyed. Our discovery of the scattered and fragmentary post-cranial remains of between six and fourteen individuals in the vicinity of the 'Boat Place' constitute materials missed by Schwatka.

One of the important contributions made by Klutschak in his own journal (in addition to a detailed map) is his set of quality drawings of some of the events and many of the locations searched by the Schwatka expedition. An example is the drawing of Lt Irving's grave at Crozier's Landing (where the Franklin Expedition crews congregated after abandoning their ships in late April 1848). The drawing of this site in Schwatka's edited journal notes does not contain much useful detail, while in Klutschak's own account it is very illuminating and important to present researchers. It shows a grave structure strikingly similar to that of one individual from the Franklin Expedition buried on Beechey Island in April 1846 (Royal Marine William Braine). Along with the account of what they found in Irving's grave (a handkerchief and some blue material), this drawing reinforces the interpretation that Lt Irving was given a formal burial similar to those performed in early 1846 at Beechey Island. Our own search of this area failed to locate the remains of Irving's grave and, as Schwatka had removed the skeleton, we were not surprised that no additional materials were found, though the camp site occupied by the Franklin Expedition crews immediately after abandoning their ships is still clearly identifiable, as is the 'clothing dump' area described by both M'Clintock's and Schwatka's expeditions. This site has been so well visited over the years that it is now difficult to resolve some of the present features with those viewed and described by Schwatka and M'Clintock.

Though it is true that Schwatka and his people failed to discover further documentation left behind by the Franklin people, they did establish some vital geographical information relating to the movement of the Franklin party along the west and south coasts of King William Island. As Schwatka's searches were so thorough, it is intriguing, perhaps astounding, that they failed to find evidence for the twenty-one Franklin Expedition individuals who perished in the northwest coast area of the island prior to the abandonment of the ships, or for the 'hospital camp' thought to be located in Terror Bay. These are areas that will require meticulous re-searching in the future, aided by modern technology. The very thoroughness of Schwatka's work, coupled with the passage of time and the visits of large numbers of people, leave slim hope for additional major discoveries on the north-west and south coasts of King William Island, though I feel that the archaeological searches should continue. With the addition of the English translation of Klutschak, readers of arctic history and adventure now have an important period in the search for the fate of Franklin represented by three viewpoints. As archaeologists continue to search for the fading evidence of the Franklin Expedition they will have to give much credit to the maps and descriptions provided by Schwatka, Gilder, and Klutschak.

Many times during our weeks of survey on King William Island I had a much stronger feeling of following the trail of Schwatka than of the doomed crews of the Franklin Expedition. These feelings were recalled and reinforced as I read the preceding pages. Schwatka accomplished a survey as complete and well executed as possible, even under modern circumstances. His military background, coupled with the obvious respect and dedication he received from his crew, gave him the energy and drive to achieve what is still considered today to be the definitive Franklin search of the King William Island area.

OWEN BEATTIE
Department of Anthropology, University of Alberta

Notes

1 Sponsored by King Henry VII, John Cabot sailed from Bristol aboard *Matthew* in May 1497. He made a landfall on 24 June, probably in the area of Maine or Nova Scotia, and sailed for home again from Cape Breton or Cape Race. He sailed again the following year with five ships, all of which disappeared (Williamson, 1962).

2 Henry Hudson sailed from Gravesend in the ship *Discovery* on 17 April 1610, sponsored by the Northwest Company. He explored the south shore of Hudson Strait and coasted south along the east shore of Hudson Bay to James Bay, where he wintered. With supplies running low, on 22 June 1611 his crew mutinied and set Hudson and 8 companions adrift in a boat. On the homeward journey 4 of the mutineers were killed by Inuit in Hudson Strait. No trace was ever found of the party which was set adrift (Asher, 1860).

3 Here Klutschak has telescoped events rather drastically. In the summer of 1818 Captain John Ross in HMS *Isabella*, escorted by HMS *Alexander*, under Captain William Edward Parry, made a circuit of the north end of Baffin Bay; he briefly examined the entrances to Smith, Jones, and Lancaster sounds and decided that none of them gave access to the Northwest Passage (Ross, 1819; Fisher, 1819). A decade later, during which Parry had proven the existence of a labyrinth of channels and islands to the west, Captain John Ross, accompanied by his nephew, James Clark Ross, sailed from England in *Victory*. The expedition was sponsored by Sir Felix Booth and its aim was to discover a Northwest Passage via Lancaster Sound and Prince Regent Inlet. *Victory* was forced to winter three times at or near Felix Harbour in southern Boothia Peninsula. During this period extensive sledge trips were made and J.C. Ross discovered the North Magnetic Pole in June 1831. In 1832 Ross abandoned *Victory* and retreated north to Fury Point, where he knew Parry had left a large cache of supplies in 1825. Having wintered here for a fourth time, Ross and his party headed north

by boat in August 1833 and on 26 August were picked up by the whaler
Isabella in Lancaster Sound (Ross, 1835).

4 Here again Klutschak has achieved a remarkable feat of elision. In 1819
Captain William Edward Parry, who had been second-in-command on
Ross's expedition the previous year, led his own expedition aboard *Hecla*
and *Griper* into Lancaster Sound. Encountering particularly favourable ice
conditions, he got as far west as the southwest tip of Melville Island before
being blocked by ice. The ships wintered at Winter Harbour, from where
an overland party crossed Melville Island (Parry, 1821). In 1821 Parry led
another expedition, this time aboard *Fury* and *Hecla*, in search of the
Northwest Passage. Having confirmed Middleton's earlier report that
Repulse Bay did not provide a route west, Parry wintered at Winter Island.
The following summer the two ships coasted north to Igloolik but were
prevented by ice from getting through Fury and Hecla Strait; hence they
wintered again at Igloolik. Parry and his men made a number of overland
trips across Melville Peninsula and during both winters maintained close
and amicable relations with the local Inuit (Parry, 1824). In the summer of
1824 Parry led yet another expedition into the Arctic aboard the ships *Fury*
and *Hecla*. The expedition wintered at Port Bowen on the east shore of
Prince Regent Inlet. Then in August 1825, *Fury* was driven ashore by ice at
Fury Point on Somerset Island and had to be abandoned; both crews
returned to England aboard *Hecla* (Parry, 1826).

5 These and the various other search expeditions prior to Schwatka's
expedition have already been discussed in some detail in the Introduction.

CHAPTER ONE:
SCHWATKA'S FRANKLIN SEARCH PARTY

1 In Galena, Illinois (Stackpole, 1965:14).

2 But prior to this Schwatka had worked as a printer's apprentice and had
attended Williamette University (Stackpole, 1965:14).

3 According to Stackpole (1965:14), after his graduation from West Point in
1871 Schwatka studied law and medicine simultaneously, was admitted to
the Nebraska bar in 1875, and received his medical degree from Bellevue
Hospital Medical College in the same year.

4 Having read of the plans being formulated by the American Geographical
Society, Schwatka offered his services to Judge Charles P. Daly, President
of the Society, and was invited to New York for an interview. On the basis
of this interview Schwatka was offered command of the expedition. Daly
then wrote to General William Sherman, Secretary of War, to request that
Schwatka be given a leave of absence; this was granted by President Hayes
(Stackpole, 1965:14).

5 Within a year of his return from the Schwatka expedition, Gilder headed for the Arctic again, this time in search of George W. De Long's missing expedition aboard USS *Jeannette*. Again representing the *New York Herald*, Gilder was aboard the search vessel USS *Rodgers* when she sailed for Bering Strait from San Francisco on 16 June 1881. After *Rodgers* was destroyed by fire in her winter quarters at St Lawrence Bay on the Siberian side of Bering Strait, Gilder made a remarkable overland journey westward, eventually reaching St Petersburg (Gilder, 1883).

6 For further details of Hall's first meeting with Ebierbing and his wife, and of Hall's sojourn in Frobisher Bay see Hall (1864).

7 Hall's journal for this expedition was published posthumously (Nourse, 1879).

8 The details of the *Polaris* expedition, including those of Hall's controversial death, are presented in Davis (1876). After exhumation of Hall's corpse, a century after his burial, an autopsy revealed high levels of arsenic in the body (Loomis, 1972). The drift of half the complement of the expedition on an ice floe from Kane Basin to quite far south off the Labrador coast is described in detail in Tyson's account (Blake, 1874).

9 Klutschak is in error as to the date of the *Pandora* expedition. It was in 1875 that Sir Allen Young mounted a private expedition aboard the yacht *Pandora*, on which Ebierbing was interpreter. The objectives were to reach the Magnetic Pole and to navigate the Northwest Passage in one season. Pushing south down Peel Sound, *Pandora* was beset in Franklin Strait in August 1875. Young managed to extricate his ship and returned to England that same fall (Young, 1876).

CHAPTER TWO:
SOJOURN IN HUDSON BAY

1 Presumably the captain's caution was due in part to the fact that icebergs commonly possess dangerous underwater rams, and also may capsize without warning.

2 This is whalers' pidgin. R.G. Williamson, personal communication

3 For an analysis of the trade between the whalers and the Hudson Strait Inuit see Ross (1975:61-3).

4 Klutschak may have meant *piilitik* (take it), otherwise this term makes no sense. R.G. Williamson

5 This occurred on 7 August; in fact the ship was boarded by a whaleboat full of Inuit which had been pursuing the ship all night (Stackpole, 1965:20; Gilder, 1881:13).

6 7 August according to Gilder (1881) and Stackpole (1965).

7 According to Gilder (1881:17), the expedition's own tents were quite

inadequate and they had to borrow a tent from an Inuk call Armow through the good offices of Captain Barry.

8 First contact with the whalers was made during the pioneer wintering of *Syren Queen* and *Northern Light* (Captains Christopher and Edward, respectively) near Depot Island in 1860–1 (Ross, 1975:37).

9 Captain Fisher (of *Abbie Bradford*), Captain Mozier (of *Abbott Lawrence*), and Captain Garvin (of *Isabella*), all of New Bedford (Stackpole, 1965:24). With them was Captain Sinclair of the whaler *A.J. Ross*, which had been wrecked on a reef between Harding Point and Cape Kendall on the east shore of Roe's Welcome Sound on 24 August. Her crew had taken to the boats and had been rescued by Captain Fisher. They were now distributed among the three other ships. The boat which Schwatka now acquired had come from the wrecked ship.

10 This incident occurred during the return from a surveying trip as far east as Birnheimer Bay and lasted from 14 to 19 September. Schwatka has described it in great detail (Stackpole, 1965:28–30).

11 Invented by Réaumur, an 18th century French physicist, the Réamur scale was based on 0^0 being the freezing point of water and 80^0 being the boiling point of water.

12 Schwatka and party moved into their ice igloo on 1 November (Stackpole, 1965:32).

13 Klutschak has mistaken pidgin for Inuktitut.

14 The head of Whitney Inlet (Stackpole, 1965:33).

15 The main reason for this trip was to interview Captain Potter, second-in-command of the whaler *Abbie Bradford*, wintering at Marble Island. A Netsilik, Nutargeark, had told Schwatka that he had obtained a spoon from other Netsilingmiut; they in turn had found it on King William Island or Adelaide Peninsula. This spoon corresponded to the one which Captain Barry had allegedly taken to the United States. Nutargeark had given the spoon to the wife of Sinuksook, an Aivilik, who in turn had given it to Captain Potter (Gilder, 1881:30).

16 In December 1860, Dr August Sonntag had set off from Hayes' ship *United States*, wintering in Foulke Fiord, to attempt to locate the Eskimos thought to be living around the shores of Whale Sound. The aim of the trip was to replace the expedition's dogs, most of which had died during an epidemic. According to his Eskimo companions Sonntag fell through the ice while crossing to Northumberland Island; he was helped out of the water, ran beside the sledge for a while, but then rode on the sledge in his wet clothes. After lapsing into unconsciousness he died within about a day despite all the Eskimos' efforts to revive him (Hayes, 1867:231).

17 A slight exaggeration; including Quartzite Island off its east end Marble

Island is less than 10 miles long.

18 *Eothen, Abbie Bradford, Abbott Lawrence,* and *Isabella.*

19 Actually quartzite.

20 Schwatka left Camp Daly on 10 February and reached Marble Island on the 14th (Stackpole, 1965:44).

21 Located on Deadman Island, guarding the entrance to the harbour.

22 To this end Gilder made quite a long trip from Marble Island into the mainland interior to a major Qairnirmiut encampment on a large lake some 70 miles northwest of Marble Island (Peter Lake or perhaps Meliadine Lake). He stayed there about a week (Gilder, 1881:41-7).

CHAPTER THREE:
TREK TO THE ARCTIC WATERSHED

1 Visited by Gilder during a hunting trip in August 1878 and named by him after Mr Thomas B. Connery of New York (Gilder, 1881:24).

2 Here Klutschak is mixing a usage from Cumberland Sound (suugami) with one from the Keewatin. R.G. Williamson, personal communication

3 This was the route followed by Schwatka on his reconnaissance trip in January (Stackpole, 1965:38-40).

4 This phenomenon also described in detail by Gilder (1881:60-1), appears to have been a special type of icing.

5 This had marked the farthest point on Schwatka's earlier reconnaissance.

6 Named Payer Pass by Schwatka, after Julius Payer, co-leader of the Austro-Hungarian North Pole Expedition of 1872-4. The snow in the gorge was so deep and soft that the sledges had to be relayed through using doubled teams.

7 Wager Bay. In fact the expedition appears to have passed to the west of the head of the bay, crossing either the narrow water body of Ford Lake or the Brown River either above or below Brown Lake.

8 Klutschak is attempting to render the very idiosyncratic sounds used for steering, ie, each man has his own sounds. R.G. Williamson, personal communication

9 Gilder (1881:67) also reported 4 animals but Schwatka reported 10, including calves (Stackpole, 1965:57). These would be the only muskoxen killed on the expedition.

CHAPTER FOUR:
THE BACK RIVER TO KING WILLIAM'S LAND

1 *Tingaujaq* or 'caribou moss,' *Alectoria ochroleuca* (Hoffm.) Massal. The

favourite food of young caribou (Wilson, 1978:191).

2 On the basis of Gilder's map (1881: facing p 73) it appears probable that this was not the Hayes River itself but a major left-bank tributary, joining the Hayes at about 67°N, 93°07′W.

3 Lieutenant George Back encountered Inuit at the Dangerous Rapids during his descent of the Back River on 28 July 1834 and sketched a man and a woman (Back 1836:379–88). Significantly, Back reported one man as wearing pants of muskox skin. Back's party, however, had only one boat. Although Schwatka (Stackpole, 1965:62) and Gilder (1881:78) reported that the white men seen previously had only one boat, there is the possibility that the reference is to Anderson and Stewart's party, which descended the river, also in search of Franklin, in the summer of 1855 (Anderson, 1940-1). Travelling in two canoes, this party encountered an Inuit encampment with numerous children at the foot of the rapids leading from Franklin Lake on 30 May 1855 (Anderson, 1940:9–10) and again on the return trip on 13 August 1855 (Anderson 1941:231). It would appear that none of the members of the Schwatka expedition had any knowledge of Anderson's expedition.

4 It is difficult to decipher the truth of this story. McClintock indeed visited Montreal Island (15–18 May 1859 – McClintock, 1860:266–70) but made no mention of leaving a cairn. At the same time, according to Schwatka (Stackpole, 1965:63) and Gilder (1881:79–80), they had been told by one of the Utkuhikhalingmiut on the Hayes River that the cairn had been built by a party in two boats which he had seen descending the Back River as a boy (presumably Anderson and Stewart's party). The latter group did indeed visit Montreal Island, but Anderson (1940-1) made no reference to leaving a cairn or any of the items mentioned here.

5 The whole of Ogle Peninsula is an area of outwash sands and gravels according to Fraser and Henoch (1959:Fig. 7).

6 According to Gilder (1881:84) this informant had seen several skeletons, books and papers scattered among the rocks, knives, forks, spoons, dishes, cans, and several watches.

7 Starvation Cove.

8 Ahgekshewah, according to Schwatka (Stackpole, 1965:74).

9 But, while reporting the gold chain, Schwatka does not indicate that it was attached to the ear rings (Stackpole, 1965:75).

10 However, a sledge named *Lady Franklin* operated from Belcher's ships *Assistance* and *Pioneer* during the Franklin search expedition of 1852-4 (Belcher, 1855). These two ships were abandoned in the ice by Belcher in the southern part of Wellington Channel in the fall of 1854. Could one of

these ships (with the sledge *Lady Franklin* still on board) have drifted to
the northwest coast of O'Reilly Island? In other words, could the ship
seen by the Inuit have been one of Belcher's ships, rather than *Erebus*
or *Terror*?

11 This cairn is located on the south coast of King William Island near the
mouth of the Peffer River. Hall built the cairn to mark the grave of one
skeleton (not two) presumably from the Franklin expedition, during his
brief visit to the area on 12 May 1869 (Nourse, 1879:401).

CHAPTER FIVE:
FROM CAPE HERSCHEL TO CAPE FELIX

1 Built by Dease and Simpson (who also named the cape) on their way back
west to the Coppermine River from their farthest east point on the west
coast of Melville Peninsula in September 1839 (Simpson, 1843:379–80).

2 According to Schwatka this find was made by Frank Melms, and it was
Tuluak who identified the skull as that of a white man (Stackpole,
1965:80). This occurred on 24 June, mid-way between Franklin Point and
Cape Jane Franklin, presumably on the south side of the entrance to
Collinson Inlet.

3 According to Schwatka this site lay about 2 miles north of Cape Jane
Franklin (Stackpole, 1965:80) according to Gilder (1881:124) about 1.5 miles
north of that cape.

4 This document was written with a lead pencil and was partly illegible due
to exposure (Gilder, 1881:127). The note was written by McClintock as he
travelled clockwise round King William Island in May 1859, to record his
finding of a note left by Lieutenant William Hobson only a few weeks
earlier (McClintock, 1859:283). It in turn reported on the finding of one of
the only two written records of the Franklin Expedition ever discovered.

5 A trench 4 feet wide and 20 feet long was dug, running north from the
cairn, but no trace was found of the document which McClintock said he
would bury (Gilder, 1881:129; Stackpole, 1965:85).

CHAPTER SIX:
THE MAIN SEARCH AND ITS RESULTS

1 This find was made on 5 July; according to Schwatka it was on a very
prominent ridge about 3 miles inland (Stackpole, 1965:84).

2 This cairn was found on the return trip by Lieutenant Schwatka, about 1
mile inland and 1 mile north of Wall Bay (Gilder, 1881:147).

3 The bedrock of King William Island consists of Ordovician and Silurian

limestones and dolomites (Fraser & Henoch, 1959:6). But although the surface of Graham Gore Peninsula consists of exposed limestone bedrock, bedrock is rarely exposed along the south shores of the island. From Douglas Bay to Washington Bay the southwest coast of King William Island is covered by a magnificent field of drumlins with a northwest-southeast orientation, representing a continuation of the large field covering most of Adelaide Peninsula (Fraser & Henoch, 1959:13–19). The numerous islands in Simpson Strait and farther west in McGillivray Bay represent submerged drumlins. Elsewhere much of King William Island is mantled by rather featureless ground moraine and in places with faint flutings. Even where bedrock is exposed as low ridges or scarps it is often barely distinguishable as such due to the effects of severe frost-shattering.

Immediately after deglaciation, when the land was still glacio-isostatically depressed, the whole of the island was submerged beneath the sea. With subsequent emergence extensive flights of strandlines and raised beaches have been formed, commonly developed on the slopes of the drumlins (Fraser & Henoch, 1959:33–5).

The present rate of uplift (Andrews, 1970:Fig. 3) is of the order of 0.8 m per century. This means, of course, that items left at high tide mark by the Franklin expedition are now approximately 1 m above sea level, and depending on the slope of the shoreline, some varying distance inland.

4 'Surrounding the drumlins ... are wide expanses of sandy plains, containing shallow lakes and narrow, winding streams. Colonized by goose grass and cotton grass, marsh areas are extensive and the level plains extend to the base of the drumlins where poorly preserved strands are manifested by lines of boulders from which the finer materials have been removed' (Fraser & Henoch, 1959:34–5).

5 On 16 July according to Schwatka (Stackpole, 1965:87).

6 The pieces included the stem, which was retrieved by Schwatka's party and is now preserved at the National Maritime Museum, Greenwich, England.

7 An incomplete skeleton, including skull, according to Schwatka (Stackpole, 1965:91).

CHAPTER SEVEN:
THE DIVIDED SEARCH

1 Here, too, what Klutschak is describing is a series of raised beaches, formed successively as the land has emerged from the sea due to glacio-isostatic rebound in postglacial time.

2 This description, along with the cross-sections, represent an excellent

portrayal of the drumlin landscape of this coast, the drumlins being modified by wave action as raised beaches were developed on their slopes.

3 According to Dr Walter O. Kupsch, Department of Geological Sciences, University of Saskatchewan, Klutschak's uppermost figure most likely represents the gastropod *Maclurites*. The figure at the bottom is a cross-section of the fossil above it which is a receptaculitid, popularly referred to as the 'Sunflower coral,' although it is certainly *not* a coral. *Maclurites* and *Receptaculites* are common index fossils of the upper Ordovician-Silurian rocks which underlie King William Island. Dr Kupsch was puzzled by the figure between the *Maclurites* and the *Receptaculites*; he tentatively wondered whether it were an overly stylistic rendering of a 'chain coral' or halysitid such as *Catenipora*.

4 This section embraces the best-developed drumlin zone, where much of the lowland areas between the drumlins is bare of vegetation (Fraser & Henoch, 1959:35).

5 The medal was barely 1 inch in diameter; on the obverse was a bas-relief of Prince Albert, surrounded by the inscription 'PRINCE ALBERT BORN AUGUST 26th, 1819.' On the reverse was a bas-relief of a six-masted screw steamer with all sails set. Above it were the words 'The Great Britain'; below it 'Length 322 feet, Breadth 50 feet 6 inches, Depth 32 feet 6 inches, Weight of Iron 1500 tons, 1000 Horsepower. Launched July 19th, 1843 by H.R.H Prince Albert.' *Great Britain*, designed by Isambard Kingdom Brunel, was a unique ship in many ways. Launched at Bristol on 19 July 1843, she was the first iron ship, the first sea-going ship to use screw propulsion, and the largest ship ever built. Having served as a passenger ship and troopship, she ended up as a hulk in the Falkland Islands. In the summer of 1970 she was salvaged and brought back to Bristol, where she is now being restored and is on display to the public (Rowland, 1971).

6 Hall in fact found only part of one thigh bone but his Inuit companions reported having seen the graves of 5 men here (Nourse, 1879:400–2).

CHAPTER EIGHT:
IN PERMANENT CAMP

1 Eta Island. Dr R.G. Williamson was unable to guess at the derivation of this name.

2 Schwatka's camp was about 10 km southeast of Gladman Point (Gilder, 1881:192).

3 For further details see, for example, Jenness (1924) and Mary-Rousselière (1969).

4 Tulugaq left on 14 October and returned on the 23rd (Stackpole, 1965:99).

According to Gilder (1881:197) the woman involved was Joe's wife, the two
men having agreed to exchange wives since it was felt that Tulugaq's
young son would suffer too much from the cold on the trip.

CHAPTER NINE
KING WILLIAM'S LAND TO THE DANGEROUS RAPIDS

1 Klutschak's geological observations are accurate. Montreal Island indeed
   consists of Precambrian gneisses, in strong contrast to the Paleozoic
   sedimentaries of Adelaide Peninsula to the west, which in any case are
   largely mantled by fluvioglacial and glacial deposits (Fraser & Henoch,
   1959:5).
2 Schwatka's party did not reach Cockburn Bay, just south of Elliott Bay,
   until 2 December (Gilder, 1881:208; Stackpole, 1965:103).
3 Until very recently (certainly as late as 1963) the Utkuhikhalingmiut still
   congregated at this site (known as Amujat) for the period November-
   March, in order to fish through the ice (Briggs, 1970:367).
4 The descendants of the people whom Schwatka's party met are still
   heavily dependent on the fish caught in this section of the river, known as
   Itimnaaqjuk, in both summer and fall. During the latter season salmon
   trout are taken by jigging and whitefish by nets set under the ice (Briggs,
   1970: 30–1).
5 Dr R.G. Williamson found this rendering unrecognizable.

CHAPTER TEN:
ON THE BACK RIVER

1 Nalijau was the Utkuhikhalik who had joined the expedition on the
   Hayes River.
2 The proposed route was almost certainly via the Meadowbank River and
   the lower Quoich River.

CHAPTER ELEVEN:
THE OVERLAND MARCH

1 The route appears to have lain southeastward between and parallel to the
   Herman and Meadowbank rivers.
2 This is pidgin Inuktitut. R.G. Williamson, personal communication
3 A reference to Payer and Weyprecht's expedition aboard *Tegetthoff* in
   1872–4.
4 A further example of pidgin Inuktitut.

5 Given the time it took the party to reach the mouth of the Connery River from this point (11 days of which at least one was a rest day) and their weakened state, it seems very unlikely that this was the Quoich River. The straight line distance from where the Quoich crosses the 64°21′N parallel to the mouth of the Connery is some 180 km.

CHAPTER TWELVE:
THE FINAL STRETCH TO MARBLE ISLAND

1 Unrecognizable, according to Dr R.G. Williamson

2 This term is also unrecognizable, according to R.G. Williamson

3 Lieutenant Schwatka set off for Marble Island on the morning of 12 March. By prearrangement Gilder, Klutschak, and Melms were to follow at intervals of five days if Schwatka did not return (Stackpole, 1965:114).

4 One wonders why Klutschak should have been so bafflingly coy about the object in question. Gilder is equally reticent (1881:206), but according to him the Inuk touched all the snow blocks inside the snow house at the level of the sleeping platform with the object, then went outside and threw it in the air. From the way in which it fell he predicted that no further deaths were imminent. Dr R.G. Williamson suggests that the object was probably a walrus baculum (penis bone).

5 Schwatka and one of his Inuit companions had left the other Inuk at Chesterfield Inlet with half their supplies (Stackpole, 1965:114). It was from this point that they had covered the impressive distance of 75 miles to Marble Island non-stop in 23 hours. At Marble Island Schwatka was very relieved to find the whaling ship *George and Mary*, under Captain M.A. Baker, and received a very warm welcome.

Gilder left Camp Daly on 17 March and that same day met an Inuit messenger coming from Marble Island with supplies and mail; the supplies consisted of bread, pork, molasses, and tobacco. Gilder took one of the two boxes of supplies (plus a bottle of whisky) for his own use and sent the rest on north to Klutschak and party at Camp Daly. Gilder reached *George and Mary* at Marble Island at midnight on the 21st (Gilder, 1881:236).

CHAPTER THIRTEEN:
THE LAST MONTHS IN HUDSON BAY

1 This return trip to Camp Daly, and indeed the entire subsequent four-month sojourn there, are totally glossed over in the other two published accounts.

2 Black Guillemot (*Cepphus grylle*).

3 The introduction of whaleboats to the Inuit of this coast has been discussed in detail by Ross (1975).

4 On 7 June (Gilder, 1881:267).

5 According to Gilder (1881:267), Tulugaq was persuaded from going south to the United States by the Aivilingmiut elders.

6 *George and Mary* called first at Marble Island for water; while her casks were being filled Captain Baker and Gilder crossed to the mainland to the southwest by boat (Gilder, 1881:272) to trade for muskox skins, etc. with the Qairnirmiut. *George and Mary* next headed back north along the coast past Depot Island, Cape Fullerton, and Whale Point. Off Cape Fullerton a female bear was spotted on an ice floe and killed. Schwatka managed to capture her cub alive, but Captain Baker decreed that it had to be shot since there was not enough room for it on board (Gilder, 1881:274).

Since the ice in Roe's Welcome Sound was still solid from Whale Point to Southampton Island, *George and Mary* now ran for home. She met *Isabella* in Fisher Strait and *Abbott Lawrence* off Charles Island, both inward-bound (Gilder, 1881:274). Calling at North Bay in Hudson Strait, Captain Baker purchased the baleen from a large whale from the Inuit but then discovered that it was at a place called Akkolear near Strathcona Island at the northwest end of Big Island. The ship's first officer, Mr Williams, took two boats and Inuit guides to fetch the baleen; he returned with it after four days. *George and Mary* then got under way again, her next port of call being New Bedford.

CHAPTER FOURTEEN:
THE INUIT OF THE AMERICAN NORTH

1 This is an outrageous statement, particularly in view of Klutschak's limited linguistic competence as evidenced by his frequently demonstrated inability to hear accurately what was being said. R.G. Williamson, personal communication

2 This is probably a man's name; *angut* is the word for man. Mrs Karla Williamson, personal communication

3 *Kuni* is whalers' pidgin; the Inuktitut word is *arnaq*. Mrs Karla Williamson

4 This is a proper name. Mrs Karla Williamson

5 This term is unrecognizable. Mrs Karla Williamson

6 Yet another unrecognizable term. Mrs Karla Williamson

7 *Qilak* is the Inuktitut word for sky; perhaps Klutschak was confused with *ublaaq* (morning). Mrs Karla Williamson

8 Another unrecognizable term: *uqartuq* is to talk. Mrs Karla Williamson
9 Yet another unrecognizable term. R.G. Williamson
10 This statement is totally indefensible and demonstrates that Klutschak's grasp of the language was extremely superficial. R.G. Williamson
11 These comparative expressions are further examples of pidgin Inuktitut, demonstrating further the superficial nature of Klutschak's grasp of the language. R.G. Williamson

References

Amundsen, R. 1908. *The North West Passage: Being the record of a voyage of exploration of the ship 'Gjoa' 1903-1907* ... London: Archibald Constable, 2 vols

Anderson, J. 1940-1. Chief Factor James Anderson's Back River journal of 1855. *Canadian Field Naturalist, 54*:63-7, 84-9, 107-9, 125-6, 134-6; *55*:9-11, 21-6, 38-44

Andrews, J.T. 1970. Present and postglacial rates of uplift for glaciated northern and eastern North America derived from postglacial uplift curves. *Canadian Journal of Earth Sciences, 7*(2):703-15

Asher, G.M. 1860. *Henry Hudson the navigator: The original documents in which his career is recorded, collected, partly translated and annotated, with an introduction.* London: Hakluyt Society

Back, G. 1836. *Narrative of the Arctic Land Expedition to the mouth of the Great Fish River in the years 1833, 1834 and 1835.* London: John Murray

– 1838. *Narrative of an expedition in* H.M.S. *'Terror,' undertaken with a view to geographical discovery on the Arctic shores, in the years 1836-37.* London: John Murray

Baker, F.W.G. 1982. The First International Polar Year, 1882-83. *Polar Record, 21*(132):275-85

Barr, W. 1985. The expeditions of the First International Polar Year, 1882-83. *Arctic Institute of North America Technical Paper, 29,* 222 pp

Beattie, O.B. 1983. A report on newly discovered human skeletal remains from the last Sir John Franklin expedition. *The Musk-Ox, 33*:68-77

– & Savelle, J.M. 1983. Discovery of human remains from Sir John Franklin's last expedition. *Historical Archeology, 17*(2):100-5

Becker, A. v. 1878. *Arktische Reise der englischen Yacht 'Pandora' im Jahre 1876: Unter Commando des Capitain Sir Allen Young* [The arctic voyage of the English yacht *Pandora* in 1876: Under the command of Captain Sir Allen Young]. Pola: Carl Gerolds Sohn in Wien

Beechey, F.W. 1831. *Narrative of a voyage to the Pacific and Bering's Strait, to* co-operate with the polar expeditions: Performed in His Majesty's Ship 'Blossom,' under the command of Captain F.W. Beechey, in the years 1825, 26, 27, 28. London: Henry Colburn and Richard Bentley, 2 vols

– 1843. A voyage of discovery towards the North Pole, performed in His Majesty's ships 'Dorothea' and 'Trent,' under the command of Captain David Buchan, R.N., 1818, etc. London: R. Bentley

Belcher, E. 1855. The last of the Arctic voyages: Being a narrative of the expedition in H.M.S. 'Assistance,' under the command of Captain Sir Edward Belcher, C.B., in search of Sir John Franklin, during the years 1852–53–54. London: Lovell Reeve

Bellot, J.-R. 1854. Journal d'un voyage aux mers polaires exécuté à la recherche de Sir John Franklin, en 1851 et 1852. Paris: Perrotin

– 1855. Memoirs of Lieutenant Joseph René Bellot . . . with his journal of a voyage in the polar seas, in search of Sir John Franklin. London: Hurst and Blackett

Bessels, E. 1879. Die Amerikanische Nordpol-expedition. [The American North Pole Expedition]. Leipzig: Wilhelm Engelmann

Blake, E.V. 1874. Arctic experiences: Containing Capt. George E. Tyson's wonderful drift on the ice-floe, a history of the 'Polaris' expedition, the cruise of the 'Tigress' and rescue of the 'Polaris' survivors . . . New York: Harper and Bros

Boas, F. 1888. The central Eskimo. Bureau of American Ethnology, Sixth Annual Report, 1884–5 (pp 399–669). Washington: Government Printing Office

Boumphrey, R.S. (trans.) 1967. A visit to South Georgia by H.W. Klutschak, 1877. British Antarctic Survey Bulletin, 12:85–92

Briggs, J.L. 1970. Never in anger: Portrait of an Eskimo family. Cambridge, MA: Harvard University Press

Burwash, L.T. 1930. The Franklin search. Canadian Geographical Journal, 1(7):587–603

– 1931. Canada's Western Arctic. Ottawa: King's Printer

Cooper, P.F. 1955. A trip to King William Island in 1954. Arctic Circular 8(1):8–11

Corby, G.A. 1982. The First International Polar Year (1882/83). World Meteorological Organization Bulletin, 31(3):192–214

Cyriax, R.J. 1939. Sir John Franklin's last arctic expedition: A chapter in the history of the Royal Navy. London: Methuen

– 1951. Recently discovered traces of the Franklin Expedition. Geographical Journal, 117:211–14

– & Jones, A.G.E. 1954. The papers in the possession of Harry Peglar, Captain of the Foretop, H.M.S. Terror, 1845. Mariner's Mirror, 40(3):186–95

Davis, C.H. (ed.). 1874. *Narrative of the North Polar expedition, U.S. Ship 'Polaris,' Captain Charles Francis Hall commanding.* Washington, DC: Government Printing Office

Dodge, E. 1973. *The polar Rosses: John and James Clark Ross and their explorations.* London: Faber and Faber

[Fisher, A.] 1819. *Journal of a voyage of discovery, to the Arctic regions, performed between the 4th of April and the 18th of November, 1818, in His Majesty's Ship 'Alexander,' Wm. Edward Parry, Esq. Lieut. and Commander. By an officer of the Alexander.* London: Richard Phillips

Franklin, J. 1823. *Narrative of a journey to the shores of the Polar Sea, in the years 1819, 20, 21 and 22 etc.* London: John Murray

– 1828. *Narrative of a second expedition to the shores of the polar sea in the years 1825, 1826, and 1827 etc.* London: John Murray

Fraser, J.K. and Henoch, W.E.S. 1959. Notes on the glaciation of King William Island and Adelaide Peninsula. *Geographical Paper* 22. Ottawa: Geographical Branch, Department of Mines and Technical Surveys

Gibson, W. 1932. Some further traces of the Franklin retreat. *Geographical Journal, 79*:402–8

– 1937. Sir John Franklin's last voyage: A brief history of the Franklin expedition and an outline of the researches which established the facts of its tragic end. *The Beaver, 268*(1):44–75

Gilder, W.H. 1881. *Schwatka's search: Sledging in the Arctic in quest of the Franklin records.* New York: Charles Scribner's Sons

– 1883. *Ice packs and tundra: An account of a search for the 'Jeannette' and a sledge journey through Siberia.* London: Sampson Low, Marston, Searle and Rivington

Gilpin, J.D. 1850. Outline of the voyage of H.M.S. *Enterprise* and *Investigator* to Barrow Strait in search of Sir John Franklin. *Nautical Magazine, 19*(1):8–9; *19*(2):89–90; *19*(3):160–70; *19*(4):230

Great Britain. Parliament. 1851. Return to an address of the Honourable the House of Commons dated 7 February 1851; – for, 'copy or extracts from any correspondence or proceedings of the Board of Admiralty . . . ,' 'copies of any instructions from the Admiralty to any officers in Her Majesty's service, engaged in Arctic expeditions . . . ,' and 'copy or extracts from any correspondence or communications from the Government of the United States . . . in relation to any search made on the part of the United States . . .' Ordered, by the House of Commons, to be printed, 7 March 1851. (Great Britain, Parliament. House of Commons. Sessional Papers, Accounts and Papers, 1851, Vol. 33, No. 97)

– 1855. Further papers relative to the recent Arctic expeditions in search of Sir John Franklin and the crews of H.M.S. 'Erebus' and 'Terror' (Great Britain,

Parliament. House of Commons. Sessional Papers, Accounts and Papers,
    1854–5, Vol. 35, No. 1898)
– 1856. Further papers relative to the recent Arctic expeditions in search of
    Sir John Franklin, and the crews of Her Majesty's Ships *Erebus* and *Terror*
    including the reports of Dr. Kane and Messrs. Anderson and Stewart ...
    Presented to the House of Commons. (Great Britain, Parliament. House of
    Commons. Sessional Papers, Accounts and Papers, 1856, Vol. 41, No. 2124)
Hall, C.F. 1864. *Life with the Esquimaux: The narrative of Captain Charles
    Francis Hall, of the whaling barque 'George Henry,' from the 29th May, 1860
    to the 13th September, 1862* ... London: Sampson Low, Sons and Marston
Hansen, G. 1908. Towards King Haakon VII's Land. In *The Northwest Passage:
    Being the record of a voyage of exploration of the ship* Gjoa *1903–1907* ...
    R. Amundsen, ed. London: Archibald Constable, Vol. 2, pp 296–364
Hartlaub, G. & Lindeman, M. (eds.) 1873. *Die zweite deutsche Nordpolarfahrt
    in den Jahren 1869 und 1870 unter Führung des Kapitan Karl Koldewey*
    [The second German North Pole voyage in the years 1869 and 1870 under
    the leadership of Captain Karl Koldewey]. Leipzig: Brockhaus, 2 vols
Hayes, I.I. 1867. *The open polar sea: A Narrative of a voyage of discovery
    towards the North Pole in the schooner 'United States.'* London: Sampson
    Low, Son and Marston
Hooper, W.H. 1853. Ten months among the tents of the Tuski, with incidents
    of an Arctic boat expedition in search of Sir John Franklin, as far as the
    Mackenzie River and Cape Bathurst. London: John Murray
Jenness, D. 1924. Eskimo string figures. In *Report of the Canadian Arctic
    Expedition 1913–1918*, Vol. 13, Pt B. Ottawa: King's Printer
Jones, A.G.E. 1969. Captain Robert Martin: A Peterhead whaling master in the
    19th century. *Scottish Geographical Magazine, 85*(3): 196–202
Kane, E.K. 1854. *The U.S. Grinnell expedition in search of Sir John Franklin: A
    personal narrative.* London: Sampson Low, Son and Co.
Kennedy, W. 1853. *A short narrative of the second voyage of the 'Prince
    Albert' in search of Sir John Franklin.* London: W.H. Dalton
Klutschak, H.W. 1881. Ein Besuch auf Sud Georgien [A visit to South
    Georgia]. *Deutsche Rundschau fur Geographie und Statistik, 3*(11):522–34
Koldewey, K. 1871. Die erste deutsche Norpolar-Expedition im Jahre 1868 [The
    first German North Pole expedition in 1868]. *Petermanns Geographische
    Mittheilungen*, Erganzungsheft 28.
Learmonth, L.A. 1969. A divergent opinion. *The Beaver, 299*:32–3
Loomis, C.C. 1972. *Weird and tragic shores: The story of Charles Francis Hall,
    explorer.* New York: Alfred A. Knopf
McClintock, F.L. 1859. *The voyage of the 'Fox' in the arctic seas: A narrative of*

the discovery of the fate of Sir John Franklin and his companions. London: John Murray

McDougall, G.F. 1857. *The eventful voyage of* H.M. *discovery ship 'Resolute' to the Arctic regions in search of Sir John Franklin and the missing crews of* H.M. *discovery ships 'Erebus' and 'Terror,' 1852, 1853, 1854* ... London: Longman, Brown, Green, Longmans and Roberts

McKenzie, W.G. 1969. A further clue in the Franklin mystery. *The Beaver,* 299:28–32

Mary-Rousselière, G. 1969. Les jeux de ficelle des Arviligjuarmiut. *National Museum of Canada Bulletin* 233 (Anthropological Series 88)

Mathiassen, T. 1945. *Report on the expedition. Report of the Fifth Thule Expedition 1921–24: The Danish expedition to Arctic North America in charge of Knud Rasmussen,* Ph.D. Copenhagen: Gyldenalske Boghandel, Nordisk Forlag, Vol. 1

Miertsching, J.A. 1855. *Reise-Tagebuch des Missionars Joh. Aug. Miertsching, welcher als Dolmetscher die Nordpol-Expedition zur Aufsuchung Sir John Franklins auf dem Schiff 'Investigator' begleitete. In den Jahren 1850 bis 1854* [Travel diary of the missionary J.A. Miertsching, who accompanied the North Pole expedition in search of Sir John Franklin aboard the ship *Investigator* as interpreter in the years 1850 to 1854]. Gnadau: Verlag der Unitats Buchhandlung bei H.L. Menz

Nourse, J.E. (ed.). 1879. *Narrative of the second Arctic expedition made by Charles F. Hall: His voyage to Repulse Bay, sledge journeys to the straits of Fury and Hecla and to King William's Land, and residence among the Eskimos during the years 1864–'69.* Washington: Government Printing Office

O'Byrne, W. 1849. *A naval biographical dictionary: Comprising the life and service of every living officer in Her Majesty's navy, from the rank of Admiral of the Fleet to that of Lieutenant, inclusive.* London: John Murray

Osborn, S. 1852. *Stray leaves from an Arctic journal; or, eighteen months in the polar regions, in search of Sir John Franklin's expedition, in the years 1850–51.* London: Longmans, Brown, Green and Longmans

Parry, W.E. 1821. *Journal of a voyage for the discovery of a North-West Passage from the Atlantic to the Pacific: Performed in the years 1819–1820, in His Majesty's Ships 'Hecla' and 'Griper'* ... London: John Murray

– 1824. *Journal of a second voyage for the discovery of a North-West Passage from the Atlantic to the Pacific: Performed in the years 1821–22–23, in His Majesty's Ships 'Fury' and Hecla'* ... London: John Murray

Payer, J. 1878. *Die osterreichisch-ungarische Nordpolar-expedition in den Jahren 1872–74, nebst einer Skizze der Zweiten deutschen*

Nordpolarexpedition 1869–70 und der Polar-Expedition von 1871 [The Austro-Hungarian North Pole Expedition in the years 1872–74, along with a sketch of the Second German North Pole Expedition of 1869–70 and the polar expedition of 1871]. Vienna: Alfred Holder

Pullen, H.F. (ed.). 1979. *The Pullen expedition in search of Sir John Franklin.* Toronto: Arctic History Press

Rasmussen, K. 1927. *Across arctic America: Narrative of the Fifth Thule Expedition.* New York: G.P. Putnam's Sons

Rich, E.E. & A.M. Johnson. 1953. *John Rae's correspondence with the Hudson's Bay Company on arctic exploration 1844–1855.* London: Hudson's Bay Record Society

Richardson, J. 1851. *Arctic searching expedition: A journal of a boat-voyage through Rupert's Land and the Arctic Sea, in search of the discovery ships under command of Sir John Franklin.* London: Longman, Brown, Green and Longmans. 2 vols

Ross, J. 1819. *A voyage of discovery made under the orders of the Admiralty in His Majesty's Ships 'Isabella' and 'Alexander,' for the purpose of exploring Baffin's Bay, and inquiring into the probability of a North-West Passage.* London: John Murray

– 1835. *Narrative of a second voyage in search of a North-west Passage, and of a residence in the Arctic regions during the years 1829, 1830, 1831, 1832, 1833, etc.* London: A.W. Webster

Ross, J.C. 1847. *A voyage of discovery and research in the Southern and Antarctic regions during the years 1839–43.* London: John Murray

Ross, W.G. 1975. *Whaling and Eskimos: Hudson Bay 1860–1915.* National Museums of Canada Publications in Ethnology 10

Rowland, K.T. 1971. *The Great Britain.* Newton Abbott: David and Charles

Schwatka, F. 1885. *Along Alaska's great river: A popular account of the travels of the Alaska exploring expedition of 1883, along the great Yukon River, from its source to its mouth, in the British North-West Territory and in the Territory of Alaska.* New York: Cassell and Co. Ltd

Seemann, B. 1853. *Narrative of the voyage of H.M.S. 'Herald' during the years 1845–51, under the command of Captain Henry Kennett, R.N., C.B.* London: Reeve and Co. 2 vols

Simpson, T. 1843. *Narrative of the discoveries on the North coast of America; effected by the officers of the Hudson's Bay Company during the years 1836–39.* London: Richard Bentley

Snow, W.P. 1851. *Voyage of the 'Prince Albert' in search of Sir John Franklin: A Narrative of every-day life in the Arctic seas.* London: Longmans, Brown, Green and Longmans

Stackpole, E.A. (ed.). 1965. *The long arctic search: The narrative of Lieutenant Frederick Schwatka, U.S.A., 1878–1880, seeking the records of the lost Franklin expedition.* Mystic, CN: Marine Historical Association Inc.

Sutherland, P.C. 1852. *Journal of a voyage in Baffin's Bay and Barrow Straits, in the years 1850–51, performed by H.M. Ships 'Lady Franklin' and 'Sophia' under the command of Mr. William Penny, in search of the missing crews of H.M. Ships 'Erebus' and 'Terror.'* London: Longmans, Brown, Green and Longmans

Walsh, R.T. 1974. Quest in the North. *Sentinel, 10*(5):23–4

Williamson, J.A. 1962. *The Cabot voyages and Bristol discoveries under Henry VII.* Cambridge: Hakluyt Society (Cambridge University Press)

Wilson, M. 1973. Sir John Ross's last expedition, in search of Sir John Franklin. *The Musk-Ox, 13:*5–11

Wilson, M.R. 1978. Notes on ethnobotany in Inuktitut. *The Western Canadian Journal of Anthropology, 8*(2, 3, 4):180–96.

Wohlgemuth, E.E. v. 1886. *Osterreichische Polarexpedition nach Jan Mayen. Beobachtungs-Ergebnisse,* Bd I [The Austrian Polar Expedition to Jan Mayen: Observation results. Vol. I]. Vienna: Die Kaiserliche-Konigliche Hof und Staatsdruckerei

Wonders, W.G. 1968. Search for Franklin. *Canadian Geographical Journal, 76*(4):116–27

Wright, N. 1959. *Quest for Franklin.* London: Heinemann

Young, A.W. 1876. *Cruise of the 'Pandora.' From the private journal kept by Allen Young.* London: William Clowes and Sons

Index

Except for *Erebus* and *Terror*, all vessels are listed under 'Ships.'

BOSTON PUBLIC LIBRARY

3 9999 03139 020 4

BOSTON PUBLIC LIBRARY